COACHING TRACK & FIELD SUCCESSFULLY

Mark Guthrie

University of Wisconsin at La Crosse

Human Kinetics

Library of Congress Cataloging-in-Publication Data

Guthrie, Mark, 1953
    Coaching track & field successfully / Mark Guthrie.
        p. cm.
Includes bibliogaphical references (p.) and index.
    ISBN 0-7360-4274-1 (pbk.)
    1. Track and field–Coaching. 2. Track and field–Training. I.
    Title: Coaching track and field successfully. II. Title.
GV1060.675.C6 G88 2003
796.42–dc21

                                                                    2002154209

ISBN: 0-7360-4274-1

Acquisitions Editor: Ed McNeely; **Developmental Editor:** Julie Rhoda; **Assistant Editors:** Carla Zych and John Wentworth; **Copyeditor:** Scott Jerard; **Proofreader:** Anne Meyer Byler; **Indexer:** Nan N. Badgett; **Graphic Designer:** Nancy Rasmus; **Graphic Artist:** Kim McFarland; **Art and Photo Manager:** Dan Wendt; **Cover Designer:** Keith Blomberg; **Photographer (cover):** Tom Roberts; **Photographer (interior):** Tom Roberts (unless otherwise noted); **Illustrator:** Roberto Sabas; **Printer:** Custom Color Graphics

Copies of this book are available at special discounts for bulk purchase for sales promotions, premiums, fund-raising, or educational use. Special editions or book excerpts can also be created to specifications. For details, contact the Special Sales Manager at Human Kinetics.

Printed in the United States of America   10 9 8 7 6 5 4 3 2 1

Human Kinetics
Web site: www.HumanKinetics.com

United States: Human Kinetics
P.O. Box 5076
Champaign, IL 61825-5076
800-747-4457
e-mail: humank@hkusa.com

Canada: Human Kinetics
475 Devonshire Road Unit 100
Windsor, ON N8Y 2L5
800-465-7301 (in Canada only)
e-mail: orders@hkcanada.com

Europe: Human Kinetics
107 Bradford Road
Stanningley
Leeds LS28 6AT, United Kingdom
+44 (0) 113 255 5665
e-mail: hk@hkeurope.com

Australia: Human Kinetics
57A Price Avenue
Lower Mitcham, South Australia 5062
08 8277 1555
e-mail: liahka@senet.com.au

New Zealand: Human Kinetics
P.O. Box 105-231, Auckland Central
09-523-3462
e-mail: hkp@ihug.co.nz

To my parents, Robert and Lois Guthrie, for their love,
kindness, discipline, and support in all of my endeavors.

To my wife, Dawn, who showed patience and love
and who understood the time and commitment
it takes to be the wife of a coach.

To Allison and Anne, my daughters, who spent
many a day going to Dad's meets and functions.

CONTENTS

Part IV   Coaching Meets

FOREWORD

Coach Mark Guthrie is not only one of the most successful track and field coaches in NCAA Division III, he is one of the most successful coaches in all of collegiate track and field. He has created a program at the University of Wisconsin at La Crosse that is a model of what sports programs are all about. His athletes are not only at the top of the class on the playing field, they are also students at the top in the classroom. The ideals that drive his program are the ideals that he holds dear.

He understands that a successful program would never be complete without primary recognition for the life processes of the student-athletes. In his words, "the successes that we share in track and field are in part the by-products of how well we teach these life values. What we do as coaches is to provide the facilities and the environment where the student-athletes can gain the maturity and the confidence necessary to enhance their talents and attain the goals they set for themselves." In this book, Coach Guthrie provides the materials necessary for serious students of track and field to enhance their opportunity for success. Coach Mark Guthrie is a man who knows how to balance life on and off the field. Track and field is all the better for it.

Jimmy Carnes

Executive Director, United States Track and Field Coaches Association
Head Men's U.S. Olympic Coach, 1976

ACKNOWLEDGMENTS

Thanks to Dr. Phil Esten, who is a contributor in this book and who is personally responsible for my being at the University of Wisconsin at La Crosse. The other collaborators of this book—Josh Buchholtz, Dennis Kline, and Evan Perkins—shared their knowledge with UW-La Crosse athletes and their friendship with me. Thanks to Joe Newton at York High School in Elmhurst, Illinois, for sharing his motivational concepts and for helping a young coach begin his journey. John Davis, former track coach at Glenbrook South High School in Glenbrook, Illinois, shared his passion for the sport and the importance of being organized and professional in all endeavors. Thanks to Dr. John Curtis at UW-La Crosse, who tutored our teams and me in *The Mindset For Winning*.

Thanks also to the coaches whose event-specific clinic notes I've adapted into my coaching including Jim Bush, for the hurdle research presented at the USTCA Convention in Los Angeles (December 1999), and Clyde Hart, for the 400-meter research presented at the USATF Convention in Dallas (December 1997). My 100- and 200-meter training has been greatly influenced by discussions I had with Mel Rosen, Track Coach Emeritus at Auburn University, at the 1999 USTCA Convention.

Finally, thanks to all the coaches who have been my assistants, the numerous high school boys and girls at Fennimore and Naperville North High Schools in Illinois, and the men of the University of Wisconsin at La Crosse track and field program who embraced the coaching methods and who are responsible for the success that has allowed me to be in a position to share this material with others.

INTRODUCTION

*C*oaching Track & Field Successfully is a compilation of shared ideas and original concepts based on a foundation of scientific, physiological, and kinesthetic knowledge. The ideas and concepts are presented in a user-friendly format for beginning, intermediate, and advanced coaches. With time management always a concern, there is a need for an informational coaching tool that enhances the coach's knowledge and presents an efficient and effective way of teaching the various skills to the student-athlete.

It is important to note that although there is not a panacea or quick fix to success, *Coaching Track & Field Successfully* provides information that, through commitment, intelligent training, and effort, will help your athletes perform at improved levels. These techniques and methods are adaptable to various climates, facilities, and equipment resources. A coach's ability to think outside the box and put forth an enthusiastic, motivational, and fun program will go a long way in increasing participation, which will result in success at the individual and team levels.

This book covers recruiting talent, establishing a philosophy, managing meets, planning practices and training cycles, utilizing staff members, coaching event techniques, correcting common errors, planning successful competition tactics, and motivating and mentally preparing athletes for competition.

The chapters that follow are presented by coaches who have been involved in the track and field program at the University of Wisconsin at La Crosse, which is one of the most successful NCAA Division III programs in the nation. The individual and team successes at UW-La Crosse are the result of the coaching techniques of several outstanding coaches. These techniques, described in this book, develop fine athletes from various levels of talent. This wealth of knowledge and its application are shared in these pages.

Part 1

COACHING FOUNDATION

Chapter 1

DEVELOPING A COACHING PHILOSOPHY

The coaching philosophy you choose is central to how you define your career and how your team functions in practices and competitive situations. The coaching philosophy is the foundation of your program; it not only guides you and your staff, but it also sets the stage for the athletes on your team. It leads them to assume responsibility for their own actions and decisions, and it encourages them to meet the expectations that affect them as individual athletes and as an entire team.

As a young coach, you will create a dynamic philosophy that will continue to evolve throughout your career until such time as you are comfortable and confident with the way you make decisions for your team. Your coaching philosophy inevitably is shaped by the experiences you gain working with different athletes in various situations. Ultimately, your philosophy comprises the values you hold in highest regard and the ones you are comfortable sharing with and teaching to the athletes that make up your team. One such value may be that the actions of one individual can affect the entire team. For example, if one relay member misses one or more practices, the athlete's absence can not only negatively affect the remaining three athletes in practice, but it may also affect the entire team. If the absence causes the relay to drop the baton during an exchange, the team may therefore lose points in a meet.

Most young people function from an individual perspective as opposed to a group perspective; this provides a teaching opportunity for the coach. The values that coaches teach may be few or numerous, but they almost always include such concepts as being on time, working as a group, accepting responsibility, and being good citizens. In short, your philosophy is composed of the same values that govern your own life; therefore, they are easy to teach and easy to use on

a daily basis. If you try to become someone that you are not or if you adopt someone else's values, you will have a difficult time representing foreign values in your own actions.

Perhaps the most significant difference in the philosophy of a track and field coach versus that of a coach in a more traditional team sport is that in track and field, an athlete can have measurable, quantitative success individually. These individual successes have to be viewed in terms of how they affect the total team performance. For example, you can easily have three or four athletes that are outstanding in one or two events but still have a losing team result. As a track and field coach, your ability to orchestrate, or blend, the egos and accomplishments of individual athletes will be an important ingredient of your philosophy. Coaches of traditional team sports, on the other hand, usually base their coaching philosophies on the performance of the athletes functioning as a unit. For example, to be successful, all 11 players in football must execute their portion of the play correctly. If one of the 11 athletes fails in his performance, it could directly affect the success of the whole team.

An Evolving Philosophy

As with most coaches, my philosophy evolved from the experiences I had as an athlete and as a coach as well as through conversations with coaches at clinics or private meetings.

A cornerstone of my philosophy on how to interact with athletes came from an experience I had while in high school. Following an indoor meet my senior year at which I did not perform well—having thrown about four feet below my personal best in the shot put—my head coach came to where I was sitting in the back of the bus and began to berate and cajole me in front of my teammates for my poor performance. My coach embarrassed and humiliated me with his words and demeanor, and more important, I was already upset with my performance because I had let my teammates down. I did not need someone to reinforce that I had failed; instead, I needed someone to reassure me. I needed someone to tell me that although the performance was not acceptable, I could learn from it and be a better thrower in the future. This experience (and others like it with this coach) shaped my own coaching philosophy. I can now separate the emotional reaction to a negative performance and turn it into a teachable moment—or, in the case of an outstanding performance, I can use that emotion for immediate positive feedback to the athlete. This experience also taught me the importance of communicating with athletes in a one-on-one setting. Athletes know when they have not met your expectations and their own. They do not need someone to climb all over them at that time; instead, they need someone to address the fact that they did not perform up to expectations and to help them learn from that performance and avoid the same result in the future. This experience, as well as others, helped to define how I would deal with athletes in my program.

I probably have learned the most and built much of my philosophy around the knowledge that I have gained from my association with Joe Newton, the legendary track and cross country coach at York High School in Elmhurst, IL. Coach Newton also has the ability to break the tension at the appropriate times to allow for personal rapport with his team, while earning their respect at the same time.

As a result of the time I spent with Coach Newton, I had the opportunity to meet and learn from other great coaches, such as John Davis, the longtime track coach at Glenbrook South High School, who taught me about meet management, organization, and professionalism as a head track coach. His enthusiasm and devotion to the sport of track and field—and more important, to the young people he interacted with—provided me with a model for how to conduct myself at all times. John always had a positive comment for both the outstanding athletes as well as the journeymen on his team. They each received reinforcement and praise for their efforts. My association with the Keebler Prep International Track Meet allowed me a firsthand view of John's organizational and management skills.

While serving as the head track and field coach for boys and girls at Naperville North High School, I had some access to Al Carius, the cross country and track coach at North Central College. He shared with me how to incorporate fun into sport and how to allow this fun to evolve into a passion for the sport, thereby helping athletes attain lofty goals. Coach Carius showed me the value of allowing the development of all athletes, and he also showed me the importance of cultivating alumni as fans and a source of financial support for a program.

Paul Olson, the coach at Augustana College in Rock Island, Illinois, is blessed with the gift of youthful enthusiasm, which enables a coach to remain excited about the sport. Paul will be the first to tell you that his enthusiasm is a God-given gift, but I also firmly believe that he continues to grow and nurture that gift on a daily basis. During my tenure at University of Wisconsin (La Crosse), I have had numerous opportunities to observe Paul in action. No matter what his day is like or what his condition is, he continues to motivate his athletes through this enthusiasm. It may come in the form of a positive comment, a humorous gesture, or a quietly shared moment that has a lesson in it. His enthusiasm is authentic, and it draws his current athletes and alumni to him, much like steel to a magnet.

Dr. Phil Esten, the former head cross country coach at the University of Wisconsin (La Crosse), taught me to think "out of the box" to reduce competitive stress and to employ strategies that allow for success at the most important meet of the year. Phil could always see the big picture or goal. He had the ability to make strategic decisions regarding training and racing so that his athletes were placed in a position to be successful when it most mattered. He was willing to concede something small so that the big prize at the end of the season was attainable. On a more practical note, he also shared with me the details that are involved with hosting major invitational meets or championship contests.

Sometimes we are too close to the edge of the forest; we often need to step back and view a situation from different perspectives so that we can assist the athlete and the team in attaining their seasonal goals. Phil was a master of being able to do this. He was willing to train his athletes through the conference and NCAA regional meets, but he only raced them once every 14 days. He did this to put them into a position to run at their best at the national championships. His plan was rarely understood by his contemporaries, who often tried to win every meet. But once the national meet came, Coach Esten's methodology became clear. His athletes always came together to run the best team-race of the season. I believe this maturity in coaching allowed him to attain the success he enjoyed at the national level.

There are some consistent principles that go into creating your own coaching philosophy, whether you are coaching track and field or another sport:

✓ Be yourself.

✓ Define your coaching objectives.

✓ Establish rules.

✓ Build and nurture relationships with athletes.

✓ Be organized.

✓ Involve your assistant coaches.

✓ Help athletes manage their goals.

✓ Help athletes manage their stress.

✓ Focus on the big picture.

BE YOURSELF

Most coaches have incorporated information into their own program that they have picked up from colleagues, clinics, videos, printed materials, or the experiences they have had as athletes with their own coaches. While continuing to collect and use this information is a valuable part of remaining current in the sport, it is important that you meld it into your existing coaching philosophy in such a way that your athletes see your approach as a cohesive whole. Young people are very observant, and they can quickly detect if you are being a phony. To build the relationships needed to be a successful coach, you must be yourself so that your athletes can accept and believe in your approach.

Over the years, I have adjusted my coaching philosophy based on the experiences I have had in my life. The largest change that I've incorporated into my coaching philosophy is that track and field (or any sport) is not the paramount focus of life. For example, while winning a national championship is important to the athletes, their families, and the school, I often remind them that there are millions of people in the United States who don't even know that this event is taking place, let alone that we have won the championship. This singular example shows them that there is a great deal more to life and life's issues than winning a track and field championship, which is why being a good citizen, developing a work ethic, and caring for members of society are ultimately more important than this brief moment of success. As I have aged and been blessed with family and children, I have learned that valuable lesson.

Exude Confidence

While no track coach, especially the head coach, is all-knowing, he or she must have a general understanding of each of the various track and field events and must develop expertise in only a few of these events. However, the confidence with which you approach all aspects of your job is critical. When assistant coaches know that you are supportive of them and their efforts and that you do not challenge or criticize them in front of their athletes, they coach with greater confidence and are willing to take more initiative and responsibility within the program.

Perhaps it takes more confidence to address the areas in which you have less knowledge versus those in which you have a great deal of knowledge. In either case, if you are uncertain about the information you are sharing, your tentative style will be noticed—and it won't be embraced by your team. If they detect that you are unsure of yourself, they will question your methods and may undermine your leadership capabilities. Therefore, make sure that you are comfortable in all aspects of your program: rules, philosophy, training concepts, and the interaction that you have with your team, parents, and staff. If you can do that, your leadership will be accepted with greater confidence and support.

Stay Calm

Your ability to retain an even temperament in all situations—especially the most critical ones that occur in the competitive setting—demonstrates to your team that they can have confidence in your plan. Even when things are

Time spent building a rapport with your athletes at practices will pay off throughout the season.

not going as expected, your composure can convince them that they will see success if they continue with what they have been taught. Even in daily encounters, your ability to retain focus and work through situations earns you the respect of your athletes, which in turn strengthens their belief in your philosophy.

Be an Example

As the leader, you must exemplify in your own life those traits that you expect to have your athletes follow. You must be positive yourself in order to have your athletes think and act positively. In other words, you need to consistently act in a positive and professional manner at all times. You cannot turn these traits on and off and expect your athletes not to notice the inconsistencies and then question your sincerity when dealing with them.

Your personal, daily grooming habits and dress, along with your punctuality, also send a message as to how you expect your team to act. While in season, our athletes are expected to present a positive image in their actions, appearance, and dress. Members of any athletic team are more visible and are therefore held to higher moral standards than the regular student body. Their appearance and behavior are always under scrutiny, and as a result, fair or not, how they look, dress, and act constitutes the perception that people will form of them. It was once said that perception is 90 percent of reality. That is the very reason that we as coaches need to talk to our athletes about how they should dress when they are both at practice and in public, how they should act when they are in a public setting, and how they should talk when they can easily be overheard.

In keeping with the example I set as a coach,

I hold people accountable for their punctuality, or lack thereof. For example, I have started meetings without people if they were late, and I have left athletes and coaches stranded if they were not where they should be on time. These acts signify to everyone on the team that they are all equal and that regardless of their status or talent, there are no excuses for being late. Someone's inability to be on time can have a negative impact on a team, especially if it happens at a critical time. If that time happens to be when the team leaves for a meet, it can affect the overall outcome of an event or the eventual team score. I find that placing such expectations on athletes and coaches in addition to leading by your own example assist in team building as well.

DEFINE YOUR OBJECTIVES

There are many forms of objectives, and yours can be either brief or in-depth. They can be team-oriented, seasonal in nature, and in the case of you and your staff, individualized.

Objectives are like goals; they are a road map for you to follow to your destination. These objectives involve all aspects of your daily programming, training, competition scheduling, motivation of athletes, and the direction of your program. Some of these objectives should be designed and outlined by you, while others may be a collaborative effort that draws on the knowledge of your assistant coaches and, in some cases, the input of your athletes. As with goals, your objectives need to be attainable, measurable, and practical. Each year presents a fresh start for setting objectives. You need to evaluate the past year, the current talent, and what the goals of the student-athletes are for this season. You can have a long-range plan for yourself and your staff, but you should focus on what the team can accomplish during the current season. A cookie-cutter approach is not available to us as coaches. In fact, this is where the real coaching begins. Each situation, staff, and team is unique and therefore should be considered in defining the objectives you are trying to attain.

Track and field offers the unique ability to challenge athletes with different body types, various speed abilities and strength levels, and a variety of interests through the many events our sport includes. The sport allows the development and individual success of lower, moderate, and highly skilled athletes throughout their time on the team. Anyone who is willing to follow the rules, attend practice, and do the things required to enhance their current skill level can leave the program with some degree of individual success.

However, with competition comes the emphasis on winning; therefore, coaches find themselves at a crossroads. They must decide whether to focus on developing a large team that emphasizes participation and individual improvement, or to focus on elite talent that can win at the dual meet, invitational, conference, and state level. Coaches then need to consider the following questions: Does the program focus on large participation numbers, or (once some success has been established) does the program focus on the accomplishments of the elite athletes and on state championships?

I am a strong proponent of stressing large participation numbers, especially at the junior and high school levels, since many youngsters develop at significantly different rates. In addition, success in dual, triangular, and conference championship meets still requires team depth.

An important by-product of having larger numbers of athletes is that it provides more opportunity for athletes to experiment and migrate to events they are comfortable with or interested in. Some simply need the time to develop the strength or skills necessary to have some measure of success in a particular event.

Your ability to manage or orchestrate the athletes can produce continued success if you allow developing athletes to step out of the shadows of the better athletes at dual meets. For example, if your dual meets do not count toward your conference championship and if you are running two meets per week, you can hold out your top two athletes per event. Doing so allows the next level of athletes to represent the school, have the chance to score points for your team, and gain experience. In the process, they also strengthen their self-confidence while giving the other athletes a chance to rest so that they are ready for the upcoming invitational meet. Another by-product of this scheduling format is that it allows for one more practice day per week for all of your athletes, which can be significant over the course of a 12-week season. In other words, your team gets 12 more practices and 12 fewer stressful situations. When the important meets at the conclusion of the season arrive, you and your staff are more prepared than your competition. All of your athletes are more rested, and you've given more athletes experience competing. You can also allow your top athletes to use dual meets to compete in their second or off event, without triggering additional and unnecessary stress.

If you decide to approach your objectives by focusing only on your most elite athletes, you dramatically reduce your developmental program, and you force yourself to make sure that you have outstanding athletes every year. This feat can be effectively accomplished by assigning certain coaches to work with each level of athlete or by splitting practice times such that different portions of your team report at different times within the practice time window. Another option is to intentionally reduce the overall size of your varsity squad to allow more one-on-one coaching opportunities for your athletes. Focusing on a smaller group of athletes does not allow you to absorb the effects of an injury, but it does provide more one-on-one experience for each athlete and allows for more repetitions during practice in the field and technical events. Usually, you will find less concern from your athletes about being neglected than when you are dealing with larger numbers. If this is your desired style, my recommendation is to compete only once per week. Fewer meets are beneficial because your athletes are asked to contribute more at each meet, which increases their stress levels.

In general, I recommend that as the athletes mature and improve, the teams should move from larger numbers to smaller, more focused groups of athletes. For instance, junior high and high school teams retain larger numbers while college and postcollegiate programs evolve to smaller numbers with more elite athletes.

ESTABLISH RULES

The rules that your team needs to adhere to daily should reflect what you are the most comfortable with. In short, you as the coach must be able to believe in these rules in order to follow and enforce them. Generally, the older the athletes are, the more of an adult approach you can use when dealing with issues in this area. This applies in direct proportion to the age of the athletes you coach. At a junior high or high school level, it is very important for the head coach to have more of a my-way-or-the-highway style with the athletes and provide more direct supervision than he or she would with collegiate athletes. The junior high and high school years are important in assisting the development of the maturity that these young people can refer to as they become young adults and professionals.

At the college level, I have found that both the my-way-or-the-highway and the shared-responsibility styles can be used successfully by coaches. The shared-responsibility style involves a dialogue between the athlete and the head coach before the start of each season. The dialogue outlines how each athlete on the team is held accountable for following the rules, and it defines what is acceptable behavior. I have used this method throughout my career, and it is the one I feel more comfortable with and the one I implement. Since college athletes are (ideally) more mature and focused on their athletic careers, this approach can be very successful and can assist in the transition between college competition and a professional career, which are separated by only one to five years.

It is important to avoid covering too much in a single meeting with the athlete or team. If team rules are the major topic, don't integrate another aspect into that meeting. Make sure that the message you want to share is heard and not lost among the clutter as a result of the number of topics you discuss.

Present your rules in writing at the beginning of the season so that there is no misunderstanding as to what the rules are. Once the rules have been presented to the athletes, it is crucial that you enforce them, no matter what the circumstances or which athlete is in violation. Many coaches have a certain softness for the young people we work with; however, my experiences have shown that you must not waiver in following your team rules, regardless of the "extenuating" circumstances athletes or parents challenge you with. Bending your rules—even once—opens the door for continued challenges and exceptions. Once this situation evolves, your credibility as the leader of the program is compromised, and it becomes difficult to lead, motivate, and discipline your athletes.

Throughout your coaching career, you will make adjustments or improvements to your philosophy. However, you should maintain a similar theme from year to year so that your returning athletes have a comfort zone with you and know generally what to expect. For example, you don't want to have mandatory attendance one year (as a prerequisite for an athlete to be able to compete), then follow that up the next year with no attendance policy at all. If you make drastic changes each year, your returning athletes—who can help promote your program to the younger athletes—will have no basis from which to assist in this process.

When creating your team's rules, keep a few of thoughts in mind.

1. Are your rules reasonable?
2. Does the punishment fit the crime?
3. Are the rules and the punishment defensible and consistent with your school's disciplinary code?
4. Do the rules cover attendance, dress code, substance abuse, and facility usage?
5. Do the rules support your team's objectives?

Once the rules have been established and accepted, it is important to have the student-athletes and their parents or guardians read and sign off on them. Table 1.1 on pages 12-13 shows an example of our team rules.

BUILD AND NURTURE RELATIONSHIPS

While we don't all have degrees in psychology and human relations, it is important to develop successful coach-athlete relationships. Athletes need to feel comfortable in approaching you without concern for reprisal, and they need to know that the information shared remains private. Once a positive relationship based on trust is established, you have a greater insight into what makes each athlete succeed and fail, and you have a better ability to motivate and assist all your athletes in attaining their goals.

One common concern athletes have is whether they are being dealt with fairly. When athletes have a concern or issue, they want to know that they can come to you and that their conversations remain confidential. Properly addressing these simple concerns goes a long way toward establishing positive relationships. From your handling of these concerns and conversations, they will know that you have their best interests in mind. Have conversations regarding aspects of their lives away from track and field, such as their outside interests or how they are doing in school. In general, show a sincere interest in them.

An important aspect of your relationships with your athletes is the extent to which you recognize and acknowledge their success. Track and field is a quantifiable endeavor because we are always dealing with an athlete's performance in terms of time, distance, or height. These numerical measurements are most often used to define success, and they are useful for establishing goals and determining when a goal has been attained. However, there is another type of success, separate from numerical measurements, and it is much more difficult to measure. That success is based on the experience that these young people have while participating in your program. Its criteria include how you have been able to assist them in their overall growth and development as a person. While this is not as easily measured and while this is the hardest to teach, it is the one that endures the longest.

BE ORGANIZED

The ability to organize is essential to any head or assistant coach, whatever the sport. These skills apply to all aspects of the sport—from recruiting and retaining athletes to devising daily practice procedures; from creating a competition schedule to developing a training program; as well as managing a meet, making travel arrangements, and assigning responsibilities to your assistant coaches. Allow yourself a long enough period of time (before the start of the season) to establish, review, and reconsider these organizational components. Have a daily plan of tasks that need to be accomplished and an order in which the tasks should be completed. Many professionals use a daily planner to set up their day and week. Once you get into a routine, it is much easier to complete tasks. You also need to plan the future so that you know what is coming and what the timeline will be. We all have daily, weekly, monthly, and seasonal tasks. Get them down in writing, and lay out a plan that includes due dates. Allow plenty of time within your plan for the unforeseeable situations that invariably come up and demand your attention. You can obtain examples of organizational methods by talking with other coaches or attending clinics.

INVOLVE YOUR ASSISTANT COACHES

Your assistant coaches are a valuable resource . . . so use them. I recommend that they become involved in as many aspects of the total program philosophy as you feel comfortable with. Assign them specific tasks for which they will be responsible. They can save you, the head coach, significant time when you allow them to use their expertise on a daily basis. Before the start of each season, I identify these responsibilities and outline the form or way I want them accomplished with my staff. This allows them time to prepare for their assignments and to provide feedback and improvements. We also meet weekly as a coaching staff for a minimal amount of time to cover any concerns, questions, or details on how we will deal with a specific issue or situation.

HELP MANAGE YOUR ATHLETES' STRESS

Today's athletes are under increasing stress, both in their athletic and nonathletic lives. There is a tremendous amount of pressure placed on being effective and efficient, meeting everyone's needs, and still having a winning team. Student-athletes try to meet the demands of their parents, teachers, coaches, and relationships with their peer groups. Seldom does a day go by when I don't have an athlete stop in my office with some concern about what is going on in his or her life.

To address those issues, I try to have an open-door policy and talk with them, not as a coach or parent, but as a sounding board where they can vent their frustrations. My office is also a place where they can seek some assistance, whether it comes directly from me or from a referral who can be of more help. This works especially well with collegiate athletes, but it can also be effective with high school athletes if the coach-athlete relationship is a safe haven for them. I am sure that initially, most high school athletes will be uncomfortable approaching a coach if the topic may be confrontational. However, if they feel secure that they can have an open discussion without negative consequences, I believe that in time they will become comfortable talking about important issues with you.

I try to be relaxed, and I also try to interject humor whenever possible during practice sessions to keep the day light and up-tempo. In meet situations, I share the importance of a particular meet, and I explain to them that

Table 1.1 Sample Track and Field Team Policies and Procedures

A. Practices

1. Indoor and outdoor practices will be held as outlined by your event coach.
2. All athletes are expected to be on time.
3. If you can't practice as a result of an injury, report to the training room for treatment, then report back to your event coach.
4. If you can't complete a **full practice** two days before a meet, you will not compete in that meet. However, if it is a home meet, you will be **required** to work.
5. The only acceptable absences from practices are scheduled classes, injury, illness (must call event coach), or a family emergency (call head coach). All other absences are considered unexcused and will result in missing that week's meet, with a maximum of two such occurrences for the season.
6. Any athlete participating in a postseason outdoor meet must attend four days of practice before that meet.
7. In-season strength training is mandatory. To be eligible to compete in a meet, you must have four stamps on your weight-training card.

B. Alcohol and drugs

Track and field team members must refrain from the following:

1. Possession, consumption, purchase, or sale of tobacco products.
2. Possession, consumption, or purchase of alcohol.
3. Possession, consumption, or purchase of steroids or other controlled substances, look-alike drugs, or drug related paraphernalia.
4. Theft, possession of stolen property, or vandalism.
5. Acts of violence, or other acts considered unlawful in this or any other jurisdiction.
6. Attending a function where there is underage drinking of alcohol or use of steroids, other illegal drugs, or look-alike drugs.
7. Sale, distribution of, or providing location for the illegal consumption of controlled substances or alcohol. (Such a violation will carry a 3rd offense penalty).
8. Hazing in any athletic/activity program or outside the program.
9. Harassment in any athletic/activity program or outside the program.

Possession in numbers 2 and 3 is considered to be any presence while illegal transportation or consumption is taking place. This code is in effect 7 days a week, 12 months a year, in season or out of season, whether school is in session or not.

NOTE: It is the obligation of the student to give notice to the school administration within 7 calendar days if civil authorities are involved with a Participation Code violation. Violations of the above are considered together in terms of determining 1st, 2nd, and 3rd levels of discipline, and are cumulative over a student's high school career.

Penalty for first offense: Suspension from cocurricular participation in **four** regularly scheduled contests. If the season does not allow the participant to successfully complete the suspension, the suspension will carry over to the next season in which participation occurs. No awards will be given until the suspension is completed. The participant may be required to practice with his or her team during this period of suspension. If the violation occurs out of season, the suspension may be satisfied by doing work assigned by the administrator in charge. Twenty hours of work will satisfy a first offense suspension.

Note 1: Self-admission of any behavior that could be construed as a violation of the code prior to the knowledge of civil or school authorities may result in the penalty for a first offense being waived. The purpose of this option is to provide a mechanism by which the student can receive assistance.

Note 2: Self-admission of a violation where the student has been involved with civil authorities and prior to the schools knowledge, may be satisfied by 20 hours of community service as approved by the administrator in charge.

Note 3: The penalty for a first offense may be reduced by one-half if the student and parent(s) participate in an assessment program approved by the school's Student Assistance Coordinator and the results of the assessment are released to the Student Assistance Coordinator.

Penalty for second offense: Suspension from cocurricular participation for **nine** regularly scheduled competitions of the next regular season of participation, or the current season. The participant must practice with his or her team during this period of suspension. If less than half of the regular season remains, this will result in dismissal from the team. The participant may not compete or practice and will receive no school award. The participant will remain suspended from interscholastic competition or activity for the balance of the suspension remaining from the season during which the violation occurred.

Penalty for third and subsequent offenses: Participant is suspended from cocurricular participation for one calendar year.

C. Equipment

1. All school equipment checked out to you becomes your responsibility. Theft, loss, or damage to the equipment will result in your paying for those lost, stolen, or damaged items in full before your participation in any more meets.

   Replacement costs

Racing top	$20.00	Warm-up	$40.00
Meet shorts	$14.00	Travel bag	$45.00
Tights	$20.00		

   Damaged items will be dealt with on an individual basis. All other equipment will be billed at its current replacement cost.

2. Uniforms and sweats will be checked out the first week of practice and returned on the Monday following the final meet. A late fee of $2.00 per item will be charged per day.

D. Travel

Travel to and from scheduled away competitions will be by the means arranged by the athletic department. All other modes of transportation are at the discretion of the head coach or his designee. Return by another means than that scheduled by the institution may be allowed, but only with a signed parental release form issued by the head coach before the date of travel.

E. Poor sporting behavior

1. This conduct will not be condoned. Your immediate removal from the meet will take place. If the conduct took place in your final event of that competition, you will be held out of the next meet. If the meet is at home, you will be required to work that meet.

2. A second offense in the same year will be grounds for removal from all remaining meets.

3. Examples of inappropriate conduct include swearing, throwing of items, inappropriate gestures, and so on.

F. Team meetings

Your attendance is **required.**

G. Team huddles

1. All team members will be at premeet huddles 10 minutes before the first event. Failure to attend will result in penalty.

2. All team members will be at postmeet huddles and will not depart the facility for any reason until released following these huddles.

3. This requirement is the same at home or away.

Outline specific responsibilities for each member of your coaching staff at the start of the season; in this way each coach can bring his or her own strengths to the coaching team.

what we are about to do is important to them, their families, and their friends. Then I remind them that in the larger scope of life, it really isn't that big a deal. The ability to manage stress and anxiety in critical situations can allow for some great performances and positive results for your athletes.

Usually in high-stress situations, I try to downplay the importance of the event. I place the meet in comparison with the size of the United States and how many people really know or care that this competition is taking place. I also try and relax them a little by joking with them. In some cases, I simply wish them good luck, well in advance of the start of their event, then leave them alone. Remember, just because it is a major event, don't overcoach or overanalyze it!

As the coach and leader, it is important to

not make every contest the *big* meet of the year. I have found that one can really only go to the well a couple of times during the season, both emotionally and physically—so let them have some fun. Approach some of your meets with a relaxed atmosphere . . . it just may pay off when you need it the most.

FOCUS ON THE BIG PICTURE

I have been asked at various times, "What do you coach?" My response varies. Sometimes I say, "Students." Other times, I say, "Athletes," or "Student-athletes," or "Young people." It's not what I coach; it's who I coach. This perspective is too often lost, but it highlights what we really do in the coaching profession. We have been charged with coaching a sport, made up of young men and women who have an interest in a particular event. This allows us a window of opportunity not afforded to the average classroom teacher, simply because of the amount of time we spend with athletes, the emotional highs and lows we share with them, and the number of personal issues that we discuss with them under the assurance of confidentiality.

This opportunity allows for personal growth and maturity that has a positive impact on athletes' lives long after the final gun has sounded and the last time recorded. This is the real mission of a coach . . . the molding of productive young people who can be a positive part of our society. Without a doubt, winning can be a fantastic experience, and losing can be a great motivator. But it is the lifelong lessons that your athletes take with them that determine the real winners and who has done the best coaching job.

Chapter 2

COMMUNICATING YOUR APPROACH

Communication is the lifeline of any successful undertaking, and the same is true at all levels of track and field. Student-athletes need to hear one clear vision for the season, and they need to know what the daily expectations are as members of your program. You must be able to communicate your philosophy and plan to the administration, as well, so that they have a clear understanding of how you lead the program. You also need to communicate in a concise and clear manner the expectations and responsibilities of your coaching staff. Staff need to be provided with the appropriate information so that they can support your philosophy and so that they become the conduit between the athletes and you. Finally, the parents need to receive the same information so that they feel comfortable in having their son or daughter become a member of your team.

Your ability to share this information with all of these groups without doubt, concern, and misunderstanding goes a long way in eliminating potential problems throughout the season. Since coaching is nothing more than building relationships and trust, your ability to communicate must receive careful attention as you put your plan together.

WITH STUDENT-ATHLETES

It is primary that you focus on improving your communication with your athletes, both in team meetings and practice settings, as well as one-on-one situations. Communicating with your athletes consistently, frequently, and personably goes a long way in building good relationships.

Hold a Preseason Meeting

For the most part, athletes come to a team with enthusiasm, with a desire for success in their event as well as a search for discipline and camaraderie with the team. As the head coach, the first priority in communicating with your athletes is to clearly outline what expectations you have of them, what your coaching philosophy is, and what the rules are with which you will govern the team (see "Establish Rules" in chapter 1). It is important to share with your athletes that all discipline is equally enforced. If you communicate these rules and consequences at a preseason meeting, your athletes will know that they will all be treated fairly and equally. Deviating from equal enforcement of the rules creates tension and turmoil within any group and may derail the entire season. So be sure that this is out in the open from day one.

Create a Winners' Council

After the preseason meeting in which the rules and expectations of athletes are communicated, one of the next early-season steps I take to facilitate communication within the team is to create a leadership group called the "Winners' Council," led by the captains and inclusive of all age groups on the team. The

One-on-one preseason meetings with each athlete provide an opportunity to discuss the individual goals—short term and long term—each athlete is reaching for.

delegates are selected by a vote of the entire team, with the seniors voting only for their senior representative, the juniors for their junior representative, and so on. I recommend a total committee size of five to eight athletes: four athletes (selected by the team as just described) and one to three captains. This council provides a way for athletes to share concerns with the coaching staff without placing any one individual in an uncomfortable situation. The team can ask questions of the council members that they may need clarification on or are uncomfortable coming to the coach with. The coaches can pass information through the council to share with the team members so that it may be received more openly or in a less threatening manner. If your team is a junior high team or if it is made up of younger athletes, you may wish to limit their involvement and supervise the council more closely than you would with older athletes.

The Winners' Council can also organize team involvement in fun-day activities and provide input on uniform designs, team T-shirts, and possible meets they would like to participate in. This small involvement goes a long way in helping to make team members feel that this really is "their" team and not entirely the coaches' team. We coaches have already had our time as athletes. It is now time for us to remember that this is their experience and that we are now the facilitators in helping our athletes to achieve some measure of success through track and field.

Communicate Daily

In addition to establishing a Winners' Council early in the season, it is important for coaches to maintain daily communication between themselves and their athletes. This daily communication can take many forms, but it must take place regularly to provide and update information relative to daily practices, to acknowledge performances or new records, to share information about an upcoming meet (i.e., departure time, the meet lineup, order of events, and time schedule), or to let athletes know they need to stop in and talk with you before practice.

Stretching Check-In

I use a team stretch to start practice. During this time, I like to move around and talk with the athletes, and when I do, the topics are on anything but sports. This is time for me to get to know them on a more social level. I also encourage assistant coaches to join the "walk-around." At the end of the group stretch, I deal with important announcements for the day, which have also been posted on the announcement board in the locker room. I allow time for questions, then I end the huddle with the "Joke of the Day," where an athlete has the opportunity to share a tasteful joke with the team.

Before the start of practice and at anytime during the day, my door is open for one-on-one conversation to take place with any athlete who has any concerns. Individual formal meetings are used on a per-situation basis and are conducted privately. My coaches and I also meet with athletes in their event groups from time to time to review their goals with them and provide some instruction if they are becoming frustrated with their progress.

Communicating during a practice or competition is different, but the teaching cues should remain the same, and they should be simple. In other words, the best method is still the KISS method—Keep It Simple, Stupid. Trying to correct too many errors or trying to teach too much at a given session only clouds the message you are trying to share. Most athletes cannot process numerous pieces of information in an error-correction mode during a competition. As the coach, it is your responsibility to identify the most important point and share only that point with them. Too much information can lead to "paralysis through analysis." Positive support and encouragement is one of the most important things you can provide an athlete during a competition. Postpractice and competition meetings are situations where you can address concerns in a lengthy manner.

If you need to have a conversation with an

athlete that may make him or her uncomfortable, select your words carefully. Do not place athletes in situations that humiliate them, and don't make them uncomfortable in front of their peers.

Various forms of this communication can involve daily exchanges at practice, notes or e-mail messages that communicate a positive message, or bulletin-board materials that honor or highlight accomplishments for everyone to see. I recommend keeping at least one bulletin board in your locker room area for daily details such as announcements, posting of lineups, workouts, practice plans, meet and travel information, status of letter points, fun-day activities, and meetings (see figure 2.1, a-e, for some examples).

UW-La Crosse Men's Track and Field

Meet: Bearcat Open
Date: Friday, May 11, 2001
Site: North Central College
Load: Van #1 - 9:15 A.M. Van #2 & 3 - 11:45 A.M.
Leave: Van #1 - 9:30 A.M. Van #2 & 3 - 12:00 P.M.

Van #1: Buchholtz (DR) - Kuntz - Wallace - McMullen - Haas - Brown - Wittleder - Lori Meyer
Van #2: Nykamp (DR) - Raisbeck - Berge - Yarbrough - Ansley - Bottorff - Stakston - Pentek
Van #3: Krahulik (DR) - Guthrie - Tutskey - Lantzy - Peter - Foos - Tomrell - Losinski

Time	Event	Athletes
1:00 P.M.	Discus	Andy Stewart
5:00 P.M.	Shot Put	Tim Amann
	110 HH	Josh Wallace
	4 x 100	
	1500	Josh Bottorff
	100	Dave Pentek
	400 IH	Jason Haas - Charlie Wittleder
	400	Kevin Yarbrough - Ryan Losinski
	800	Nick Ansley
	200	Dan Tutskey - Dave Pentek
	Steeple	P.J. Lantzy - Tony Peter
	4 x 400	Jesse Reed - Jason Haas - Charlie Wittleder - Kevin Yarbrough
	5000	Tyler Foos - Jason Tomrell
	10,000	Justin Stakston

This is a Rolling Schedule

Notes:
1) Bring sport drink, refueling snacks, healthy food.
2) Bring your own towels, locks, soap, shampoo, spikes (1/4"), uniform, sweats, trainers.
3) Be prepared for various weather conditions—make sure you have **warm clothes as well as sunscreen and rain gear.**
4) Bring batons, poles, implements, tape measures, chalk, carrying cases, etc.

Make sure you stay out of the sun (when that is an issue) and drink plenty of fluids!

Figure 2.1a   We post the upcoming meet schedule on the team bulletin boards to let athletes know the departure times, event schedule, and athletes participating.

Long and Triple Jump Workouts

Date: _____
Team Meeting: Room:_____ Time:_____
_____Pick Up Uniforms Today
_____Return Uniforms Today

Warm-Up Drills (All drills to be done twice—each leg.)
__High knees __Butt kicks __Paw-skip __FTD's *(small)
__Extended FTD's __Skip for height
__Skip for distance __Goose steps (triple jumpers only)

Box Drills
__Run-paw-run-paw on 6" boxes at 10' apart (alternate legs)
__Hop-hop-hop drill on __" box for frosh and __" box for vets
__FTDs at __', __', __', frosh __" and vets __" boxes
__Knee-up drill stepping up onto a 15" box (with partner)
__Hop into step on __" box and jump into high-jump pit
__6" box to 12" box jump into high-jump pit
__Toe-toe-toe-flat-flat from __" box into pit

Ground Drills
__Arm motion drill for triple jump
__Mini triple jumps
__Hop-step-hop-step…
__Hop-step-step-hop-step-step…
__Goose-goose-hop-step-goose-goose-hop-step-goose…

Running Workout
__Report with the short 400 group today
__Single-file run (last person sprints to front) over __meters of running
__Sled pulls over __meters with __ % of BW
__Meter accelerations or straights and curves
__Meters at :__with _____rest between sets
__(Stadium/Mitchell) steps with :__between sets
__Timed runs through zones (outdoor season only)
__Cheese wedges
__Declining cheese wedges
__Cheese wedges with a lunge walk back
__Run-throughs checking the board

*FTD's are bounding drills in which the athlete pushes off from the toes

Notes:

Figure 2.1b We also post daily workouts for each event group on the team.

400 Meters

Date: _____
Team Meeting: Room:_____ Time: _____
_____Pick Up Uniforms Today
_____Return Uniforms Today

Warm-up: On reverse side of this form
Main Workout:

___ x 200 @ PR Pace +:0 ,+:0 ,+:0   Rest:_____

___ x 200 @ :___-__:_____ standing rest

___ x 200 @ :___-walk 200, __x____ @ +:___-walk ____-1x 200 @ :____-walk 200

___ x 200 @ :___-walk 200, __ x 320 FAST -15:00 walk - ____ -3 x 200 :27 - 5:00 walk

___ x 200 @ :___-walk 10:00, - 1 x 200 @ :___ -walk 200

___ x 200 @ :___-walk 200, 6 x 150 @ +:___-walk back to the start - 1 x 200 @ :___-walk 200

___ x 200 @ :___-walk 200, ___ x 450 @ +: ___-15:00 walk - 3 x 200 @ :___, :___, :___ -3:00 rest

___ x 200 @ :___-walk 200, 3 x 150 @ +:___-walk back to the start - 1 x 200 @ :___-walk 200 - 1 x 320 fast
       - 15:00 walk- 3x200 @ :___ - 5:00 walk

___ x 200 @ :___-walk 200 - 1 x 600-400-200-400-600 @ :38 per 200 - 5:00 walk - 1 x 200 @ :___-200 walk

___ x 150 accel   - 150 walk - ___ x 500 / 450 / 350 @ +:___ - 15:00 / 10:00 walk - 1 x 250 @ +:3-10:00 walk
- 1 x 200 @ +:2-10:00 walk-1 x 200 @ +:7 - 200 walk

___ x 150 accel   - 150 walk -350 fast - 10:00 walk - 3 x 200 @ :___ - 200 walk

___ x 150 accel   - 150 walk -1 x 350 @ +:05- 15:00 walk - 1 x 300 @ +:04-10:00 walk-1x 250 @ +:3-10:00
walk-1 x 200 @ +:2-10:00 walk-1 x 200 @ +:7 - 200 walk

___ x 150 accel   - 150 walk - ___ x 350 @ +:___ - 10:00 walk - 1 x 200 @ :___ -200 walk

___ x 150 accel   - 150 walk - ___ x 300 @ +:___ - 5:00 walk - 1 x 200 @ :___ - 200 walk

___ x 150 accel   - 150 walk - ___ x 300 @ +:___ - 9:00 walk - 3 x 80 meter accels - 3:00 stand

___ x 150 accel   - 150 walk - ___ x 200 @ +:___ - 3:00 walk - 1 x 200 @ +:29 - 200 walk

___ x 150 accel   - 150 walk - ___ x 200 @ +:___ - 3:00 walk - 1 x 450 / 350 @ +:___
       - 15:00 walk - 1 x 200 @ :___ - 200 walk

___ x 150 accel   - 150 walk - ___ x 200 @ +:___ - 3:00 walk - 3 x 300 @ +:___ - 5:00 walk - 1 x 200@ :___
       - 200 walk

___ x 150 accel   - 150 walk - ___ x 200 @ +:___ - 3:00 walk - 1 x 350 @ +:5 - 15:00 walk - 1 x 200 @ :___
       - 200 walk

___ x 150 accel   - 150 walk - ___ x 200 @ +:___ - 2:00 walk - 4 x 150 @ +:___ - 250 walk

___ x 150 accel   - 150 walk - walk back to start

___ x 150 accel   - 150 walk - x 150 @ +:___ - 1:50 walk - 1 x 200 @ :___ - 200 walk

___ x 150 accel   - 150 walk - x 200 @ PR Pace +:0 ,+:0 ,+:0 ,+:0 - 200 walk

___ x 150 accel   - 150 walk - x 200 m - run 5 man relay style @: per man

___ x short hill runs in Myrick Park after the main workout - all recovery is walk down - use the short steep hill

___ x sprint drills (on back of form)

Workout Speeds by Training Groups:							
Indoor PR	Outdoor PR						
47	46						
48	47						
49	48						
50	49						
51	50						
52	51						

Figure 2.1c   Another idea is to post multiple copies of the workout sheet on the board. Athletes can take them and mark their own notes or split times from the session.

Announcements

May 10, 2002

Meet setup will be at 12:00 P.M.
TODAY. . . we need everyone.

1) Ring deposit: I need a deposit of $100 toward your ring by
   TODAY. . . make the check out to: Jostens.

2) Training Room times for Final Exam week:

   2:00—5:30 P.M.

3) Last day for lockers will be: Monday, May 13—unless you
   are qualified for the NCAAs.

Bring Rain Gear For Saturday's Track Meet!

Make sure you report on time to the meet for Saturday...
assignments were sent on Tuesday!

Figure 2.1d   Be sure to print announcements on a color of paper that will stand out on your bulletin board.

2000 Indoor Practice Times

Practice Times	Monday	Tuesday	Wednesday	Thursday	Friday
2:10 P.M. - 3:40 P.M.	Javelin/Discus	Hurdles	Hurdles	Hurdles	
3:10 P.M. - 4:40 P.M.	Long & triple jump Pole vault (4:00-6:00) Shot put (west end) 800/Distance (outside)	High jump Weight throw (east end) Shot put (west end) 800/Distance on track	High jump Weight throw (south end) Shot put (south end) 800/Distance (outside)	High jump Weight throw (west end) Shot put (west end) 800/Distance on track	Shake-out for the entire team at 3:30!
4:45 P.M. - 6:00 P.M.	100-400 Meters Hurdlers running	100-400 Meters Lj/Tj/Hj/Pv Running Hurdlers running	100-400 Meters Hurdlers running	100-400 Meters Lj/Tj/Hj/Pv Running Hurdlers running	Team meeting as posted on calendar.

2000 Outdoor Practice Times

Practice Times	Monday	Tuesday	Wednesday	Thursday	Friday
2:10 P.M. - 4:00 P.M. 2:10 P.M. - 3:30 P.M.	400 Hurdles Javelin throwing High jump technique	110 Hurdles Steeplechase (barriers) High jump technique	400 Hurdles Javelin throwing High jump technique	110 Hurdles Steeplechase (barriers) High jump technique	Team shake-out for all Saturday meets at 3:30!
4:00 P.M. - 6:00 P.M.	Pole Vault		Pole Vault		4 x 100 Relay Zone Work
3:00 P.M. - 4:00 P.M.	Long/Triple jump	4 x 100 Relay stick work	Long/Triple jump	4 x 100 Relay stick work	Team meeting at 5:00 P.M. on premeet days.
3:15 P.M. - 4:45 P.M.	Shot put (NW) 800 Meters	Hammer throw Lj/Tj/Hj running work 800 Meters	Shot put (NW) 800 Meters	Hammer throw Lj/Tj/Hj running work 800 Meters	
4:45 P.M. - 6:00 P.M.	100-400 Meters Hurdlers running Distance	Discus throw 100-400 Meters Hurdlers running Distance	100-400 Meters Hurdlers running Distance	Discus throw 100-400 Meters Hurdlers running Distance	

Notes:

All times listed above are start times for the main body of the workout. All warm-up work should be completed by these start times for those events on the track.

All changes in schedule should be cleared at least one week in advance because they will affect our women's team and Aquinas High School.

Figure 2.1e Practice times are a standard item on the bulletin board as is a copy of the team roster.

Instruct your team to look at this board on a daily basis. To make sure this happens, I post a motivational saying on the board every day, then at practice, I ask my athletes what it says. If I call on an athlete and he gets it right, he receives a piece of candy. If the athlete does not know what it said, he has a duty following practice, such as picking the towels up, helping to put the hurdles away, and so on. If a second board is available outside the locker room, use it to promote your team and keep others informed as to what successes your athletes are having that season.

The most important thing in keeping communication open with athletes is showing that you sincerely care about them. Initiate one-on-one conversations that may or may not deal with what is going on in their event. Make sure that you initiate conversations about what is going on in their lives in general. Once you understand the motivation behind an athlete, you will have a better understanding of what his or her needs are and how you can assist him or her in meeting them.

These conversations about who athletes are and what they are involved in are an excellent way to maintain communication during the summer and off-season. Showing a genuine interest can provide a comfort zone that allows for open conversation with the athletes during the season in areas that they would not normally feel comfortable.

WITH ADMINISTRATION

The school's administration has the task of overseeing the safety, welfare, and success of the student-athletes, coaches, and support staff under its supervision. It is important for administrators to clearly understand how you manage and direct all aspects of your program. If a concern does arise during the season, they are then equipped with the appropriate knowledge to answer the questions at hand and protect you and your staff from any misinformation, alleged actions, or disciplinary concerns brought from within or outside your program.

Schedule an annual meeting well in advance of your season with your athletics director to share your personal goals, team goals, coaching staff assignments, team rules and discipline procedures, practice times, competition plan (i.e., which meets you will focus on and why), and the equipment or uniform needs. At this same time, you can review together any changes that the school district has instituted that may affect your plan. This also is an opportunity to express concerns that you may have about the direction of the program.

I have found that the more organized and detailed your approach is in this area, the more support and understanding your administration has for you, your staff, and your student-athletes.

I find that in-season meetings with administrators really don't need to be formally set up, since most administrators should stop by your competitions and practices to monitor or informally evaluate what and how you are doing. Casual conversations also can maintain open communication between the coach and the superiors. However, if an important

Presenting Your Needs

During one such preseason meeting, when I was coaching high school, I presented a detailed plan on why we needed to purchase new pole vault and high jump pits. (Track and field may be the second most expensive high school sport—behind football or hockey—to properly equip, conduct, and support.) In the meeting, I was successful in defending why we needed the two pits and was able to assist in the formulation of a capital equipment plan. This plan eventually included all of our teams so that we could have a sense of the costs that would be incurred on an annual basis and so that we could logically defend the proper funding. Having such a meeting early in the year allows you to place an order in a timely manner so that you ensure that the equipment you require is on location before the start of the season.

Administrators and coaches of other sports at your school can provide valuable help as officials at home meets.

concern arises, you should always deal with it immediately by scheduling a private meeting with your administrator.

WITH ASSISTANT COACHES

Since track and field is by nature large in numbers and spread out over a large space, it is important that your assistant coaches have a complete understanding of all aspects of the program and your expectations of them. The assistant coaches, to support your decisions and demonstrate loyalty to you and the program, must believe in your philosophy or plan of action. The longer a staff is together, the easier this becomes. In other words, there is a direct correlation between the success of a program and the longevity and consistency of a staff's working together.

If you review the history of the most successful teams, regardless of the sport, one of the common denominators of successful teams is that the staffs have been together for

an extended period of time. When a group of coaches work together, it results in several positive by-products. The coaches feel more comfortable engaging in open discussions, and they are willing to challenge past practices and current literature. Coaches who work together understand and establish a team philosophy, and they tend to think along the same lines. Additionally, the veteran staff already understands their various responsibilities each year, so there isn't a need to take time at the beginning of each season to outline these assignments. The time saved can be used to accomplish tasks that would not otherwise have been able to be addressed, which results in greater productivity and an enhancement to the team.

Similar to the meeting you hold with your athletic director, schedule a preseason meeting, or meetings, with your staff. Discuss some of the same details, but also include more of the daily coaching issues, technical aspects of the events, the rules and results of noncompliance, the meets you plan to train

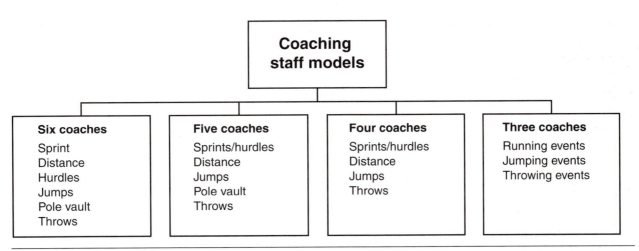

Figure 2.2   Track and field requires expertise in a number of events; split coaching responsibilities according to the size and individual strengths of your staff.

through and the ones you will focus on, and with whom certain decisions will rest. Outline the specific support duties among the staff and allow for some give-and-take so that you can meet individual preferences among your staff (see figure 2.2).

You should also discuss which clinics you plan to attend as a staff. Attending clinics as a group not only provides continued education for each person in the group, but it also gives you a time when you can get together, away from campus, brainstorm new ideas, and become closer as a group.

The length of your preseason meeting depends on how well the year before went, the number of new staff members that joined your staff, and whether there have been significant changes at the state, conference, or local levels. At the start of each year, I present and discuss the daily, weekly, and seasonal responsibilities that I have assigned to each assistant so that they are clear on what I expect. Following discussion with the staff, I then make coaching assignments, which are reflected in figure 2.2.

Once the season starts, coaches should establish a weekly meeting time to cover certain topics, which may include evaluations of practice and athletes, disciplinary issues, upcoming meet planning, and meet entries for the upcoming contests. Since time is valuable to all of us, you want to be as efficient as possible. If there is a significant

item to be discussed, let the staff know in advance so that they can come to the meeting prepared to have valuable input into the discussion and final resolution.

Assistant coaches should be a direct reflection of your program's vision. They can make the head coach's experience pleasurable and satisfying, or they can create concerns or issues that the head coach has to deal with. Remember, you can't do this job alone, so be sure to publicly and privately recognize the accomplishments of your assistant coaches along the way.

Utilize the numerous ways to communicate with your staff, but remember that the most effective way is still face-to-face. With e-mail readily available, you can also now easily communicate with staff members who may not teach in your building or who come from the community to assist in your program.

WITH PARENTS

Almost all parents have some information on track and field available to them—perhaps now more than ever with the accessibility of the Internet—and they may have formed opinions on how their children should be trained. It is becoming increasingly more challenging to coach in this environment; therefore, the communication link between the parents and coaches has also increased in importance. Fortunately, technological breakthroughs such as e-mail and team Web sites have provided unprecedented access between the parents and the coach. Using e-mail to send parents information such as meet times, driving directions, fund-raising activities, team functions, and home-meet assistance requests allows you to communicate quickly and inexpensively, as opposed to "snail mail."

Some coaches may even be proficient in Web site development (or know a student who is), and they can set up their own team site to share their program history, meet results, honors, records, and more. If updated regularly, a Web site is a great way to keep parents and others who are interested in your program in tune with what's going on with your team.

Embrace new communication tools such as Web sites and e-mails to build relationships with the parents and maintain an open line of communication, but don't discontinue using the old-fashioned, most reliable communication tool available . . . meeting face-to-face. Start each season with a meeting with the parents or a potluck dinner. This gives you and your staff the opportunity to meet and greet all the parents and make positive comments about their sons and daughters, which really starts the season on a positive note. In this relaxed, informal environment, you can introduce your staff, clearly outline your expectations of the athletes, share your code of conduct, communicate what tasks the parents can assist you with, detail the outlook for the upcoming season, and perhaps have small group meetings per event so that the parents can learn more about the sport their children are involved in. Another positive outcome of this event is that parents have a chance to meet other parents. In my experience, this can go a long way in avoiding embarrassing situations in the stands when parents comment about an athlete other than their son or daughter. This event also allows for interaction between the new participants and those who have been associated with the program for one or more years so that they can establish new friendships and share fresh ideas.

I have also used this opportunity to create a parents' leadership group of five to seven parents, who act as liaisons between other parents and me and who secure volunteer officials for all of our home meets and any necessary away meets. This alone removes a major burden from the head coach's shoulders. The chairperson for this group is the person that is in direct communication with the head coach and assumes the greatest amount of responsibility for securing the officials.

This group can also become involved with activities such as the parents' play-day. While coaching in high school, I combined a picnic with a mini-meet that had the athletes coaching their parents in their own event in a clinic setting; the athletes then assisted their parents in an abbreviated meet in which the parents participated in their sons' and daughters' events. One of the positive results of this activity was that the parents gained a small appreciation for the work their children do in practice, the difficulties associated with the events, and the stress that is involved with the actual competition. I was surprised at how willing the parents were to allow themselves to become kids for a short period of time, to let their inhibitions go, and to really get involved in this event. Initially, the turnout was average, but throughout the years that we did this, it continued to grow to almost 100 percent participation.

Remember this: Effective communication can prevent unpleasant situations, resolve concerns, and foster the growth of relationships that go far beyond the competitive years of the athletes, their parents, and the coaching staff. Developing this skill is well worth the investment of your time.

Chapter 3

MOTIVATING TRACK & FIELD ATHLETES

There is no *one* way to motivate athletes. As coaches, we may sometimes feel that we should be the ones who provide the impetus for motivation to our athletes. In reality, it is the athlete, regardless of his or her age, who must *want* to be motivated, and most successful athletes have a certain amount of self-motivation before we ever lay eyes on them. While older athletes tend to be better self-starters (even high school athletes can learn what motivates them), it sometimes takes a coach to assist in bringing it to the surface. But rest assured, it is there to be tapped.

When most people think of motivation, they think of the dramatic locker-room speeches that coaches use to motivate athletes to compete against all odds. But motivation takes many forms, and the big premeet speech is not always the best motivator. While we are all aware that a certain arousal level needs to be present in athletic competition, it is easy to drive that arousal level over the top, which can result in the athletes' incapacity to perform at their optimal levels. In fact, I have found that a very effective way to reach the desired outcome is to have a calm, rational discussion with the team as a whole about the challenges we are up against, what the goal is for the competition, and what plan needs to be implemented to achieve this goal. I then hold individual conversations with those athletes who may be more stressed than others or who might try to place the entire weight of the competition on themselves. The last thing you want as a coach is to have any athlete using precious energy worrying about what

needs to be accomplished, rather than using that energy to perform during the competition.

So how do you motivate your athletes to prepare them for optimal performances? Motivation starts in the daily practice setting, with the athletes' desire and excitement about going to practice to learn and improve their event techniques. My staff and I work to keep the motivation running high at practice by staying positive ourselves, being clear about our expectations of athletes, working with athletes to set realistic goals, providing opportunities to improve, empowering athletes, and setting up an incremental awards system.

BE POSITIVE

One of the easiest ways to motivate athletes is to be positive in everything you do and say on a daily basis and to encourage your team members to do the same. No matter how bad a situation seems, there is always a positive

Motivation begins at daily practices; its foundation is frequent positive communication.

Keep It Positive

A young man once came into our program as a thrower, but he failed to make the team as a freshman. His hard work and our continued support of him and his efforts allowed him to make the team his second year in school. He had success at the lower level meets but struggled in major competitions. However, by always being supportive of him and trying to always find the positive, we helped him evolve into a national caliber athlete who won the NCAA III national title in the hammer throw on his final competitive effort of his career.

In my career, I have only had one athlete with whom I could use negative motivation to get positive results; therefore, I strongly recommend that whenever possible, say something positive to your athletes.

side to it—even if that side includes nothing more than learning from the mistake and not repeating it again. Thus, being positive doesn't mean being untruthful about a situation, but rather it means viewing it from the perspective of what an individual can learn from it to improve.

I talk with my athletes about how every competition leads to a culminating event—a "learning experience." In each competition, athletes may do something positive or something negative (and sometimes both), but regardless, they can learn something from it that will assist them in attaining their goal. Each learning experience reinforces positive actions while teaching athletes to eliminate the negative.

Recently, we had a steeplechaser who raced aggressively early in a race but would fade near the end. After discussion, the athlete and I together identified a strategy of patience, and we determined how he could build his momentum throughout the race. He eventually became a NCAA Division III three-time all-American and ran to a runner-up finish his senior year with a lifetime best performance in his final race.

Every day I try to make one positive comment or personal communication to the athletes on my team, and it does not always deal with something athletic. Sometimes it is as simple as calling an athlete by her name or nickname and shaking her hand. Other days it might be a short conversation about something positive an athlete did in a meet or practice or something that he was recognized for in a class or club. The important thing here is that you enhance your athletes' self-image and make them feel important.

COMMUNICATE YOUR EXPECTATIONS

One of the earliest motivation techniques I used with high school male athletes was to call them "men." That singular word changed how they viewed themselves, just as society has a different view of and different expectations for boys and men. The use of the word "men" implied that they were more mature than "boys"; as a result, they handled themselves more like adults, showed more confidence, and accepted responsibility for their actions. I believe that it also showed my respect for them and what they were doing, as opposed to their being referred to as "boys" and interpreting it as a lack of respect. Since 1975, I have continued this reference with all of my male athletes, no matter what their age. Of course, the same applies to calling female athletes "women."

Communicating your expectations of athletes starts at the preseason meeting in which you cover team rules. It continues throughout the season in how you communicate daily with athletes and in how you help them achieve the goals they set for themselves.

SET GOALS

Before you leave on a driving trip, one of the first things that you do before leaving home is to get out a map and plot a course to your final destination. In a similar vein, goal setting by athletes in sport is their map toward achieving the big goal they are striving for as a culmination of their season or career.

• Coaching goals. A coach's goals usually involve the growth of his or her own career. What level of coaching do you aspire to? What is your timeline for accomplishing your goals? Much like the athletes, coaches need to continue to evaluate where they are and whether they are still on course to accomplish the task within the time frame they've allowed. In my mind, it's inappropriate for a coach to set goals for his or her team's seasonal success since it is not the coach's team, but rather it is the athletes' team. The coach should, however, guide, facilitate, and assist athletes in meeting the seasonal goals that they have established for themselves, individually and as a team.

• Team goals. The head coach and staff must be secure enough in who they are to allow the team leaders and team members to establish the goal or goals for the team. The coach can provide guidance or data to the team that allows them to make appropriate decisions in this process. In most high school settings, athletes have either an indoor and outdoor season, or just an outdoor season. In either case, the team can have a seasonal goal that can be reviewed at the midpoint of that season to see if they are still on track to accomplish that goal or if they need to consider amending it.

• Individual athlete goals. As with the team goals, the coach should allow each student-athlete to determine his or her own goals. The coach may have to provide some guidance but should avoid becoming the dominant personality in this process. Goals can be medium- (seasonal) or long-term (career). Both forms require continued reevaluation since numerous factors can impede or enhance the attainment of these goals. More time should be devoted to the development, progress, and attainment of the seasonal goals than to the long-term goals. An annual review of an athlete's career goals is sufficient at all levels.

When setting and guiding athletes in setting goals, ensure that all goals are measurable and realistic, and include incremental or intermediate (short-term) goals that you can check off along the way to long-term goals.

The first thing I have athletes do when we sit down to establish their goals is to see where they have come from. The more athletic or coaching experience you have, the more data you have to help you determine realistic goals. In other words, you can see how much improvement has been made from year to year, which gives you a guide for the current years' goal.

I always keep the goal-setting conversations somewhat relaxed and unstructured. Keeping this meeting informal ensures that the athlete won't be intimidated and won't see the process as laborious.

The measurability of a goal is much easier in track and field because events are measured objectively in time, distance, or height. Thus, athletes should avoid vague goals such as "I want to be better than last year." While such a goal is somewhat measurable, the athlete has not clearly defined what performance is acceptable. Will a six-inch improvement in the shot put be enough to meet the goal? Is this improvement realistic or too easily attained? Much like the trip analogy, you want to measure how far you have gone on your trip by referring back to the map to see where you are "now." In goal setting, this is achieved by establishing incremental goals that can be broken into smaller segments of the season.

The biggest problem most athletes have is that once they write down their goal or goals, they never revisit them. Many things can interfere with a goal from the time it is written down until the day you have set to accomplish the goal. Injuries, bad weather, and illness can all play a role in whether it is achieved or not. It is therefore important that the athlete, with support and counseling from the head coach or an assistant coach, create a seasonal goal, intermediate goals, and reevaluation dates to review the progress, or lack of progress, to determine if the original goal is still attainable or appropriate. There is nothing more discouraging than to struggle through a season with the sole purpose of attaining a goal that has been moved beyond

Focused Goals

I once had an athlete who came into our program and participated in two events. He evolved into a decathlete, but as a senior, he decided to return to his original two events. His goal all along was to be an all-American first, but he also had an ultimate goal to be a national champion. After his junior year, he had accomplished the first goal but was fatigued with the workload necessary to continue in the decathlon and maintain his academic success. After a conversation with me, he revised his goal and decided to leave the decathlon to focus on winning a national championship in his best event—the long jump—while maintaining his academic success. During the indoor season of his senior year, he jumped to an 11-foot lifetime personal record, won the conference meet, was selected the conference scholar-athlete, then culminated his season by winning the NCAA III national championship in his event.

reach. Not only will the seasonal goal not be attained, but the entire season may be such an incredibly negative experience that the athlete will choose not to continue in the sport.

For example, if I were a shot putter who currently had a personal best of 50 feet, my goal might be to throw 55 feet by the end of the season. My three incremental goals throughout the season might be to throw 51 feet, then 53 feet, and then 54 feet by a certain date, leading up to the end of the season. I could also use other measurements to determine if I were ready to meet these marks, such as meeting specific criteria in the strength center.

It is important to write down acceptable seasonal goals, along with the intermediate steps an athlete must take to achieve these goals. Once they are written, the athlete should keep them visible throughout the day. Research has indicated that written goals are attained at a higher rate than those goals that are not visible. We have had athletes post

their goals in numerous locations in their rooms or apartments, at school, and in their lockers—we have even had them take them with us on the road and put them up in their hotel rooms.

At the beginning of each season when I meet with athletes one-on-one, I ask them each to have a singular seasonal goal for their main event, and I request that they evaluate their progress on a weekly or semimonthly basis. Once they have established their seasonal goal, the coaching staff helps establish the incremental goals that are necessary to get them there. An important factor for coaches to remember is that we are only *assisting* in this process. To have significant meaning and therefore be motivating to the athlete, the goal must be each athlete's own personal goal—and not ours. Since meets are used as our measurements, the athletes can, on their own, process the information and determine their progress. If athletes develop some frustration, they are always encouraged to stop in and talk with their event coach or head coach.

PROVIDE OPPORTUNITIES TO IMPROVE

In track and field, you have opportunities early in the season or during less intense meets to run your third and fourth runners in open events. Doing so gives them the opportunity to step out of the shadows of better athletes, and it also allows them to be your scorers for the day. This not only increases these athletes' feelings of importance to the team, but it also provides motivation to continue to work to improve themselves so that they do better next time. In the process, it strengthens your team for that year and for years down the road. I use this technique primarily in dual and triangular meets to provide athletes who are not normally point-scorers with an opportunity to compete and score points, while giving our better athletes an additional training day. This also limits the number of stress days all of the athletes have during the season.

© Mary Langenfeld Photo

Relay participation is a great way for athletes to gain confidence and experience improvement.

Another good way to allow for developing athletes to have success with minimal stress is to incorporate them into relay races. They can be part of the four-member team or part of a full relay team made up of developing athletes. This allows success for the relay participants as well as the open athletes who can then be more rested for their main events.

EMPOWER ATHLETES

The team captains and leadership groups are given responsibilities and opportunities to provide input on various items that deal with the program, such as rules, the meet schedule, team T-shirt designs, fun activities, speaking to the team regarding a meet, or the overall team goal. As I have moved into the college level, this group plays an even greater role within the program, but I recommend going slowly into this venture with junior high and high school athletes. You can allow them to

act as a sounding board as you prepare the team rules and regulations, letter points, and similar items. You want to retain the final decision in most of these areas, but by allowing their ability to share ideas, you assist in their buying into the program. Areas in which they can play a more integral part would be the fun days and the premeet meals. This participation allows them to feel your respect for them, which again provides an opportunity to improve their self-image.

PROVIDE INCREMENTAL AWARDS

The ability for team members to receive some form of recognition for positive accomplishments assists in the overall development of their self-esteem. A simple accolade can serve as a small motivator in helping them maintain focus on their goals and continued improvement, which will eventually help them and their team to reach the seasonal goal.

The PR Bar

During one season, the father of one of my athletes worked for a national candy company and gave me two large bags full of candy bars to give to the team. This started the "PR Bar" every day following a meet. To receive a PR Bar, an athlete has to obtain a new season or lifetime personal best in an event. The day after the meet, during the team huddle and in front of their peers, the PR athletes stand up and share their PR with the rest of the team, after which they receive a PR Bar from me. While this is a simple thing to do, it allowed for all levels of talent to receive recognition from their teammates, and it reinforced why they were working so hard. This single motivational technique became a big deal to the team, and when I see some of the athletes today, many years later, they still talk about the PR Bar.

Special T-Shirts

Coaches have been using T-shirts since day one to promote their team, gain recognition for their program, advertise their individual or team success, and motivate their athletes. Nothing has changed in this area. You can have a T-shirt made for almost anything today, and you can establish your own rules for the awarding of them. You can have the perfect attendance T-shirt, the all-state T-shirt, the state qualifier T-shirt, the champion T-shirt, the strength T-shirt, and so on. This visible motivational technique allows for the athletes to receive something for their efforts. It encourages positive comments from their peers, and it provides you with an opportunity to say something positive about each athlete as you present the shirt.

Fun Days

While working to achieve goals, I try to involve fun at least once per week. These days can be extravagant or very simple, and they usually result in some team building as a by-product. Our fun days include Hawaiian-shirt/grass-skirt day for practice, Coach Guthrie look-a-like day, kindergarten-games day, slow-bike-ride day, and bear-hunt day. Since we typically have one meet a week and it is on Saturday, we usually do something fun on Friday to forget about the work we did that week and start focusing on the next meet as a team. Additionally, these types of activities allow for good recovery and a light day, both mentally and physically. Most of these activities apply to various ages of athletes.

If a fun activity is used as a distraction the day before the meet, it is important to make this a part of the day, not the entire day. Physiologists remind us that we cannot allow the athletes' metabolic rate to drop too far on the day before a competition or else they might struggle in the early stages of the competition to reestablish the normal metabolic rate. Also, it is important to note that I do not recommend doing this the day before the conference, state qualifying, state championship, or national meets.

Silly Awards

At the end of the season each year, we have awards presented by our seniors to members of the team for crazy or dumb things that occurred during the year. This is usually a big production and one that the athletes organize. At the same time, we have the handing down of legendary items to the returning athletes for next year. These items vary from socks, shoes, signs, shirts, coats, medals, and so on. This process, while humorous, also provides a connection to the history of the program and is always a topic of conversation when our alumni return in January to spend a day with the team.

Food Bets

Food bets started with our throwers and are now used across the team equally. I use these bets with a training group in a hard workout to assist them in getting through the workout. The principle is simple: If they achieve a daily goal, they get some food. We are not talking about a meal here, but rather a soda, candy bar, some jellybeans, cookies, and so on. It allows them to lock their focus on the bet and not what they are enduring. It also motivates them to be able to successfully complete the workout individually or as a group. This small reward goes a long way in getting through a difficult situation. Once the task has been completed, they see an accomplishment, which strengthens their belief that they can accomplish more in their next contest.

Chapter 4

BUILDING A SUCCESSFUL TRACK & FIELD PROGRAM

© Human Kinetics

Success at any level of track and field depends on the ingredients that make up your team; thus, the recruitment of athletes into your program is the foundation on which your program is built.

NURTURE THE TALENT

If you are a high school coach who is fortunate enough to have a junior high school track and field program in your school district, it is in your best interest to help cultivate these young athletes through numerous events and experiences. The first is to connect the junior high coaching staff with your staff. Take time to share your training methods and philosophy as they relate to each event, and involve the coaches in miniclinics by inviting them to attend coaching schools and clinics with your own high school staff.

While coaching in high school, we would invite the junior high coaches to attend at least one clinic annually with our entire staff. We would get a block of rooms, one being a suite, and we would discuss how to implement the ideas and concepts that we had just listened to into our own programs. We would also discuss ways to refine what we were currently doing and how we might enhance the track and field experience for both the junior high and high school athletes.

With the junior high coaches on the same page as the high school staff, you can then turn your attention to the athletes. Try holding single-day technique clinics before the start of the junior high season, using the current high school athletes as clinic coaches for the younger athletes. The clinic can provide several positive results. First, the junior high athletes have the opportunity to meet the high school athletes whom they have heard about and look up to. Second, they begin to feel comfortable with athletes who may be their teammates in the future, and finally, both the junior high and high school athletes have an opportunity to gain knowledge or reinforce techniques they are already familiar with.

At the end of the day, it is important to do something that is fun. That way, athletes learn that by being a part of your high school program, they will have the opportunity to participate in fun activities as well as the chance to do the work that will make them better.

If a junior high school program is not available to you, then it is important that a track and field unit be a part of your junior high physical education program. At the conclusion of that unit, you might want to suggest and help plan a field day where the students have the opportunity to participate in the various events.

Whether you schedule interscholastic competitions or a field day, the involvement of your high school student-athletes as the meet officials can once again allow the junior high students to be exposed to the high schoolers. This type of competition provides you with an opportunity to see potential talent, and it also assists with the development of relationships between the high schoolers and junior high students that will be important to your program year after year.

I always took an opportunity to meet with the junior high athletes as a group in whatever setting was best for their program—such as a postseason wrap-up meeting, where I would assist with handing out awards, or a postseason banquet, where I would give a short talk or assist them in any way possible. Either occasion would provide yet another chance for my future athletes to meet me in a relaxed setting as well as give me an opportunity to meet their parents before making contact in their high school years.

RECRUIT ACTIVELY

How many times have you heard one coach tell another that a particular school or coach always has better talent than is available at their school? Each school has potential greatness walking its halls, going to work after school rather than participating in a sport, or going home to do absolutely nothing. The difference is that some individuals have the ability to recruit and retain these potential athletes into their programs.

As the peer group to these potential athletes, your current student-athletes are a very powerful lobby. If the athletes currently involved in your program are having fun and experiencing success, they can be your best recruiting tools. They can get the attention and the respect of their fellow students much more easily than you can. I have often had our seniors stop by lockers and lunch tables to talk with potential athletes and share the excitement and fun they are having. Sometimes I have asked our seniors and juniors to actively share their excitement with prospective athletes, and other times they have been so excited about their experience that they just naturally initiate those conversations with fellow students.

Another recruitment opportunity is to assist other coaches in your school with the development of their programs and in turn ask for their support with your team as either an assistant coach or a volunteer at a meet. At one point, I had the head soccer coach, the head volleyball coach, and a football coach as assistant coaches on my staff, which made it much easier to have access to their athletes.

All coaches want to maintain contact with their athletes in the off-season. A perfect opportunity to do just that is to be an assistant coach in a sport that involves speed, jumping, and throwing techniques on the field and strength and conditioning concepts off the field. In fact, I was even willing to allow one or two drills or training aspects from those other sports to become a part of our daily warm-up stations. A by-product is that these crossover athletes can then develop more physical skills than just their sport-specific skills.

If I could convince other head or assistant coaches to be a part of my program, I would offer my services in return. I would assist them in game management, conditioning ideas, or in any other way I could to help them and their team. The spirit of the relationship is to give them what you, and all the athletes, receive in return—support.

On the high school and junior high level, I recommend speaking one-on-one to young people who have the potential to benefit from being in your program and to contribute to the team. Meet with the physical education classes for a couple of minutes to invite students out for the team. Another time to speak with potential athletes is when other teams make their final cuts. This is a difficult time for young people, as everyone wants to be a part

The Good All-Around Athlete

One of my athletes at University of Wisconsin (La Crosse) was Bill Schroeder, who was recruited into our program because he was an all-conference football player and basketball player. He could hit a softball or baseball forever; he was an excellent golfer; and he was an excellent field athlete. He was simply an outstanding *athlete*. Following a track and field career that included two NCAA Championships and 13 all-American awards (6 in one national meet), he was drafted by the Green Bay Packers as a wide receiver. After playing just one year of Division III college football, he even became a starter. Athletes like Bill, unfortunately, are becoming a thing of the past. These athletes, however, are many times the best ones to get into your program because of their upside—being well rounded and highly accomplished in lateral, vertical, and horizontal movements. This well-roundedness may often translate into an athlete's having more potential to excel or improve.

of something and wants acceptance. While an athlete may not have made the team they were trying out for, your track and field program can provide them with the acceptance they seek in a nonthreatening way.

As a follow-up to approaching a potential athlete in the hall, make phone calls to prospective athletes and their parents to share your thoughts about their involvement in your program.

PROMOTE YOUR EVENTS

It is important to get your sport in front of the students at your school and the community. This awareness can be done in a variety of ways.

✓ Maintain a bulletin board, at least during your season, and if possible, throughout the year. If you can, make the board available so that anyone moving through the halls of the school can read it. Share your successes on that board with attractive, eye-catching components, and above all, change it often so that people will take the time to look at it and see what is new. Include news articles, pictures, team points, meet results, team records, and photos of your fun-day activities. Keep this team-promotion board separate from the team bulletin boards, which are usually in the locker room and are reserved for specific information for your athletes. In other words, one board is a team-promotion piece, and the other one is for team functions and information-sharing.

✓ Place flyers around the school on days of meets to let people know who, what, where, and when athletes will be in action. These flyers can be designed and distributed by members of your team.

✓ Have the school's daily announcements include meet information and the results following competitions. This method can also be used to announce upcoming meetings or honors that were received by your athletes.

✓ Mail letters to incoming high school students as well as athletes that are already in your school's sport program. Share with them how impressed you are with what they have done in another sport, and invite them to be a part of your program.

✓ The week before your first team meeting is scheduled, place posters (made by your current athletes) in the halls and locker rooms of your school.

✓ Be proactive about scheduling interviews with your school newspaper and radio station as well as the local media outlets. They will not only provide accolades to your current athletes, but they may be the stimulus for athletes' joining your team. Congratulating athletes in other programs on their performance during their season may initiate an interest in you and your program when spring rolls around.

KEEP ATHLETES INVOLVED

Now that you have these newcomers to the sport, how do you keep them interested in staying on, especially during the first few tough weeks they need to build their fitness? Make the first weeks of practice so easy for them that they can't believe it.

While all athletes are required to follow the same team rules, the workouts that newcomers experience should at first be substantially less strenuous than those for returning athletes. Once a physical fitness base has been established, you can gradually raise your expectations of the rookies until they eventually work their way into doing almost all of the work for their age. This growth process may take three to four weeks of small increases. As a general rule, I start newcomers out at 25 percent and add about 15 to 20 percent more work each week until they have established a base. If you take the time to explain to athletes how newcomers are integrated into the regular training program that returning athletes experience, your team chemistry should not be negatively affected.

Interject fun into these early practices, and let newcomers go home feeling good about themselves and feeling that they could have done a great deal more. As they grow to like the sport, gradually increase their workload over the entire season. The biggest mistake you can make is to increase their workload too quickly and either place them in stressful situations that they are uncomfortable with or place unrealistic expectations on them too soon. Take extra time to nurture these new athletes into your program so that they will still be competing in years to come and realizing the long-term goals that evolve from the annual participation in your sport.

In early meets, place new athletes in events in which they can have easy success. Place them in heats where they can easily run out front, then share with them what a great job they did and how proud you are of them as well as what aspects they can focus on to improve in their next race. Reinforce the positive, and evaluate them as you would any of your athletes, but spend a bit more time on what the athletes did well. Be selective as to how many events newcomers participate in during a meet. You want them leave the competition wanting more and feeling as though they could have done more.

If one of your newcomers starts to immediately show promise, don't rush things by changing this approach and by working that athlete harder than other newcomers. Doing too much too soon can place new athletes in a situation in which they feel pressure to live up to expectations before they have really had a chance to grasp and embrace the sport. This is true even in collegiate sports.

Avoid Too Much, Too Soon

Just recently, we had a very talented first-year 400-meter runner enter our program. We didn't talk about expectations in terms of the winning and losing. Because he was new to the collegiate scene, we didn't want to constrain him with expectations. I limited his competitions to one or two events per meet, with a couple of weeks off of competition in between meets. As a freshman, this youngster placed second at the NCAA Division III Indoor and Outdoor Championships at 400 meters with one of the top-ten times ever run, 46.52 seconds. Once he had some positive experiences, we began to use the more traditional goal-setting program with him, as we do with all athletes, to assist him in continued improvements. Now we discuss his goals and expectations in one-on-one conversations, since his teammates look to him more as a leader. Because of his talent and accomplishments, he has become the "go-to person" in the critical situation. My task is to assist him with managing the expectations and team pressures that can come with being successful at an early point in a career.

CHOOSE YOUR STAFF

You may work with a staff that you inherited from a previous coach during your initial days and years at your new school. If that is the case, you need to have individual meetings to learn what they have been doing, what they are comfortable with, and what support you can provide them if they feel some transition time into your program is needed. The need for this transition phase occurs at all levels of coaching because we all have feelings, egos, and our own most comfortable way of coaching athletes. I have always believed that the head coach should allow his or her assistant coaches to coach to their expertise while the head coach fills the remaining event vacancies.

If you can hire assistant coaches, it is important to have a plan in place to take an aggressive role in putting together a position that will meet your needs and the academic requirements of the assistant's position. For example, if you are aware that you will be losing an assistant coach, then have a meeting with your athletic director and possibly the department chair. That way, you can have an active role in writing the position description for the replacement. You might be seeking a person with specific event expertise; therefore, you would naturally like to have that in the description. In addition, take an active role by sharing the fact that an opening exists with people you know and by recruiting qualified applicants. Also, look at the needs of your school's other athletic coaching staffs. You may be able to hire someone who fulfills the needs for not only your sport but other sports and their coaching staffs as well. I believe that cooperation within a school district and its athletic department can produce strong ties, camaraderie, and support for what everyone is trying to accomplish.

Another aspect that is important in putting together a coaching staff is to create an atmosphere where everyone can flourish and develop their relationship with one another, as well as provide a positive experience for the athletes. This is not always easy. One way that I tried to bolster our staff's camaraderie and tolerance was to have a family get-together following our invitational meets most weekends. These socials involved their spouses and their children, with everyone

Blending Old Ideas With New

When I took over as the head track coach at Naperville North, I inherited a staff that was made up of coaches who were involved in other sports, had been together for a period of time, and ranged in experience from a few years to many years. This staff had produced several conference championship teams for both boys and girls. The first thing I did was to meet them and talk about their other assignments and interests, as opposed to having an initial track conversation. This allowed all of us to get comfortable with each other in a nonthreatening way. As time passed, I began to ask questions as to how things were done previously and what they would change if they had an opportunity to do so. I sought the opinion of the eldest coach and listened to his advice and experiences. My final decision was to make few changes for the first year, except in the area of discipline and meet scheduling. Then over the next few years, I gradually implemented my vision. The fact that the program was relatively successful and that there were no major issues allowed for this gradual transition. If you are faced with having to rebuild from the foundation, you may need to take a more aggressive approach with the staff and many aspects of the program.

pitching in to bring food and drink. Even though these socials traveled from home to home, it really wasn't much work for the host because of the group cooperation. I found that as we grew closer socially, we became closer and more supportive of each other in the coaching arena as well.

As the head coach, you need to assist your assistant coaches in their professional development. This might include encouraging them to attend coaching clinics, holding regular one-on-one coaching conversations, visiting college coaching staffs, and providing them with technical articles related to their event areas.

FOCUS ON THE TEAM

While a team is made up of individual athletes, its success depends on how well they support each other to achieve a common good. The military uses boot camp to teach and create the ultimate team atmosphere. It removes the individualization from its ranks for the good of the entire group. While I don't think that boot camp is required in track and field, I have always coached the sport from a team perspective for the following reason—it is the easiest way for a large number of athletes to win. There have been years when we have had athletes win individual conference and national titles, yet the majority of our team members were not individual champions. By creating a well-balanced and supportive team atmosphere, all of our athletes, through a unified effort, have been able to obtain a conference or national championship.

We have done several things to assist in developing a team concept in track and field. We've encouraged, for example, having each team member know every other member's name and event. We have also tracked the points scored by each event-group to build camaraderie within events and to help athletes understand the contributions of each team member. That is, we've tracked the points contributed by the throwers, jumpers, distance runners, and sprinters, and the points by field events versus track events. I have also had prediction meets where we would identify one person per event area and have the rest of the team predict what their performance would be. This facilitates the athletes' interacting with one another to find out how they are feeling and what strategies they are using. As a result, team members follow each other's results and victories throughout meets and share in other team members' performances and experiences.

I believe that athletes in general compete and act in much the same way as they dress. Clothes and appearance are ways that people project who they are and what their confidence level is; therefore, I have very specific expectations regarding my athletes' appearances.

Our team's success depends on each athlete supporting the others and understanding that every individual contributes to the whole, in practice and competition.

By asking that your team dress neatly, wear appropriate clothing, and not act out in an individual way, they can solidify a team concept that produces individual and team success, which becomes contagious and enhances your program for future years. It also goes a long way in creating acceptance among those in your school district who make the critical decisions regarding the support your program will receive.

For instance, I ask our college athletes to adhere to a dress code when we are in public and when we travel as a group. When I was a high school coach, we had our athletes dress up on competition days. Initially, there was some concern that they would be laughed at by their peers; however, the more they dressed up, the less concern there was. When our best athletes complied—and these athletes were also some of the best overall athletes in the

school—it became a very okay thing to do. This one simple act allowed everyone to know when we had a meet. Teachers started to wish their students good luck, which triggered conversations about how they were doing and how the season was going. In other words, we increased our visibility while bringing our athletes additional support and recognition, thus enhancing their self-image.

ASSESS YOUR TEAM'S COMPETITIVE LEVEL

It is important to evaluate the condition of your program and the level of competition at which your team can be immediately successful. While I discuss this in greater detail in upcoming chapters, it is important that you create a feeling of success as soon as possible, especially when the goal is to build a successful program that has winning meets as one of its primary goals. Don't simply run the same teams in the same order from year to year. Create a schedule that fits the talent level of your current team, one that allows time for proper training and one that prepares you for the championship meets at the conclusion of the season. Each year this schedule may change significantly until you have developed your team into a consistent winner (see chapters 5 and 9 for more information).

Reward Success

It is important that you take time to reward the successes of your coaches, athletes, and team, no matter how small the achievement or how small your gesture may seem. As the saying goes, "You catch more flies with honey than you do with vinegar." In our program, we focus on commenting on or rewarding success of individual athletes at all levels in front of the peer group whenever the occasion presents itself. What may seem like a small acknowledgment to you may be a pivotal event that keeps an athlete or team motivated to continue toward a goal. These rewards can also develop the personal pride and team pride needed to overcome the struggles encountered throughout a season.

I would even encourage you to try to view athletes' accomplishments through the eyes of these young people, since they are less cynical in their youth than we may become as we age. This youthful enthusiasm for success and accomplishment can be contagious and motivating—that is, it can become a significant part of the team's success and a building block for continuing a strong program.

Part 2

COACHING PLANS

Chapter 5

PLANNING FOR THE SEASON

Perhaps the single easiest thing a coach can do to assist staff and athletes in attaining their goals is to prepare for as much of the season as possible as far in advance as possible. We all know as coaches that on any given day, numerous distractions, demands, and conversations pop up that reduce the time available to prepare workouts and travel plans, to script lineups, to produce meet workers and key officials, to edit and publish pre- and postseason books, and to review and print any materials needed to function for the upcoming year.

Reviewing the Season

Two situations come to mind when I consider discussing changes for the upcoming season at a postseason meeting with staff. The first occurred when I was a new coach. At the postseason meeting that year, we realized that our training had been based on the major culminating meet for the year, which at the high school level is the state meet. Although it is true that this is the biggest meet, it is only such for only a limited number of athletes. In other words, athletes who do not qualify for state championships have their training peak at least two if not three weeks past their own major meet of the season—the conference meet. After realizing this problem, we developed alternate training programs that diverged from each other about four weeks before the conference meet, thereby ensuring that each group of athletes had the opportunity to be rested and to peak for their own major meet of the year. This change resulted in significant performance improvements. As a result, the team grew in strength, and the results indicated that we had made a positive adjustment for all members of our team.

In another instance, we realized at the conclusion of the season that our freshman class, soon to be sophomore class, was very talented and had just completed a very positive campaign. As we looked ahead at the incoming freshmen from our two junior high feeder schools, they too had a significant amount of talent. Originally, we had planned to move the current freshmen up to the varsity level when they became sophomores to improve a weak varsity team and to make them more competitive at the conference meet the following year. However, after long discussions, one of my assistant coaches—who had more years of experience than his head coach or any of the other assistants—proposed that we hold the sophomores at the frosh-soph level for one more year to allow them to experience a great deal of success. Then we could move the majority of these two classes up together and continue to feed that success as a varsity team. The end result was that this group started an extended conference championship win streak and garnered a third place finish in the state meet.

These are just two examples of how the evaluation process can benefit your athletes. Good things happen when a staff sits down together, without time constraints, and looks at the program from various aspects, with the end result being marked improvement for your athletes and team.

REVIEWING THE PAST YEAR

Since track and field is a spring sport, summer provides an excellent opportunity to review the past season, make adjustments to your plans and schedules for the upcoming year, learn more about the sport, and listen to recommendations for the upcoming year. In other words, time exists to meet these demands before you have to address the routine demands of the school year. In reality, with the technology that is now available, you are only looking at a couple of hours of work per day for a few weeks to plan for the next season. Using this time allows you to deal with those situations that arise and demand your full attention during the season while maintaining your calm and not looking as though you were caught by surprise. Much like the duck, you can paddle frantically beneath the surface but remain calm and smooth above the water line.

Since summer vacation follows right after the season, it is a great time to hold a short staff retreat to go over items that are currently on their minds and that may require changes for the planning of the new season. During this time, you may wish to talk about moving athletes into different events and the rationale for such moves. You can discuss the workouts from the past year and how you can tweak them so that they are more effective for next year. Some questions you may want to discuss include the following:

✓ What meets do you feel need to be added or dropped, based on changes in talent level?

✓ What coaching responsibilities need to be addressed, and what possible event changes must be made to better accommodate your staff knowledge?

✓ Did you make a mistake with an athlete by asking too much during the season or during an important meet?

Multiple issues can be addressed at this time. While all of them won't be solved during this singular retreat, there is time to sit back and look at several options that might be available to create a better situation. The retreat also provides an opportunity for your assistant coaches to give input into next year's plan.

PLANNING YOUR MEET SCHEDULE

The first thing you need to do is to put together your competition schedule for the upcoming year. From this schedule, you can build your training plan and other events. Using a calendar, I like to work from the end of the season to the beginning of the season. The reason we do this is that we all want to do well and plan toward the conference, state, or national meets; therefore, everything we do during the season is timed with those championship meets in mind. For example, I like to have an easy meet followed by a challenging, invitational-type meet when we have a championship-caliber team.

This hard-easy meet approach has the same benefits as the hard-easy practice plan, which is to allow opportunities for an athlete to run

© Mary Langenfeld Photo

Many parents enjoy being involved in their child's home meets—they can help the team and get to know other athletes and parents.

an off event (not their main event) or take a meet off to freshen up mentally. Your management of the athletes and their efforts is important since most high school and college track seasons cover many weeks and months. So, I start by marking on a calendar the state meet, then I add the regional or sectional meets, then the conference meet, and finally I start alternating easy and challenging meets, with the meet before the first major meet being an easy one. This alternating of stress and nonstress meets also matches our stress weeks and light weeks of training for most events.

Most state and national associations have calendars that are two, three, or more years out, so you can easily anticipate those dates. Most invitational meets have settled into a yearly schedule and don't change very much over time. At the collegiate level, the Internet is a great resource you can use to find other programs' schedules or to locate coaches and their contact numbers so that you can ask questions about their home meets.

As a college coach, I also look at the distance traveled to get to particular meets and the time student-athletes must take away from their normal lives when I consider if a meet is an easy meet or a stress meet. Traveling, sleeping in a motel, and being away from your normal routine is stressful and must be taken into consideration.

I started this tactic of working from the championship meet backward when I was a college athlete. Since I had a goal to go to the NCAA Championships, I first needed to determine when this meet was going to take place. Once I knew that date, I next needed to know when the conference meet was scheduled. Any event or sport requires hard, intelligent work, and athletes need to taper their training for the major meets. I knew that I needed

Do Unto Others . . .

While coaching high school, I volunteered to work and provide coverage at sporting events that took place during the fall and winter so that I could then go to those coaches for assistance during our home meets. This allowed me to develop head officials that I could count on for each of our home meets. I also created a parents' liaison group made up of a small number of parents. These parents were responsible for securing additional workers for all of our home meets, as well as for handling other supportive responsibilities such as a postseason social, parents' day at the track, snacks for the team, and so on. I provided the meet schedule, the starting and potential end times for all home meets, and the number of officials needed by event or area of responsibility. Then I handed that off to the liaisons to fill in the spaces, inform the workers of their assignments, and provide them all with the rules they would need to know to do their job.

This process was born as a result of a lack of parental support at a conference meet early in my career. My assistant coaches and I had to provide four workers for the conference meet, as per conference rules, and since we were not able to get assistance from other sources, we coaches had to serve as officials. As a result, the mother of a discus thrower came running over to me, asking for help for her son and we were not able to provide assistance because we were serving as meet officials. After that situation, parents understood that if they wanted their children to receive coaching at meets, they needed to assist with the officiating so that the coaches would be free to coach. This single form of support has saved me a tremendous amount of time and anxiety, and it has allowed me to focus on actually coaching the boys and girls in my program. Usually, I could persuade parents of a junior to stay around and assist as a leader the next year when their son or daughter became a senior. By doing this, you don't have to completely retrain new parents each year. The selection process of recruiting volunteers can also be very informal. I ask for volunteers when I can, but often I have current parents make suggestions or make initial contact with potential liaisons.

to determine when I was going to work hard and when I needed to back off so that I could have success at these major competitions. It was at that time that I began to work in reverse from the goal to the start of the season.

Away-Meet Logistics

Once you have your schedule in place, you need to make sure that your transportation is scheduled, and you need to allow for plenty of time at the meet site before the start of competition. I like to be on-site at least 90 minutes before the start of the first event so that the athletes do not feel rushed getting ready. Also, if something does go wrong with the transportation, this allows time to deal with it.

When meals are involved, coaches need to create a plan as to where, when, and what everyone will eat, especially since most track teams involve large numbers of participants. If it is postmeet and if fast food is acceptable, all you need to have is a contact name, phone number, and address so that the restaurant is prepared for your arrival. Calling ahead eliminates a lot of potentially lost time. If you give them enough lead time, many of these fast food restaurants can have your food ready for you when you arrive. With cellular phones, you can call when you are 20 or 30 minutes away. On the other hand, if your plans involve a meal before or during competition days, you need to pick a restaurant with a suitable menu and make reservations far enough in advance to ensure that you and your team are taken care of in the way you require.

Most meets also involve some form of an entry fee. During the summer months, you can put together check requests for your meets so that they are processed well in advance of when they are needed. Remember that it is always easier to cancel at the last minute than to rush at the last minute.

Home-Meet Logistics

Securing the key officials as early as possible ensures that you have the preferred starter, referee, and key officials available to work your home meets. It is also important to get your schedule completed early in the summer so that your team has scheduling priority if you share a multiuse facility with other sports or programs.

You need to produce meet information and either get it in the mail or make it available to be distributed electronically (Internet or e-mail) to those teams attending your meet (see figure 5.1, a-c). All of this can easily be done in an hour or less, simply by changing dates and a making couple of computer entries. Order medals, ribbons, or other awards if appropriate at this time. You can also fill out the paperwork for processing checks for those officials who receive an honorarium for their service.

MAINTAINING EQUIPMENT AND UNIFORMS

Preparing the equipment and uniforms for the upcoming season starts at the end of the previous season. At the conclusion of your last meet of the year, have a team wrap-up meeting to review the season with the athletes, hand out some fun awards, and begin the process of collecting equipment and uniforms. Since the academic year for the two cities in which I coached high school track and field went beyond the state meet, I had a captive audience that included our juniors, sophomores, and freshmen. The seniors, once they returned their uniforms, sweats, and any implements checked out to them, were released.

Everyone else participated in the wrap-up phase. Each of my assistant coaches was assigned to a type of equipment or to soft goods as one of their areas of responsibilities. They were in charge of the repair, storage, and inventory of the items that were needed to run the program.

We had storage boards made for the throwing implements. When they were returned, they were inventoried, inspected, and stored. Hurdles were oiled; all nuts and bolts were tightened; damaged hurdle boards were replaced with those made and painted in our

Meet:	La Crosse Quandrangular
Date:	Saturday, January 26, 2002
Teams:	Luther College (M/W), St. Norbert's College (M/W), Wartburg College (M/W), Winona State (W)
Schedule:	An updated schedule will be posted ***http://perth.uwlax.edu/Athletics/Mens-track-field/*** by noon on Friday, January 25, 2002. A schedule is also enclosed.
Fee:	$100.00 per team—payable the day of the meet.
Entries:	Four (4) per individual event and one (1) 4 x 200 relay and multiple DMR and 4 x 400 relays will be permitted.
Entry Form:	The entry form is enclosed and entries are due on Wednesday, January 23 at 12:00 P.M. (CST). Please fax to Mark Guthrie at 608-785-8674.
Scratches:	You can e-mail changes to ***guthrie.mark@uwlax.edu*** by noon on Friday, January 25, 2002. Only scratches will be taken on the meet day.
Scratch Mtg.:	A scratch meeting will be run at 12:00 P.M. in the French Conference Room, which is adjacent to the main entrance to the fieldhouse.
Rules:	2002 NCAA Rules will be in effect for the meet.
Eligibility:	Only college athletes on a current eligibility form will be allowed to compete.
Track:	The track is a Martin ISS System that will allow 1/4" pyramid spikes or "trees." The infield is a NON SPIKE SURFACE! The pole vault will have a rollout runway that will handle 1/4" or "tree" spikes. The long and triple jump can also accommodate spikes. The shot and weight throws will be contested on plywood.
Timing:	*Finishlynx* will be the primary timing system.
Scoring:	As per the NCAA rules.
Parking:	Parking is available in the Veteran's Memorial Stadium Lot across from Mitchell Hall.
Lockers:	Locker room #5 for the men and #13 for the women are located on the lower level of Mitchell Hall and are unsecured. You need to provide your own locks.
Weigh-ins:	Weigh-in of implements for all throws will take place from 12:00-12:20 P.M. next to the throwing cage.
Trainers:	UW-La Crosse will provide Certified Athletic Trainers for the meet.
	Contact Mark Guthrie at 608-785-8679 or at ***guthrie.mark@uwlax.edu***

Figure 5.1a The most useful meet flier includes general information (date, teams, schedule, and fees) as well as parking and facilities information.

La Crosse Quadrangular Meet
Saturday, January 26, 2002

Field Events:

1:00 PM	High Jump	Women
1:30 PM	Long Jump	Men
1:45 PM	Pole Vault	Women
2:00 PM	Weight Throw	Men
2:15 PM	High Jump	Men
2:30 PM	Weight Throw	Women
2:45 PM	Long Jump	Women
3:45 PM	Pole Vault	Men
4:00 PM	Shot Put	Men
5:00 PM	Triple Jump	Men
5:15 PM	Shot Put	Women
6:00 PM	Triple Jump	Women

Track Events:

1:05 PM	55 Hurdle Trials	Women
1:17 PM	55 Hurdle Trials	Men
1:29 PM	55 Meter Trials	Women
1:45 PM	55 Meter Trials	Men
2:01 PM	5000 Meters	Women
2:19 PM	4 x 200 Relay	Women
2:27 PM	4 x 200 Relay	Men
2:32 PM	5000 Meters	Men
2:50 PM	55 Hurdle Final	Men
2:55 PM	55 Hurdle Final	Women
3:00 PM	55 Meter Final	Women
3:05 PM	55 Meter Final	Men
3:10 PM	1500 Meter Final	Women
3:20 PM	1500 Meter Final	Men
3:33 PM	400 Meter Final	Women
3:53 PM	400 Meter Final	Men
4:11 PM	800 Meter Final	Women
4:41 PM	800 Meter Final	Men
5:01 PM	200 Meter Final	Women
5:25 PM	200 Meter Final	Men
5:50 PM	3000 Meter Final	Women
6:14 PM	3000 Meter Final	Men
6:34 PM	4 x 400 Final	Women—Running Heats #3 and 4
6:48 PM	4 x 400 Final	Men—Running Heats #3 and 4
7:00 PM	Distance Medley	Women
7:12 PM	Distance Medley	Men
7:23 PM	Exhibition 4 x 400 relays	(women first—start in alleys)

UPDATED SCHEDULE — Friday, January 25th.

Figure 5.1b Draw up a schedule of events for your home meets and stick to it!

Team Entry List Form

Please type all entries along with each performance.
All hand-timed marks should be converted to FAT by
adding the autoconversion of .24 seconds. Indicate
field event performances metrically.

Entries and Final Declarations

Due: _____

by e-mail at: _____

or fax to: _____

Date: _____ School: _____ Coach: _____ Phone (o): _____ (h): _____ e-mail: _____

	Name(s), seed time	Name(s), seed time	Name(s), seed time	Name(s), seed time	Name(s), seed time	Name(s), seed time
100 m						
100 hurdles						
110 hurdles						
200 m						
400 m						
400 hurdles						
800 m						
1500 m						
3000 m						
5000 m						
High jump						
Pole vault						
Long jump						
Triple jump						
Shot put						
Discus						
Javelin						
Hammer						
4 x 100						
4 x 200						
4 x 400						

Figure 5.1c Make the entry form as clear as possible and include the deadline as well as a fax number or e-mail address.

school shop (or ordered from the manufacturer); then all hurdles were inventoried. All of our jumping pits were checked for damage, then cleaned and placed into storage, unless they were being sent out for repair or being destroyed to make room for new pits.

Performance indicators, flash cards, and the sign were checked for damage before storage. All starting blocks were evaluated for damage, with repairs made and parts ordered, then stored for the summer.

All small items, such as finish string, starter's guns, shells, lap counters, and watches, were inventoried and stored. During inventory, all uniforms and sweats were checked in, sorted by size, then sorted a second time for repair. All clothing was then repaired, washed, folded, and put away for the upcoming season.

At the conclusion of this process, I knew exactly what needed to be ordered for the upcoming year, what items we had lost (and who was responsible for them), and what purchase orders could be prepared and held for the start of the new fiscal year.

Taking care of your equipment needs at the end of each year ensures that you are fully prepared once the season starts. When the athletes report for their first day of practice with all of that enthusiasm, you don't want their first experience to be fixing equipment or being handed old and tattered clothing. If it is, they may assume that you are not organized and that your program is not well-thought-of.

MAINTAINING THE RECORD BOARD

If you have a record board (or another board that honors accomplishments of your athletes) make sure that it is good-looking, legible, and up-to-date. Summer once again provides an excellent opportunity to make updates and make any repairs needed to show that your program does matter and that your athletes' accomplishments do not go unnoticed. This should also include any display areas that you have available to you. Make sure they have current photos, that items are dusted, the brass shined, and the glass cleaned. While many of these items seem like small details, they present an image to people about your program, and you cannot afford to present less than your best image.

Since most associations and governing bodies have strict requirements against a coach being involved in the conditioning of athletes during the off-season, any off-season conditioning an athlete does is often informal and unplanned. Sometimes athletes have a general idea of a basic training program to do during each off-season through previous experience or information passed down from older athletes. At the high school level, I feel most track athletes need to be focusing on just being a kid during the off-season or, if they are involved with a fall sport, training for that. Coaching at the collegiate level, however, I send out three letters to athletes over the summer to keep in touch or provide start-up information.

Your organizational skills and the ability to plan during the summer months for as many situations as possible can free you up to manage your team and interact with the parents and athletes instead of always being rushed into the next "emergency."

Chapter 6

PREPARING FOR PRACTICES

The challenges of planning track and field practices face all head coaches. Practice preparation is a multidimensional task, and as a coach, you must take into consideration the time and facilities available, the size of your staff, the amount of equipment that is accessible, and your competition schedule. Your practices also depend on whom you coach. Practices will likely be different if you are the head coach of a coed program rather than the head coach for just the boys or just the girls. If you are not a coed coach, your practices may need to be compatible with those of your counterpart's team.

COED VERSUS ALL-GIRL OR ALL-BOY PROGRAMS

I have had the opportunity to work with both single-sex and coed track and field teams, and having learned from both experiences, I can share ways to make both situations successful. If you are the head coach of a coed team, your workload is obviously increased; however, there are benefits to this position. For example, when you are coaching a coed team, it is easier to administrate a practice because one philosophy, one coaching staff, and all of the facilities are available to you.

If you are the head coach of just the boys or just the girls, then you need to have a meeting with your coaching counterpart, preferably in the summer or early fall, to establish a practice plan that can accommodate everyone's desires and facility needs. It's important to compromise, whether you share assistant coaches between the two programs or not. If the assistants coach by gender only, then the planning becomes even more important, especially if you have limited facilities available. The fewer your facility options and the less time that is available, the greater the potential for problems between the two teams.

SCHEDULING THE FACILITY

Constraints that could be placed upon your practice plan include the amount of space and equipment that is available and the physical

Coaching Coed

When I coached the high school girls' and boys' team, we always started practice 20 minutes following the dismissal bell. We started each practice with a complete team stretch. This stretch took place at the starting/finish line with our girls' team on one side and the boys' team on the other side, facing each other. The captains, usually four in total, were between the two groups, and they led the activity as instructed by one of my assistant coaches. During this time, we'd take attendance, and coaches would move throughout the group and interact with the athletes. This was the only static stretching that was done during the practice, and it included only about four to six stretches, held for 15 seconds each.

Following the static stretching session, we'd break into six coed groups of multiple athletes (because that was the number of assistant coaches that were in the program). The athletes then reported to an assigned station where they would spend five minutes going through a dynamic warm-up that involved light plyometric activities and technical running drills. Athletes would be allowed 20 seconds to jog to the next station, and they would continue this rotation until they had visited every station. The static stretch and the station drills used 40 minutes of practice time. Afterward, we had optional station time, which meant that my assistant coaches who coached other sports could have eight minutes to include drills specific to their sport before starting the regular track practice. This plan was introduced to make being an assistant coach in my program worthwhile, and it provided a way for them to maintain contact with their athletes and monitor their progress.

On days before meets, the warm-up is all we would do, with a short practice of 15 minutes that focused on each athlete's main events for the next day.

After the stretching and stations, we began event-specific practices that rotated through two 30-minute sessions. The entire team would receive coaching in their events, with a primary day in one event and an off day or a follow-up day in another event. Following the workout, the athletes reported to the strength center for their lifting program, which was divided by event, gender, and years in the program. We ended each practice at 6:00 P.M. sharp so that their parents knew when to pick them up or so that they could make the late bus sponsored by the school district.

Making Do With What You Have

In my first coaching position, we didn't have a track so . . . we drilled holes in the sidewalk to place a set of blocks; we painted hurdle marks on the sidewalk; and that's where we conducted our practices. We measured out a 200-, 300-, and 400-meter loop on the streets in front of the school and did interval work there. I formed and poured two cement slabs and created throwing rings. I bought take-off boards, anchored them to the ground, and used the school's tractor to dig a hole; then I filled it with sand and made a jump pit. The biggest tool or stumbling block you have for maximizing your current facility is your imagination.

layout of your track and field facility. Since most high school tracks are incorporated into stadiums that are used for other sports, limitations may exist.

In field events, have small groups organized with multiple activities going on so that when the actual facility is being utilized by a person or group, your other athletes are still working. For example, while the triple jumpers are doing a drill, the long jumpers are getting a drink and walking 200 meters to recover from their drill—then the groups switch. In the throws, you can have a person or group in the ring while the others are working on a part of the technique on the side without an implement. Have the running lanes on the track identified for use. One option would be to have lanes 1 and 2 for speed work, lanes 3 and 4 for recovery running, and lanes 5 and 6 for hurdle work. You will also want to stagger your times on the track and in the field so that your entire team does not arrive at the weight room at the same time. When that happens, everyone just stands around, and nothing gets accomplished. Your distance team can benefit from a circuit program that allows for maximum work in a minimum amount of time before the arrival of your power event athletes, who will need to spend more time in the weight training facility.

On the other hand, if you are lucky enough to ever have the opportunity to enhance your existing facility or to become involved in the construction of a new facility, do so with practice efficiency as well as outstanding competitive venues in mind. Since the field-event venues tend to be the areas that are most limited, lay out throwing and jumping areas so that multiple athletes can be working safely at the same time. Your athletes can then perform more repetitions, and you can run a more effective and efficient practice. In the long jump, triple jump, and pole vault, runways should be designed to accommodate wind from any direction. If your choices here are limited, consider the primary wind direction during the spring when creating these areas. If possible, lay out the running track so that you have at least eight lanes (and preferably nine) so that in a meet, athletes have to compete to place, rather than just automatically earn points in an invitational, conference, or at a state-qualifying meet. In practice, this additional lane allows coaches to work an event or set up equipment for drills.

ENCOURAGING PRESEASON CONDITIONING

Most, if not all, state athletic associations and national governing bodies limit the number of weeks you can interact with your junior high and high school athletes in a structured manner. Therefore, I feel it is important to suggest to your athletes that they become involved in other sports during the off-season to maintain a reasonable level of fitness, provide a healthy distraction from your sport, and enhance their total body development in ways other than those they are exposed to in track and field.

For those not involved in other sports, many schools offer a general conditioning program to all students after school or as part of a physical education unit. You need to encourage your athletes' participation in these areas at least six weeks before the start of your season. By doing so, the athletes will not experience initial soreness. They will also be ready to get involved in the technical aspects of the field events or begin at a higher fitness level if they are involved in the running events. If such programs are not available, recommend to your athletes that they run three days a week. Also encourage them to get into the strength center as well. If they do so, their transition into the season will be much easier.

Once the season starts, focus on overall conditioning components such as flexibility, strength training, proper running form, and aerobic and anaerobic work.

Don't rush into competitive settings! Allow at least 14 to 21 days of practice before competing. During the early weeks, keep practice fun and light, and make sure that the athletes leave practice feeling as though they could have done a lot more.

PLANNING IN-SEASON CONDITIONING

Just as I set up my seasonal competition schedule from end to start, I also work in reverse when writing my actual workouts for the various events (see figure 6.1). Once I have the meets on the calendar, I develop my practices by working backward from the championship meet to the first day of practice. Like some other coaches, I use a system of hard/easy days so that the athletes are exposed to a certain level of training stimulus one day and then have a lower level the next day for recovery. I even use a word processor to color-code my calendar to indicate which days are hard (including meet days, which are both physically and emotionally intense), medium, and light, and which days are off days. With this system, you can quickly count the number of stress days that you have placed the athletes in simply by counting the colors.

Along with tracking stress days, you can count the volume of work, as measured by the meters of running, the number of foot plants in jumping events, and the total throws for the shot and discus athletes. This also shows you if you are progressing too quickly or if you have placed too many stresses on your athletes during that week or training cycle. As a general rule, I only increase the workload by 5 percent per week. Remember not to increase more than one aspect per week. For example, don't increase speed and the quantity in the same week. As you gain experience, you develop a "coach's eye" where you can watch practice and not be a slave to the clock yet still evaluate the effects of training on your athletes. Remember, not every athlete is the same, and each reacts to a workload differently.

I have come to believe that most American coaches ask too much from their athletes in practice and competition. Injuries as a result of overuse seem to be one of the best indicators of overtraining, as are small bouts of illness and a decline in competitive performance. If you review the literature from our European counterparts, you'll find that they have developed a long-term, methodical, and calculated approach to developing their athletes over a period of many years rather than a single season, which many coaches in our country tend to do.

Each year you should slightly increase the workload of your athletes so that they experience a gradual increase that allows their bodies to adapt to these incremental changes. While there is not a specific formula that you can apply here, your experience and personal judgment will assist you in establishing a pattern. As a general rule, though, I look at an increase of about 5 to 10 percent. It is always better to slightly undertrain athletes than to overtrain them and have them wind up physically unavailable for the most important meets at the end of the year. This system holds throughout the season until you begin tapering for the major meets at the end of the year. Your athletes should not compete in more than two meets per week, and you should limit the number of events they participate in at each meet. One meet per week is ideal, especially if, as a team, you are trying to be successful at the end of your season. Allow your third and fourth runners on your depth chart to run in your midweek meet, and schedule your top two athletes to compete only on Saturday.

April 2003

Sunday	Monday	Tuesday	Wednesday	Thursday	Friday	Saturday
		1 8 x 100 @ :12 30:00 trail run Weights	**2** 40:00 run on roads	**3** 1 x 100 - goal pace 1 x 600 @ 2:00 1 x 100 - goal 4 x 165 accels	**4** Check out gear Team warm-up Premeet workout Team meeting	**5** Bearcat Invite Maryville, MO St. Thomas Inv. St. Paul, MN
6 5-6 miles	**7** 1 x 600-500-400-300-200-100 3 miles on road	**8** 30:00 run Weights	**9** 12 x 100 @ :12 5 x 300 cutdowns 20:00 run on trails	**10** 3 x 400 - (400 rest) 20:00 run on trails Weights	**11** 11 Check out gear Team warm-up Premeet workout Team meeting	**12** Esten Challenge Memorial Stadium
13 5-6 miles	**14** 1 x 500-300-165 at goal pace 5 x 200 at goal 15"00 grass run	**15** 12 x 100 @ :12 25:00 trail run Weights	**16** 1 x 600 goal pace 5 x 300 cutdowns from date to goal	**17** Check out gear Team warm-up Premeet workout Team meeting	**18** Pomono Invite Claremont, CA	**19** Carleton Relays Northfield, MN
20 5-6 miles	**21** 1 x 600-500-400-300-200-100 3 miles on road	**22** 3 x 165 A-F-A 3 x 165 F-A-F 20:00 on grass Weights	**23** 5 x 300 - pass 200 at: 29-27-25-24-23 25:00 trail run	**24** Check out gear Team warm-up Premeet workout Team meeting	**25** Drake Relays Des Moines, IA Simpson Twilight Indianola, IA	**26** Drake Relays Des Moines, IA
27 5-6 miles	**28** 1 x 600 goal :03 5 x 200 at 25-27	**29** 5 miles on the trails Weights	**30** 5 x 200 at :25 (200) 15:00 shag on grass			

Figure 6.1 Planning pays off. Many of the best programs plan out practices for each day or week of the season before the season starts.

Some coaches may balk at this strategy, claiming that it is too light for your high-caliber athletes. But consider it this way: Let's say that you have a meet on Tuesday and Saturday. You then have a light day on Monday to get ready to compete on Tuesday, followed by a light day on Wednesday to recover from Tuesday (light-Monday, hard-Tuesday, light-Wednesday). With Thursday being the only day to really work (hard), you would have to follow with an easy day on Friday (light) to get ready to race on Saturday (hard). If you review this week, you have three stress days out of six (two meets and one hard workout), with three easy days. Not much is getting done with regard to the coaching and development of your athletes. So let the third and fourth stringers run during the week, and have your elite athletes focus on the Saturday invitationals.

In other words, if your better athletes don't have to compete midweek, then they are able to get five days of practice, with one day being a premeet day and only one day of competitive stress. This allows you to give them more teaching repetitions and a greater period of conditioning and training, and it spares them the emotional stress and damage that all-out efforts produce on the central nervous system. Over a period of only four weeks, the athletes in the second example receive 12 more solid workout days and four less stressful competitions, with the result of being fresher and more fit when it matters the most.

DEVISING DAILY WORKOUTS

I like to review the past season immediately after it has been completed. I make some notes on possible changes for the next season, and at a later time I begin to put together the workouts for the upcoming season. This way, I can lay out a plan and have plenty of time to review and edit it. Although I enter the season with a script for each event I coach, I always retain the flexibility to make alterations based on weather, injuries, illness, or anything else that might arise.

If I am comfortable with one or all of my assistant coaches, I allow them to put to-gether their own workouts for their athletes. I do expect them to conform to the philosophy of our program, which means ensuring that the athletes are rested and competitive at the end of the season—and when exactly the season ends may change from year to year. The key meet may be a state or national championship one year, and the next year we might set the goal of winning the conference meet while trying to be competitive at the state or national meet. This shift in goals may mean changing the entire workout season by two or three weeks.

Remember that practice constitutes a majority of the time our athletes spend with us. It must be organized, meaningful, motivational—and it must also include some fun.

Posting or Not Posting Workouts

The question of whether or not to post the practice agenda has been debated for years. At the college level, we post the workouts by 10:00 A.M. so that students who have a class or lab can still get their workout in when they have time available. At the junior and senior high school level, you may create some sense of anticipation about the practice if you don't post the workouts. By not posting daily or weekly workouts, you may also eliminate some unexpected illness or small injuries that tend to arise on heavier workdays.

If you do decide to post your workout, develop a clear and concise form. Without spending too much time, you want to put together the posting so that it is meaningful and clear to students and assistant coaches.

ESTABLISHING A PRACTICE FOCUS

The KISS method—Keep it Simple, Stupid—produces benefits. I apply it to our sport in the following way: Each practice should have a focus for each event, or (if you want to take it a step further) each athlete should have a particular focus per event. Too often we confuse the athletes by sending multiple signals and overloading them with several items to work on. It is better to ensure improvement by having the athlete focus on one item and stay with that concept as a single component of the event. Athletes always try to keep the coaches happy by meeting their demands, and in the process, they may be overloaded on cues and miss the proper techniques that can assist them in their improvement. Stick to a single task, and you and the athlete will be rewarded.

I place a time limit on the duration of this teaching moment. I conclude it at the posted ending time of practice, regardless of the success or lack of success at that moment. Continuing the work usually results in repetitions of improper techniques and increased frustration that makes achieving correct form take even longer. If the athlete masters the skill, leave it and allow the athlete to feel good about accomplishing that task—it will provide some stimulus to return tomorrow and learn more.

Personally, I do not record precisely what an athlete does at practice; rather, I look to competitions for performance results. Many coaches get so involved with documenting great workouts that they miss the point of the competition, which is to see improvement.

Much like a math or science class, coaching an athlete involves layered levels of knowledge. Reasonable progression produces the desired results at the appropriate time—at the end of a season or career. If you rush the development of an athlete before a skill is well ingrained and before a neuromuscular pattern is established, it only results in improper learning and an ineffective foundation on which to build the next skill.

Part 3

COACHING EVENT TECHNIQUES AND TACTICS

Chapter 7

SPRINTS AND SPRINT RELAYS

© Human Kinetics

Perhaps the greatest misconception about training sprinters is that they need to do a large volume of work and that they can compete in three or four events each meet without it negatively affecting their future races. Typically, most coaches tend to race their sprinters too much while taking care (as they should) not to overuse their middle-distance and distance runners. When a sprinter runs at top speed, as in a race, it places a significant amount of stress on the neuromuscular system. The body needs time to repair itself after such stress. If the athlete is overraced without adequate recovery time, he or she may experience injury or tired legs. It took me almost 15 years of coaching to fully understand this concept.

Many people feel that sprinters are lazy—they assume, right or wrong, that sprinters rely on their God-given ability, as opposed to having to spend significant time at practice developing their talent. Similarly, many coaches feel that sprinters should be given longer workouts and be worked out at a higher intensity than is appropriate. In my opinion, this is the wrong way to build a team that is deep in excellent and healthy sprinters who can contribute to the team's overall success.

A reasonably sized training group of 8 to 12 athletes allows you to make competition decisions that benefit each sprinter (as well as your team). For example, you can let your fastest short sprinter handle the 100 meters for you; then you can let the sprinter who shows the ability to carry his or her speed longer focus on running the 200 meters. If your depth is solid, you can even develop a 4 × 100 or 4 × 200 relay team that does not affect your top two sprinters. Four solid sprinters who may not exhibit exceptional individual speed can become a very effective relay team by learning to pass the stick well and by embracing this event as their way to contribute positively to the team. These athletes can use this pride to provide the depth you need to score in each speed event.

100 AND 200 METERS

It is easy to find athletes who want to race the 100 and 200 meters, mainly because these events are short and considered the "glamour events" of track and field. When considering candidates for these events, remember that athletes who demonstrate quickness and speed in one sport, such as football, basketball, or soccer, may or may not necessarily have track speed. These athletes are good candidates to start with, but be open to letting others surprise you with their speed.

Before 100- and 200-meter runners do any practice, it's important for them to warm up for at least five minutes. Our athletes use the same basic warm-up for competition that they use in daily practice. This warm-up has been adapted from Loren Seagrave and Kevin

O'Donnell's *Speed Dynamics Instructional System* (Lilburn, GA: Speed Dynamics). Please refer to that work for details on the drills, or you may structure your own workout using a similar combination of warm-up drills, mobility exercises, and accelerations.

1. 10 to 30 repetitions of each of the following drills: prisoner squat, highland fling, front lunge, side lunge, speedskater. Follow each exercise with a 50-meter acceleration and 50-meter walk.
2. 10 repetitions of the following hip mobility circuit exercises: hamstring reach, leg circle forward and back, fire hydrant.
3. 2 × 100-meter accelerations, focusing on correct sprinting body position.
4. The following static stretches held for 15 counts: cross-legged hamstring, stork stand, calf stretch.
5. 10 repetitions of each exercise in the dynamic mobility circuit: head circle, trunk circle, hip circle, lead leg pick-up, trail leg pick-up.
6. 2 × 100-meter accelerations, focusing on recovery mechanics. Follow this with side slide back (changing directions every 30 meters).
7. 3 × 20 meters of each sprint exercise: ankling, butt kick, a-skip, carioca, straight-leg bounding.
8. 2 × 100-meter accelerations, focusing on recovery mechanics followed by 6 × 50 meters; alternate straight-leg bounding and fast legs.

Sprinting Mechanics

All runners, not just sprinters, need to understand and develop solid running mechanics and techniques that allow them to use their talent to the fullest. I recommend that all coaches focus the core of their sprint training here. A good source for techniques is the program by Loren Seagrave and Kevin O'Donnell called *Speed Dynamics*.

Coaches need to instruct athletes on running mechanics and technique because incoming junior high and high school athletes have usually received no previous structured education regarding how to sprint. Although we all began to run soon after we mastered walking, many of us do not know how to run correctly. Good running form is the foundation of track and field. Therefore, I recommend that a significant part of your daily training program at the start of each season feature relevant techniques and drills and that a large part of your time be spent in this area with your younger runners.

It takes many repetitions to improve a technical skill, let alone master it, so I strongly recommend that coaches continue to emphasize technique drills throughout an athlete's career. These drills can be incorporated into an athlete's competition warm-up so that the athlete's body can become familiar with both the techniques and the warm-up protocol. The primary areas that the athlete needs to focus on are head position, arm carriage, foot plant, foot action, and pelvic alignment.

Head position: The head should remain in neutral position, with the chin level and the jaw relaxed (see figure 7.1a). There should be no horizontal or vertical movements.

Arm carriage: The arms should maintain a 90-degree angle at the elbow throughout the upswing as well as the backswing (see figure 7.1b). Athletes can imagine the arms rotating around a dowel rod that runs through their shoulders. During the running phase, their arms should not elongate or shorten.

Figure 7.1, a and b   Solid sprinting mechanics involves proper positioning of the head, arms, feet, and pelvis.

Foot plant: The foot should always be in a toe-up/heel-down position (see figure 7.1c) to allow for the clawing effect explained in the following section on foot action. This plant helps prevent a breaking effect that results when the toe is pointed downward during the running phase. By keeping the toe up and the heel down during the recovery phase of the stride, the length of the lever is shortened, resulting in a fast motion.

Foot action: The clawing action that results from a toe-up/heel-down foot plant (see figure 7.1d) is critical in all distances run. As the foot strikes the ground during the plant phase, you should hear a scraping sound on the ground when doing the "claw drill" from a stationary position. The heel-down aspect assists in the foot plant, but it is also important in the recovery phase of the run.

Pelvic alignment: To assist with the lower body action, the pelvis should be tilted in an upward direction. This position is somewhat unnatural and is not used in everyday walking.

Starts

Any start should come from a position that enhances the acceleration pattern of the athlete. To accomplish this goal, the sprinter, at the moment of the start, must apply maximum force against both starting pads in the

Figure 7.1, c and d   Sprinters of all levels should continue to drill their mechanics.

shortest period of time possible. The main areas your sprinters should learn to focus on at the starting position are

1. block placement,
2. the set position, and
3. clearing the blocks.

Block Placement

Three variations of block placements result in three types of starts: the bunch start, the medium start, and the elongated start. The power leg should always be in the up-position or closest to the finish line, since this is where the first energy is developed. To determine which leg is the power leg, some coaches use a test in which the athlete stands with feet parallel and then falls forward. The logic is that the stronger leg steps out to save the athlete from landing face down. Another option is to have the athlete perform single-leg hops on each leg. The leg that allows the athlete to cover the most distance is considered the strongest leg. Other coaches simply allow the athlete to experiment and go with what feels most comfortable.

In the bunch start, the athlete is close to the line, with recommended pad placements approximately 16 inches behind the line for the front pad and 11 inches behind the front pad for the back pad (see figure 7.2a). The medium start has the front pad approximately 21 inches from the starting line and the back pad about 16 inches behind the front pad (see figure 7.2b). The elongated start places the front pad at approximately 21 inches from the start line and the back pad about 26 inches behind the front (see figure 7.2c).

You can have your sprinters try these various placements, but most are best served by using the medium start position. This position provides the athlete with maximum force because the body angle from the toe to the head is between 41 and 45 degrees when clearing the blocks, which translates to high velocity (see figure 7.2b). In races that start on a straight, make sure that the athlete has the entire starting block centered in the lane so that the runner is not leaving the starting line on an angle. Remember that the foot must

Figure 7.2, a-c   Sprinters should try the bunch start *(a),* the medium start *(b),* and the elongated start *(c)* positions, but most find the medium start position most comfortable.

be touching the starting pad as well as the track throughout the starting process. Once a comfortable starting position that produces the proper velocity and attains the required angles in the knee joint has been established, have your athletes take a tape measure and measure the exact distances for both pads from the starting line. This tape measure should be at every practice and meet as part of the required equipment since there are many different types of blocks.

Set Position

The pad settings that you and your athlete settle on should create a set position for the starting block (figure 7.3a) in which the angle of the front knee is 90 degrees and that of the back knee is 120 degrees (figure 7.3b). The athletes should apply equal pressure to both pads, and they should "roll" their weight over their arms slightly so that their weight is supported comfortably by their arms. The athletes should place their hands slightly wider than shoulder-width apart, with the thumb and forefingers creating a bridge position. The arms are straight, and the head comes to rest in a comfortable position, with the neck neutral and the hips rising to slightly higher than the head and shoulder area.

Block Clearance

Once the gun has sounded, the athlete should push against the blocks with both feet and drive out and up. The arms should drive quickly as well, and the athlete should literally run out of the blocks, not jump up or jump out (figure 7.3c). You are looking for a powerful, fluid motion.

After clearing the blocks, the athlete should continue to drive forward from a 45-degree angle, plotted from the ground, through the ankle, through the knee joint, hips, and then through the head (figure 7.3d). The toe must be up so that it can "claw" against the ground when it is applied. After covering about 30 meters, the sprinter gradually becomes more upright, with the arm drive traveling between the height of the shoulder and back to the side seam of the uniform top, never crossing the midline of the torso (figure 7.3e).

Figure 7.3, a-d From the blocks (a) to the set position (b), the athlete rolls his or her weight onto the arms and raises the hips so that they are slightly higher than the shoulders, then leaves the blocks (c) and drives forward (d).

Figure 7.3, e and f Moving into a more upright position *(e),* the athlete becomes light on the feet *(f)* and powers through to the finish.

As the race progresses, the runner should continue to claw against the ground, begin to run tall and become light on the feet, and maintain relaxation in the face and arms (figure 7.3f). At the finish, the sprinter can either lean or run hard through the finish line. I used to teach the sprinter to lean, but I found that more times than not, the athlete would slow down slightly to set up for the lean. I now ask our sprinters to run beyond the finish line before slowing down or taking any other action.

200-Meter Starting Considerations

There are a couple of starting considerations for athletes who are preparing to run the 200 meters. All sprint-starting mechanics, drive phase, and angles that occur in the first few steps are essentially the same for the 100 meters through the 400 meters—but they are more critical in the shorter races than the longer. In the longer races, the athletes start on a curve. They need to adjust the starting block so that the outside hand is just behind the line and the inside hand is about four inches behind the line (figure 7.4a). The starting block pads remain set at the same position as they would for the 100-meter race.

Figure 7.4a For a 200-meter start, the block is set at an angle to the starting line.

Figure 7.4, b and c The athlete must maintain the line through the curve while sprinting out of the block.

Once the gun is fired, the athlete runs to a point on the inside of the curve, leaving the blocks in a straight line. The left shoulder should lean in slightly (figure 7.4b), and the right arm should just drive across the midline of the torso. As the runner comes out of the curve, he or she must not float to the outside of the lane but must instead maintain the line established in the turn (figure 7.4c). The strength of your athlete determines how hard he or she runs the turn and whether it is a controlled acceleration into the straight. Either way, the goal is to maintain form and speed through the finish line.

Preseason Conditioning

Before the start of the season, I encourage a general overall conditioning program that includes a lifting program with some use of Olympic-style lifts for high schoolers, such as cleans, snatches, clean and jerks, deadlifts, stability work for both lateral and straight-ahead movement, integrated sled pulls over

30 to 40 meters, hill sprints with a sprint-up and walk-down format, and stadium stairs. If runs are going to be incorporated in your preseason conditioning, focus on aerobic power sets:

- 6 × 100 at 70 percent of race pace with 30 seconds rest
- 2 to 3 sets of 6 to 8 × 300 at 70 percent of race pace with 3 minutes rest

Or include some tempo endurance workouts, such as sets of 200 meters or more at 65 percent of race pace, with 45 seconds of rest between intervals and two minutes of rest between sets. Use these examples, and schedule a hard day followed by an easy day for a 7- to 14-day cycle. The athletes should leave practice feeling as if they could do more work.

Early to Midseason Conditioning

While at the 1999 USA Track and Field Convention, I had the opportunity to sit and discuss in-season sprint training with the 1992 Olympic head coach and former head coach at Auburn University, Mel Rosen. Mel was the first to really share with me the program that I now use and outline here. I adopted this plan because coach Rosen said that no matter the talent level or age, his athletes all improved during their four years under his coaching—from Harvey Glance to a young man whose 100-meter personal record was 10.50. This simplicity lured me to try this program, and it has resulted in more 100-meter, 200-meter, and 4 × 100-meter all-Americans in three years than I had coached in the previous ten years of coaching at the college level.

A sample week from the early to midseason program is shown in table 7.1. Note that the table shows a pattern, and that it suggests that you can make changes and keep the athletes' attention by being creative in what you do. For example, you can mix up the distances, but you should try to maintain the total meters run in a day and keep the same corresponding times. In the relay stick work, we work at only 50 percent effort. The time of the season and your program's philosophy dictate how much time athletes spend in the strength center. Weight work ranges from three or more times per week early in the season to no sessions at all late in the season (during the taper phase).

Late Season Training

Late in the year, we reduce the volume of training. However, we might increase the speed on a day with less volume so that athletes focus more on feeling fast and leave practice excited and ready for more. The racing itself will sharpen the runners' performances. Shorter practices that cover half to two-thirds of the racing distance and demand 90 to 95 percent of each athlete's personal best are enough to provide quality late season training.

You certainly can take a more scientific approach to sprint training, but consider the age of your athlete, the number of athletes you need to train and monitor, and the time you have to complete the entire practice. There are outstanding coaches who deal with elite athletes and place a great deal of emphasis on physiology and technical aspects of the sport, but they work with their athletes on a one-on-one basis, over an extended period of time. Their athletes are much more physically and emotionally mature than the average junior high and high school athlete.

Perhaps your greatest contribution to your athletes is to provide them with the technical foundation that I spoke about earlier in this chapter so that they are prepared and injury-free to make that next step in their progression

Table 7.1 Sample Week of Early to Midseason Workouts for 100- to 200-Meter Specialists

Monday	3 to 4 × 300 meters in 45 to 47 seconds, 6-minute walk recovery or 5 to 6 × 200 in 30 seconds, 4-minute walk recovery
Tuesday	Block starts Relay passes for all three passes
Wednesday	Relay passes at 50 percent speed 6 × 150 in 22 seconds, 5-minute walk recovery
Thursday	15 minutes block work Light accelerations 2 × 120 in 14 to 15 seconds, 6-minute walk recovery
Friday	Premeet practice (athletes choice; must include some light start work)
Saturday	Competition

Sprinters of all levels benefit from performing regular sprinting mechanics drills.

to excellence. They will perform well for your team and have strong performances at high-level meets. As I discuss in chapter 14, getting them mentally prepared to perform may be more important than having them complete one last great workout.

400 METERS

Athletes who specialize in the 400 meters can be the cornerstone of a successful track program. They can provide good coverage in the 100, 200, 400, 4 × 100, 4 × 200, and 4 × 400 events, and in an emergency, either at the 800 meters or a 4 × 800 relay. Many slower short-distance sprinters can find a new home in the 400-meter group where they experience newfound success. An easy way to predict a male runner's potential in the 400 meters is to take his best open 200-meter time, double it, and add 3.5 seconds. To predict a female runner's time, add 4.5 to 5.0 seconds to the doubled 200-meter time. As an example, look at your 200-meter runners who run 23.0. Apply the formula, and you have a candidate who could run 400 meters in 49.5 in an open race. Four athletes of this speed in a 4 × 400 relay could produce a time of 3:18.0 without even subtracting time for being on the roll as a relay member. These two numbers would most likely score higher at your conference and state series meets than a 23.0 in the 200 meters would.

The reason most sprinters run and hide when their name is mentioned in the same breath as a 400-meter race is that they are afraid of the pain they think is involved. Or, sometimes, they have been thrown into the race without being trained for the event and have thus had a very negative experience. In addition to preparing athletes for this event, make sure you really *sell* this event. Do it in a positive and enthusiastic manner, using current examples of key people such as Michael Johnson and taking advantage of the attention he has brought to it.

Conditioning for the 400 Meters

The key to success in the 400 is in the training for the event. Athletes should never run faster than race pace during training; they should build strength, and they should use relaxation to maintain speed or reduce the diminishment of speed. We know that athletes who are working reasonably hard will encounter lactic acid build up once they have run for 40 seconds. You'll never need to have them run faster than 400-meter speed since the main energy sources used in the 400 meters are the ATP-PC (adenosine triphosphate–phosphocreatine) and lactic acid systems. Therefore, all of your work will be to maximize the development of these systems; this does not involve running at speeds faster than race pace.

Take into consideration the time versus the distance that is covered in 300- and 350-meter efforts. A slower 400-meter runner still incurs lactate at 40 seconds, but it occurs several meters before a faster runner would incur lactate. Therefore, the time run at 400-meter pace is more important in some cases than the meters run. For example, an effective workout might be 3 to 4 × 300 at race pace plus 5.0 seconds, with a walking recovery of five minutes between runs. A 48-second 400-meter runner should arrive at the 300-meter mark at 41 seconds, while the 52-second runner would arrive at the same distance in 44 seconds, having thus been in lactate 3 seconds longer while running the same workout. The cumulative effect of being over the lactate threshold longer is much greater for the slower runner, who therefore requires a different workout the next day.

This logic also applies to girls, who still arrive at lactate after 40 seconds of sustained work. But in the case of the aforementioned workout, a 60-second 400-meter female runner would cover the 300 meters in 50 seconds—in other words, she would be in lactate for 10 seconds, as opposed to the 1.0 or 3.0 seconds that the male runner was exposed to lactate. Therefore, when determining whether to base your practices on meters or time, consider your runners: While a 48-second runner makes it to 300 meters at 41 seconds, an equal effort for a 60-second runner places them at 240 meters.

The athletes' ability to remain relaxed during the 400-meter run is strengthened by running 600-, 500-, and 450-meter runs at paces that range from their race pace plus 15 seconds early in the season to their race pace plus 4 seconds later in the season, followed by a 15-minute walking recovery and hill work. This workout provides the needed endurance work to complete the 400-meter race in good running posture while staying relaxed through the finish line.

Over time, I have assigned a race-pace plus time system to athletes' workout speeds to have consistency in the tempos that the athletes run. I then run practices by ability groups to eliminate racing in practice. Samples of this concept are demonstrated in the sample training program shown in table 7.2.

Along with the running portion of these sample workouts, I have athletes lift two to three times per week in the early season and taper off the weight training completely as we get into late season. The workouts shown in table 7.2 are for a runner with a 47-second personal record in the 400-meter run. To modify the sample workout shown in table 7.2 for a junior high group, reduce the number of repetitions as well as the speed of the runs, based on your athletes' 400-meter race pace.

Warm-Up Change-Up

It used to be that our 400-meter group would do 3 to 6 × 100 meter accelerations during practice. One year, one of our runners, who had a history of hamstring problems, ran slightly faster 200 meters than normal in place of these accelerations. At the NCAA Championships, he felt the best in the race and ran a lifetime, outdoor personal best, while our other runners felt a little heavy. During the next couple of years, I experimented with this difference and had the same results. We eventually adopted this change into our program and have since had fewer hamstring injuries.

Table 7.2 Sample Workout Weeks for 400-Meter Runners

	Preseason
Monday	8 × 200 in 34 seconds, 5-man relay style
Tuesday	4 × 500 at race pace plus 22 seconds/400, 3-minute walk recovery
Wednesday	15-minute easy run on trails
Thursday	4 × 350 in 57 to 59 seconds, 10-minute walk recovery between runs
Friday	200 in 33 seconds, 5-minute rest
	600 at race pace plus 14 seconds/400, 15-minute rest
	3 × 300 at race pace plus 9.5 seconds, 3-minute rest
	Early to Midseason
Monday	7 × 200 in 27 seconds, 5-man relay style
	200 in 30 seconds, 200-meter walk
Tuesday	200 in 28 seconds, 3-minute walk
	2 × 450 at race pace plus 5 seconds/400, 15-minute walk
	4 × short hill sprints
Wednesday	1600 of ins/outs in 29 to 30 seconds
	200 in 30 seconds, 200-meter walk
Thursday	6 × 150 in 21 seconds, 150-meter walk
	200 in 30 seconds, 200-meter walk
Friday	3 × 200 in 30, 29, and 28 seconds
	Relay stick and start work
	Late Season
Monday	5 × 200 in 26 seconds, 3-minute standing recovery
Tuesday	3 × 150 accelerations, 150-meter walk
	3 × 200 in best time plus 4, 3, 2 seconds, 200-meter walk
Wednesday	3 × 150 accelerations, 150-meter walk
	3 ×300 in best time plus 5.5 seconds, 5-minute walk
	1 × 200 in 28 seconds, 200-meter walk
Thursday	3 × 150 accelerations, 150-meter walk
	4 × 200 in 27 seconds, 3-minute walk between runs
Friday	3 × 150 accelerations, 150-meter walk
	3 × 200 in 29, 28, and 27 seconds, 3-minute walk between runs

Racing Tactics

When planning strategy for the 400 meters, remember that runners never make up in the last 200 meters what they lost or sacrificed in the first 200 meters. A classic example of this maxim is the 1988 Olympic final in Seoul, Korea, when Butch Reynolds got out slow, tried to make a move over the final 200 meters, and never got up to win the race. On the other hand, the two accepted ways to achieve success in the 400-meter race are to run an evenly split race or to run within one second of a personal best 200-meter open for the initial

200 meters and then run off of that tempo through the finish.

Evenly paced racing is very difficult to teach and even harder to execute. This racing style asks a 48-second 400-meter runner to run 12 seconds per 100 meters, for splits of 12.0, 24.0, 36.0, and 48.0. In theory, the equal disbursement of effort should physiologically produce the optimal result; however many emotions, psychological effects, and physiological factors are involved with a successful race. I support—especially for younger runners—getting into a fast rhythm over the first 50 meters, getting into a free-wheeling rhythm that allows for quick turnover without seeming to work as hard, running the first 200 meters within 1 second of a personal best, then beginning an acceleration over the next 100 meters to reduce the loss of speed related to being in a curve, which should then set up an athlete for a strong finish.

SPRINT RELAYS

The sprint relays are some of the most exciting events in a track and field program. Runners combine speed, coordination, and teamwork to accomplish the task. They also allow four athletes, who may or may not be your four fastest runners in a single event, an opportunity to get to a sectional or state final by becoming efficient in their baton-handling and sprinting. These relays are always a favorite among the runners. When asked, they will tell you that they enjoy the open events but have a special feeling for running with the baton in their hand with their teammates.

4 × 100 Relay

This event is the track equivalent of Russian roulette in many people's eyes. A coach can remove a lot of uncertainty by having the runners practice many repetitions of the actions that have to take place in the race.

Selecting Your Team
The first concern is your selection of runners and their running order. Your first and third legs should run with the baton in their right hand, and the second and fourth runners should carry it in their left hand. If you mandate this, you ensure that the stick or baton will always remain in the middle of the running lane. The main idea is to prevent the athletes from stepping on each other and from passing the baton across their body. One of the first questions I ask my runners who are being considered is whether anyone is left-hand dominant. If you don't have a lefty, you need to spend time developing left-handed technique with right-handed athletes. The second question I pose is whether anyone has ever (or never) taken a baton. These two questions may quickly establish your running order, by establishing who has (or lacks) experience.

All things being equal, I believe that coaches have many options for putting a successful relay team together. The old standard is to have your best starter lead off, use your second-fastest runner and good baton-handler second, have your best curve-runner handle the third leg, and use your fastest sprinter for carrying it home.

However, there are other possibilities. I would always agree that the first runner needs to be your best starter, someone who can run a fast turn, who is perhaps shorter in stature than the other team members and an individual who is not going to panic on you in the major meets of the year. I would look at your second runner as someone who can maintain speed longer. You would want the second runner to take the baton early in the zone and carry it deep into the second zone. This may be a 400-meter runner who has good acceleration skills or a high top-end speed that will carry past the end of the second zone. If you feel a need to apply pressure on the other teams, you may want to put your fastest runner in this second position. By the second exchange, you can be clearly in the lead and create nervousness in the other teams' runners. On the third leg, I like to use my best 200-meter athlete, if not my fastest 100-meter runner, since these athletes are used to running this turn (it also gives them more repetitions on the turn). Stature may be a concern. A shorter athlete may handle the turn better, especially if your team draws the first lane. The anchor runner is the person who can handle pressure while leading or being closed on. This person has to have supreme confidence in his or her ability and be a runner who can remain focused and relaxed if the race should become close.

In my opinion, coaches have many options available to them when establishing the running order. One major consideration you may want to seriously focus on is trying to match up with your main competition at the biggest race of the season, whether that is the sectionals, state, or national meet. After all, in the major meets, place is everything, and performance doesn't matter if you don't get the points. So review what your competition has traditionally done and think about how you can match up to gain an advantage.

Understanding the Exchange Zones

Once you have selected your team, see that your athletes understand two important concepts. The first is that they have to run through the entire zone while maintaining as much speed as possible; it is unacceptable to slow down once a runner has made the call to take the baton. The second concept is that the outgoing runner has to wait until the appropriate time to leave the starting position and begin acceleration. Failure to execute these two concepts creates problems in these and all other aspects of your relay.

The sprint relays are given an acceleration, or international zone, of 10 meters and an exchange zone of 20 meters. Equations are available for establishing "go-marks"; however, with the junior high and high school athlete being somewhat immature and not always giving you the same look from day to day, I recommend using the trial-and-error method. Start with 20 steps backward from the start of the acceleration zone, and work from that point to get the final go-mark. The athletes must have their spikes on when walking off this distance, since they will be wearing them on race day. The second and fourth runners walk back on the inside lane line for their lane, while the third runner walks back

on the outside lane line. They do this so that their mark is on the same side of the lane as the incoming runner. I have used playground chalk, half-cut tennis balls, and short and long pieces of tape to establish our go-marks. In addition, I have come up with the following ritual for our relays before a meet.

As soon as we arrive at the facility on the day of the meet, I find out which lane we are running in. I then have all of our runners walk their steps back, in their spikes, and make a small chalk mark on the inside and outside of their lane at their go-mark. Then, just before their race, they lay down athletic tape all the way across the lane at the proper location. Doing this relieves the stress and pressure of having to do all of this just seconds before running the actual race. Instead, they can focus on their task and remain relaxed while everyone else is scurrying about getting ready. Once the race has started, the outgoing runner is focused only on the next teammate and go-mark. Once the incoming runner is at or on the go-mark, the outgoing runner accelerates in a normal fashion and continues to accelerate throughout the zone. It is the incoming runner's responsibility to catch the outgoing runner, not the job of outgoing runner to slow down for the incoming runner.

The only time we have a safety mark, which is located four shoe-lengths beyond where the stick is usually passed for each zone, is in championship meets, and even then, we usually use it only in the finals. If you are forced to slow down at any point during the race, unless you have exceptional talent, you will probably not advance to the finals. However, once you are in the finals, you always want to make sure that you will score the points. It is for these races only that I would recommend that you employ a safety mark.

Polishing the Pass

In the 4 × 100 relay, the baton always remains in the middle of the lane, no matter who is carrying it at any given time. The incoming and outgoing runners are staggered in the lane so that their hands match up for the pass and so that they do not step on the other runner's foot or leg.

Runners have used several types of passes throughout the years, and surprisingly, those early forms of passes, while less efficient, are still being coached and used today. The original pass was the cradle, where the incoming runner would pull up next to the outgoing runner and place the baton in his hand, which was anchored at his waist (figure 7.5a). This approach does not allow for much "free zone" (the distance between the runners that the stick covers when being passed), and it was used during the early years of the modern era by the United States (since we usually had four superior sprinters as compared with the rest of the world).

Following that was the upsweep pass, where the outgoing runner would extend the proper hand behind the hip with the palm facing down toward the track. The incoming runner would then pass the baton up into the outgoing runner's hand (figure 7.5b). This allowed for some free zone, but the runner always had to adjust the baton forward while on the run to prepare to pass it to the next runner.

Figure 7.5, a-c
The cradle (a), upsweep (b), and downsweep baton passes are all still being coached and used today.

The down-sweep pass evolved from the up-sweep because it allowed the runners more free zone and allowed them to place the baton in the proper position to pass it to the next runner. This pass has the outgoing runner drive the proper arm behind the body, palm up and everted (away from the body), while the incoming runner brings the baton down into the outgoing runner's hand (figure 7.5c).

The down-sweep method is highly used today as is the snatch pass, which is the most modern method. The snatch pass provides all of the benefits of the down-sweep pass, and has the advantage of allowing the outgoing runner to drive with both arms to help in the acceleration process rather than having to run with one arm driving and one arm locked in the receiving position.

The snatch technique is what I use and recommend for your team. I had success with this pass at the high school and the college level, but it can also be used in junior high programs. In fact, this is a clear example of

Figure 7.6, a-c I recommend the snatch pass, which has the advantages of the down-sweep pass but also allows the outgoing runner to use both arms to accelerate.

Catching Relay Splits

I never give splits to the runners of the 4 × 100 relay and 4 × 200 relay. The first reason is that I am not that good, and I don't have the exact middle of the exchange zone marked. Secondly, the 4 × 100 relay is a teamwork event, and I want them to work together to attain the desired outcome.

However, with technology and precise markers, you may be able to get split times. First, check your rulebook for the number of markers you can have in your lane. Then, if the markers are permissible and if you are able to, determine the exact center of the zone. You may be able to get the splits if your camera has a timer that is visible on the screen so that you can see the exact splits when you play the tape in slow motion. Personally, though, I prefer to focus on teamwork, baton skills, and speed to get to the finish line.

how you can use your feeder program to teach the techniques that will eventually be used in your program. It gives athletes more repetitions of the skills that you will expect later so that they can master the skills sooner than those just learning in high school.

In the snatch pass, the outgoing runner leaves when the incoming runner hits the go-mark. The advantage of this technique over all the others is that it allows athletes to run through the acceleration and exchange zone driving both arms. The incoming runner holds the arm straight out, with the baton vertical and slightly forward, aimed at the outgoing runner's elbow (figure 7.6a). When given the signal, the outgoing runner takes the receiving arm back (figure 7.6b). Rather than swinging it out and away from the torso, the outgoing runner sweeps the arm directly backward, grazing the thumb along the running shorts. The baton is in a perfect position to be received; the runner's arm motion drives forward in a normal running motion, and the runner continues onward (figure 7.6c). In the

event of a miss, the incoming runner holds the stick in the receiving position, and the outgoing runner, using a normal arm swing, goes back for it again.

Making the Call

Many teams use what is called an *auto-drop*, which means that after a prescribed number of paces, the outgoing runner automatically reaches back for the baton. The auto-drop can be helpful when every team is calling for their outgoing runners to take the baton, possibly using the same call and thus resulting in an unexpected pass at the wrong time. The downside to the auto-drop is that the incoming runner can be in trouble and the outgoing runner would have no idea. Instruct your runners to indicate their readiness by calling the first name or nickname of the outgoing runner, as long as it is short (ideally one syllable). Runners can also use the old standby calls of *stick*, *go*, or *take*.

Once our team used the word *stop* in the 2001 NCAA III Championships 4 × 100 relay final for the men. When our second runner screamed *"Stop!"* as our call to our third runner, two teams outside of us slowed considerably as the oncoming runner ran up on them, a fact that was clearly visible in the videotape of the race.

4 × 200 Relay

The 4 × 200 relay is now becoming more popular in high school championship meets, and it presents some different challenges than the 4 × 100 relay. I recommend that you look toward your 400-meter runners to handle this relay. Select sprinters can be involved in this relay in the proper order, possibly running the short leg (less than a full distance; i.e., 180 to 190 meters). However, your 400-meter athletes will be able to maintain their speed and carry the baton through the zone without as much speed loss as shorter sprinters.

The pass can be either a visual (4 × 400 pass) or a blind exchange. I have used the blind pass, but I rely on our running to make up for differences on the speed of the pass. Since we run this event only at our conference and indoor

Figure 7.7 For the 4 × 200 relay pass, I have runners pass from right hand to left hand to allow the incoming runner to run on the inside of the lane.

We use an auto-drop strategy here after six complete strides with the same leg. This usually results in a safe pass, keeping the baton moving, and it allows the race result to rest on the speed of the runners.

The order of your team will vary considerably. My only suggestion is to be sure that your first two runners are mentally strong because they run a long stagger and must maintain their focus on what they are doing (and not become concerned about the distance between runners). If you run this event indoors, it is imperative that you lead with your best 200-meter runner as most 4 × 200-meter relays run a three-turn stagger indoors. Having the clear track to run on is more advantageous than having speed at the end and trying to get around slower runners. In an indoor 4 × 200 relay, I would run in the following order of speed: first, second, fourth, third. The only time I would lead off with speed in an outdoor setting is if you draw the outside lane and you want to get away from the field so that by the time your opponents see what has happened, they cannot run you down with their speed.

4 × 400 Relay

The 4 × 400 relay focuses on the strength of each runner's race, rather than the excellence of the baton work. It is important to maintain the speed of the baton through each of the exchanges, of course, but this can be accomplished by incorporating a visual passing technique into 200-meter repetitions during practice. The workout I am referring to is the five-man relay over 200 meters. We run 200s anywhere from 10 repetitions at the beginning of the season to 5 repetitions as the season progresses, with the speed increasing as I drop a repetition. The athletes are required to use the passing technique I expect for a meet, without the baton slowing down. Each athlete's rest during this drill is the time it takes the other four runners to run their 200 meters. I also use a whistle to keep everyone on pace, with the baton being passed at the whistle.

The baton is carried in the right hand by

championship meets and at relay meets such as the Drake and Kansas Relays, we spend a minimal amount of time with the pass.

Therefore, we use what I consider a safe technique. First, we always pass the baton right hand to left hand with the outgoing runner switching hands four to five strides after the pass is made (figure 7.7). This technique allows the runner with the stick to run on the inside of the lane, which is the shortest distance, to set up the next exchange. Second, we use the go-mark, which is the track mark indicating the start of the international zone. The outgoing runner counts forward 16 steps from that point and begins to run at that location. This distance may vary based on the strength of the incoming runner. If the incoming runner is weaker than the outgoing runner, I want the outgoing runner to get the baton immediately inside the exchange zone. In that case, I would push the outgoing runner farther back from the start of the exchange zone for the go-mark and starting point.

each runner and is passed to the outgoing runners by the left hand, which means that the outgoing runner faces the infield when preparing to accept the baton (figure 7.8). The responsibility for making a solid pass falls on the outgoing runner, since he or she is fresh and the incoming runner is dealing with fatigue. The only responsibility of the incoming runner is to present the baton as a good target, by holding it vertically in the right hand and by running through the pass (i.e., not slowing down).

The outgoing runner needs to judge the speed of the incoming runner so that the outgoing runner leaves on time, takes four fast-driving strides, looks down the track, then turns the upper body to the left, extends the left arm, and accepts the baton from the incoming runner. The outgoing runner does not switch hands before getting clear of the congestion created by the exchange area. The outgoing runner then proceeds to run the relay leg as if it were an open 400 meters.

Selecting the Relay

The runner you select for the leadoff leg should be accustomed to running the entire distance within the lane and should be able to determine location at all times, a skill based directly on running a three-turn stagger. This runner should have the strength and speed to put your team squarely into the race. With three legs to go, I like to be in a position to challenge after the first leg.

The second runner runs the first 100 meters within the lane, then makes the gradual cut from the lane to the pole that initiates the start of the second turn. As the runners begin the cut process, you runner will have to make adjustments based on how close the race is. Even if the runner is in one of the outside two lanes, that runner should still take the majority of the back straight before making this diagonal cut.

It seems that most relay teams have been coached to put their slowest or weakest runner in the third position, and you can do the same or use this leg to make a move. The anchor leg is usually, but not always, the fastest of the quartet. However, I think that it

Figure 7.8 In the 4 × 400 exchange, the outgoing runner faces the infield before the exchange and is responsible for taking a solid pass from the tiring incoming runner.

is also important to have a great competitor on this leg, someone who has the ability to remain focused in the critical situation, who doesn't try to win the race too soon, and who continues through the finish line.

Here are some additional things to consider when selecting your 4 × 400 relay team.

• With the indoor race, there is some logic to running a fast athlete on the leadoff leg so that you are able to win the cut and run in the first lane the entire way without obstruction.

• You may want to run a different order if you are trying to run a qualifying time. By leading off one of your two top runners, you get a great start and a fast time on the clock. Then you allow all of your other runners to run from a rolling start, thus running faster. Again, this strategy is best when you are striving for a specific qualifying time rather than place.

• In the trials of a championship meet, you may want to anchor your fastest runner if your other three are strong enough to put you into a qualifying position. All your anchor has to do then is get the baton around the track while expending the least amount of energy. You could also lead with and instruct your fastest runner to put the team into the top two positions, thereby assuring yourself that the runner won't sell out during the first leg (this also forces the other legs to be attentive and compete).

• I sometimes employ a switch call by my anchor runner when the meet or race is on the line during a championship or major relay meet. This means that the anchor runner has the right to switch to the third leg, depending on the team's position when the second runner has 80 meters to go. This move can get a team back into a race so that the new anchor runner can be pulled through the final leg. The thinking is that if you are way back and everyone is anchoring their fastest runner, your athlete may run a great race but barely move up; however, if you pass to the anchor runner while still in contention, it may get you a couple of more places by dragging this runner out and pulling him or her to a faster split.

• Match up in championship meets. You will need to get the splits of all of your top competitors so that you can match up personnel in the finals to give your team the best opportunity to win the race and possibly the meet.

Taking Splits

Questions and concerns often arise after the race about how splits were taken. The appropriate way to take splits in the 4 × 400 relay is by timing the baton when *it* crosses the starting-finish line, not when the runner crosses the starting-finish line. You take the split no matter which runner has the baton at the line because the race is really about how fast the baton gets around the track, not the runners.

Chapter 8

HURDLE EVENTS

©Mary Langenfeld Photo

Two basic hurdle events occur in most levels of track and field: the high hurdles and the intermediate hurdles. The hurdle heights, the distances between the hurdles, and the number of hurdles vary depending on the level of competition, whether the meet is indoors or outdoors, and whether the competitors are male or female. Most high school hurdlers can be competitive in both the high and intermediate hurdle races. However, it becomes more difficult to compete in both races in college when the height for men moves to 42 inches and the intermediate distance for men and women is 400 meters. As athletes improve, they tend to focus more on one race; if they continue to run both races, they spend less time on their second race.

High Hurdles

The sprint hurdles are different for men and women at all levels. It is because of these technical differences that these events are addressed separately in this chapter.

Both the men's and women's high hurdle races begin in very much the same way as a 100-meter race would start (see chapter 7, pages 70-73). After three quick powerful strides out of the blocks, the hurdlers raise their head and focus on the first hurdle at step four. At this point in the race, they are in more of a sprinting angle than a 100-meter runner would assume.

Men's High Hurdles

Most male hurdlers use an eight-stride approach to the first hurdle and therefore place their lead foot on the front pedal of the starting block. If the hurdler is exceptionally tall (six-foot-five-inches or taller) and has a tendency to chop his strides to the first hurdle, look at using seven steps out of the blocks, and have him put the lead foot on the back pedal of the blocks.

The athlete takes off between 78 and 90 inches from the hurdle. The takeoff distance depends on a few factors, including the

- stride length,
- speed, and
- height of the hurdler.

Having your hurdlers experiment with their takeoff points is the surest way to figure out what is most appropriate for each hurdler. You do not want your athlete to "float" way over the hurdle because this does not lead to fast times. It is best if the athlete remains tall before driving up to clear the hurdle (figure 8.1a). The hurdler cannot swing the lead leg

Figure 8.1, a and b The athlete remains upright with shoulders square as he drives to and clears the hurdle.

out to the side to clear the hurdle but must lead with the knee and unfold the leg so that he is hurdling with a bent leg. In fact, the athlete should actually be coming down *over* the hurdle and not coming down after he clears it.

Other concerns include having the hurdlers remain on their toes at all times and in all aspects of the race and having them avoid laying out their lead leg too soon. Doing so stops their clearance height and leads to hitting the hurdles.

Throughout the race, the shoulders must remain square to the direction that the athletes are running. The trail arm cannot float behind the athlete's back, and the lead arm should be bent, with the hand in front of the opposite shoulder but not outside of the shoulder. The lead arm needs to return to the sprinting action as soon as possible and therefore cannot go beyond the side seam of the jersey (figure 8.1b).

The trail leg foot should be pointed away from the torso (figure 8.1c), with the calf touching the back of the thigh. The knee should come up to the armpit area as the lead leg extends to the ground, placing the hurdler in a good position to sprint off of the hurdle (figure 8.1d).

The lead leg should be driven straight down toward the track for speed and should contact the track around 45 to 54 inches after the hurdle (figure 8.1e). The first stride after clearance should be initiated by a high-knee action, triggering a full-sprint stride. The athlete should keep the shoulders square and the eyes focused on the next hurdle bar.

In most cases, the final hurdle is the difference between winning and losing a race. The momentum established after clearing that hurdle, along with the runner's getting back into sprinting form as quickly as possible, can

Figure 8.1, c-e   As the athlete clears the barrier, the trail leg points backward and the lead leg is driven to the ground to maintain speed for the next hurdle.

secure the win. We have all watched races where a hurdler who was clearly in the lead throughout most of the race hits the final hurdle or clears it in an awkward way. The transition back into the sprint technique is delayed, and the runner thereby loses the race to someone who has good clearance, who returns to the sprint form more quickly, and who is able to carry the resulting momentum through the finish line.

Women's High Hurdles

With the lower height in the women's sprint race, speed becomes more of a factor than the ability to efficiently and effectively raise the center of mass, the primary concern of the male high hurdler.

It is because of this lower height that the lead leg should lock out on top of the hurdle, thus initiating a stretch reflex action that actually accelerates the lead leg off of the hurdle (figure 8.02, a and b). The trail leg action is also different in the 100-meter hurdle race than in the 110-meter race in that the knee is actually brought through on a downward angle. There is also not as much forward lean with the torso; therefore, the action is closer to the sprinting action in women's races than in the men's race (figure 8.02, c and d).

Figure 8.2, a-d   The leg action of the women's low hurdles is more similar to sprinting than to the men's high hurdle race.

The takeoff and landing distances before and after the hurdle are also significantly reduced in the women's race, with the acceptable takeoff range being 66 to 72 inches and a landing area between 36 and 42 inches. Sprint speed should be a strong consideration when you evaluate possible candidates to run the women's hurdles, with strength and flexibility as supporting traits.

High Hurdle Practice and Drills

The first thing to remember as a coach is that hurdlers apply much greater stress to their legs and body than do normal sprinters; therefore, you cannot expect them to run hurdles on back-to-back days. This does not eliminate, however, the need to work on the daily flexibility that is associated with the hurdling technique.

Hurdlers should always do a majority of their warm-up work in flats to protect their legs. They will need to be in spikes when they actually perform on hurdles and work on technique drills.

Because it is difficult to simulate "competitive adrenaline" during practice, you may want to consider running most or all of your practices on shortened distances between the hurdles. Doing so makes it easier for the athletes

to hit the proper strides each time and to avoid struggling to get to the hurdle. Shortened distances ensure that throughout the workout, the athlete has the best chance at using proper technique on the hurdles. At the beginning of the year I shorten the distance to the second hurdle by half the length of my shoe, the distance to the third by a full shoe length, the distance to the fourth by one and a half shoe lengths, and so on. Later in the season, I close up the space between each hurdle by a shoe's length, or even a shoe and a half per hurdle, to help the athletes produce a faster neuromuscular memory pattern.

Likewise, I like to have athletes practice over hurdles that are three inches lower than the competition height to assist in their speed development in this race. The shorter, closer hurdles enhance the athletes' "quickness" of the technique on the hurdle, first step after the hurdle, and speed between the hurdles.

I like to use the following three lead-leg drills with the hurdlers in a break-out practice setting. These same drills can be used to work on the trail leg.

Wall drill. The athlete places the hurdle up against the wall at competition height. He or she backs up and walks three steps into the takeoff position, then drives the lead leg toward the wall by leading with the knee and placing the calf up against the hamstring (figure 8.3a). He or she hits the wall with the ball of the foot, keeping the shoulders square and the arms in proper position (figure 8.3b). To drill the trail leg, place the hurdle about 30 to 36 inches from the wall. The athlete places both hands on the wall and steps with the lead leg so that the heel is in line with the vertical tube of the hurdle. Then the athlete pulls the trail leg through. Athletes can also modify this drill by doing cycles of trail-leg drills, such as five in a row without stopping, and by leaving the grounded foot stationary.

Clearance drill. With one or up to five hurdles set up in a sequence, the athlete starts from a jog. He or she approaches the hurdle and completes the lead-leg

Figure 8.3, a and b The wall drill can be used to work on upper body positioning as well as lead and trail leg action.

Figure 8.4, a and b   This athlete performs the clearance drill using one hurdle to focus on proper trail leg action.

action over half of the hurdle. The athlete then focuses on leading with the knee and remaining on the ball of the foot, with the shoulders and arms in proper position (figure 8.4, a and b). As the athlete becomes more efficient, he or she can also focus on the speed of the lead leg to the ground and the arm drive into a sprinting motion while clearing the hurdle.

One-step drill. The athlete is again working on half of a hurdle. With a sequence of up to eight hurdles set 8 to 10 feet apart and using the previously described lead-leg technique when the lead leg touches the ground, the athlete takes a single stride and clears the next hurdle. To work on the trail leg, the athlete starts from a jog, clears just half of the hurdle with the trail leg, then focuses on the everted foot and drives the knee up to the armpit. The runner then focuses on the stepping away and the high-knee drive for the next step (figure 8.5).

Figure 8.5   Using the one-step drill and athlete can perfect the sprint upon landing by emphasizing the high-knee drive.

Another trail-leg drill I like to use is a buddy drill. One hurdler rests the trail leg on the hurdle board lengthwise, then steps forward, past the support tube, down the board, pulling the trail leg down the board while a partner assists him or her in keeping the foot everted and lifting the knee into the armpit area.

To get the athlete accustomed to seeing the hurdles at faster speeds, you can do one of two things. You can either shorten the hurdles as I described earlier, or you can lengthen the distance between the hurdles and have the athlete take five or seven steps between the hurdles, thereby generating more speed. While you may have to experiment to find the right distance for your athletes, a reasonable starting point would be 12 or 13 yards between each hurdle for both male and

female hurdlers.

A good drill to use with more advanced athletes is to have the hurdlers work on all short marks. Another good drill for such athletes is to have them start from the blocks and hurdle the first three hurdles, then sprint to the sixth or seventh hurdle, then hurdle one or two more hurdles. I started using this drill after watching several national- and world-caliber athletes on television; it became obvious that they developed a great deal of speed following the third hurdle. In an effort to simulate this trend, I began to use this drill with my own hurdlers.

Another tool I use is to count the number of foot contacts that a hurdler has while running and working with the hurdles during an entire practice. I break these contacts into

Table 8.1 Midseason Workout Week for High Hurdlers

Monday	Report with the sprinters and do their sprint workout. Snatch passes Hurdle flexibility Cool-down, abdominal work, weights
Tuesday	Flexibility, sprint drills 2 × 5 hurdles of fast lead-leg drill (3 steps on 8 to 9 meters) 2 × 5 hurdles of trail-leg drill (39 inches on 9 yards) 2 × hurdle #1 2 × 8 hurdles on short marks 1 × 6 hurdles on short marks 1 × 10 plus 2 drills on 39-inch hurdles on short marks (3 steps) Cool-down, abdominal work, weights
Wednesday	Report with the sprinters and do their sprint workout. Snatch passes Hurdle flexibility Cool-down, abdominal work, weights
Thursday	Flexibility, sprint drills 2 × 5 hurdles of fast lead-leg drill (3 steps on 8 to 9 meters) 2 × 5 hurdles of trail-leg drill (39 inches on 9 yards) 2 × hurdle #1 3 × 6 hurdles on short marks Cool-down, abdominal work, weights
Friday	Report with the sprinters and do their sprint workout. Hurdle flexibility Cool-down, abdominal work, weights
Saturday	Meet day
Sunday	Rest day

- touches during drills,
- touches during the main segment of the workout, and
- touches during the endurance or strengthening segment at the end of practice.

Keeping a record of these contacts may help you see patterns in problem areas that a particular athlete is having. This habit of tracking foot contacts is similar to that of maintaining a log of total meters run in a workout for nonhurdlers. It provides information that may define or clarify a problem (e.g., too many touches resulted in an injury), and it may also provide information that helps you to gradually increase or decrease the workload for the athlete. It becomes useful as you taper your athletes' workouts for major races at the end of the season. In addition, if your team has always had injuries at a certain part of the year, this may highlight the problem area.

High Hurdle Training

Since hurdlers perform sprints with interruptions, they should train along the same lines. They do not need a lot of aerobic work, but they do need some recovery on their nonhurdle days late in the year. They cannot sprint hard during their hurdle session and plunge into an aggressive sprint workout the next day. If they were to do so, they would have four stress days out of every six, with a meet constituting another stress day during the competition season.

Knowing this, I train hurdlers by including some sprint work on one of the hurdle days and specific speed development on only one of the remaining days. I usually have my athletes do volume hurdle practice early in the week. The second hurdle day is geared more toward speed development, with less volume and drill work—we go for more quality and less quantity. A sample week from the middle of an outdoor season is shown in table 8.1

As the season nears the taper period, think less about how much and think more about how; that is, focus not on the volume but on quality repetitions of the whole technique, with speed and efficiency being the major considerations. For example, that second hurdle day might cover only the start through the first hurdle and an extended flexibility session. Remember, more mature or experienced hurdlers require less drill time and need to be given more rest following the quicker and shorter workouts. Table 8.2 shows a sample week from our taper period.

Table 8.2 Late-Season (Taper) Workout for High Hurdlers

Monday	Evaluation meeting/rest day from practice
Tuesday	Flexibility, sprint drills 2 × speed drill (5 hurdles, 6 feet apart) 3 × 8 hurdles on short marks; time touchdowns 3 × 8 hurdles on 13 yards using 5 steps (focus on speed) Cool-down, abdominal work, weights
Wednesday	Report with the sprinters and do their sprint workout. Hurdle flexibility Cool-down, abdominal work, weights
Thursday	Flexibility, sprint drills 2 × hurdle #1 1 × 6 hurdles on short marks; time touchdowns 1 × 4 hurdles on short marks; time touchdowns Cool-down, abdominal work
Friday	Rest day before meet

INTERMEDIATE HURDLES

While similar to the 400-meter hurdle race, the 300-meter hurdles do have several differences. The first and most obvious is the distance run in the race and the energy systems used. The second is that the 300-meter hurdles start on the straight and the 400-meter hurdles on a curve. The 300-meter race also has fewer hurdles and less run-in space following the last hurdle. The final difference is that a strong 100- or 110-meter hurdler, who can also run a good 200 meters, can have success in the 300-meter hurdles without significantly changing the entire training focus, as he or she would have to do if doubling in the 100- and 110-meter hurdles. It is for this reason that most high school hurdlers can successfully run both the high and intermediate races.

Intermediate hurdlers must be able to alternate lead legs, with the left leg being their preferred lead leg. While fatigue is not as great a consideration in the 300-meter race, it does become a factor in the 400-meter hurdles. With wind conditions always a part of outdoor racing, it is imperative that intermediate hurdlers have confidence using either leg as a lead leg.

Table 8.3 provides touchdown times and foot-strike times for different finishing times for the 100-, 110-, 300- and 400-meter hurdles for men and women.

300-Meter Hurdles

One of the first skills that 300-meter hurdlers must accomplish is to get their steps to the first hurdle. Most male athletes use either 21 or 22 steps to accomplish this task while most female athletes use 23 to 24 steps. It is important to note that with an even stride pattern, the lead leg should be on the front block pad, and for an odd stride pattern, the lead leg would be on the back pad.

Since this race starts on a straight, the only factors that can create problems are the wind and the hurdlers themselves. The degree of mastery of the first hurdle determines immediately the potential for success in this race.

The next task is to establish a consistent stride pattern and speed for the first two hurdles. If the hurdlers cannot clear these two hurdles, they will have problems with the next two as the curve becomes a factor in the race. Intermediate hurdlers must determine which lead leg they will use to clear the next hurdle when they are about four or five strides from the hurdle. This recognition can eliminate reaching or chopping as they prepare to clear the hurdle. Both of these actions have a negative effect on the total time.

Once hurdlers have acquired the ability to clear the second hurdle with control and to execute strong runoffs, they can focus on the hurdles on the curve. Having a primary left leg lead helps keep a hurdler from floating to the outside of the lane. Hurdlers can adjust the route they take through the curve, remaining within the lane, to improve their stride pattern for these hurdles. If the hurdler is always coming up too close to the hurdle, he or she can float to the outside of the lane, thereby adding distance to achieve a better stride pattern. Similarly, if the hurdler is always reaching to clear the hurdle, cutting closer to the inside of the lane helps to decrease the distance between hurdles. The optimal stride pattern for the 300-meter hurdles is 13 to 15 strides between each hurdle for males, and 17 to 19 strides between each hurdle for females, with adjustments made along the race.

Entering the home straight, the hurdler may need to add a stride; this is another reason it is necessary for hurdlers to be comfortable leading with either leg. If they were not, they would need to add two strides between each hurdle, as opposed to a single stride. The hurdler needs to focus on each hurdle as it comes up. Otherwise, the runner might hit the hurdle bar. If this happens going into the hurdle, it could cause the runner to lose balance and form, and thus decrease speed. If it happens later, it could cause the runner to straighten up and fail to have a good runoff. During the last third of the race, any factor that impedes speed will have a severely negative impact on the race's outcome.

Table 8.3 Touchdown Times for Various Hurdle Races

				110-Yard High Hurdles							
1	2	3	4	5	6	7	8	9	10	Finish	
2.5	3.6	4.6	5.6	6.6	7.7	8.8	9.9	11.0	12.2	**13.6**	
2.5	3.6	4.6	5.7	6.8	7.9	9.0	10.1	11.2	12.4	**14.0**	
2.6	3.6	4.7	5.8	6.9	8.1	9.3	10.5	11.7	12.9	**14.4**	
2.6	3.7	4.7	5.8	7.0	8.2	9.4	10.6	11.8	13.0	**14.6**	
2.6	3.7	4.9	6.0	7.2	8.3	9.5	10.7	12.0	13.2	**15.0**	
2.7	3.8	5.0	6.2	7.4	8.6	9.8	11.0	12.3	13.6	**15.5**	
2.8	3.9	5.1	6.4	7.6	8.8	10.1	11.3	12.6	14.0	**16.0**	

				100-Meter High Hurdles							
1	2	3	4	5	6	7	8	9	10	Finish	
2.5	3.6	4.6	5.7	6.8	7.9	9.1	10.2	11.0	12.2	**13.8**	
2.5	3.6	4.6	5.7	6.9	8.1	9.3	10.4	11.2	12.4	**14.0**	
2.6	3.6	4.7	5.9	7.1	8.3	9.5	10.7	11.7	12.9	**14.3**	
2.6	3.8	4.9	6.0	7.2	8.4	9.6	10.9	11.8	13.0	**14.8**	
2.6	3.8	4.9	6.1	7.3	8.5	9.7	11.0	12.0	13.2	**15.0**	
2.7	3.9	5.0	6.2	7.4	8.7	9.9	11.2	12.3	13.5	**15.3**	

					300-Meter Intermediate Hurdles					
1	2	3	4	5	200	6	7	8	Finish	
6.0	10.3	14.4	18.6	22.8	24.3	26.7	31.2	35.4	**36.6**	
6.3	10.6	14.8	19.1	23.2	25.2	27.7	32.2	36.8	**38.0**	
6.5	10.9	15.2	19.5	23.9	25.9	28.5	33.2	38.0	**39.4**	
6.8	11.2	15.6	20.1	24.6	26.7	29.4	34.3	39.3	**40.8**	
7.1	11.6	16.1	20.8	25.5	27.6	30.4	35.5	40.7	**42.2**	
7.3	12.0	16.7	21.5	26.4	28.6	31.5	36.7	42.1	**43.7**	
7.6	12.4	17.3	22.2	27.3	29.5	32.5	38.0	43.5	**45.2**	
7.8	12.8	17.8	22.9	28.1	30.5	33.6	39.2	44.9	**46.6**	
8.0	13.2	18.4	23.6	29.0	31.4	34.6	40.4	46.3	**48.8**	

				400-Meter Intermediate Hurdles (Women)							
1	2	3	4	5	6	7	8	9	10	Finish	
6.5	11.1	15.7	20.3	25.0	29.8	34.7	39.7	44.9	50.1	**56**	
6.7	11.5	16.3	21.1	25.9	30.8	35.9	41.1	46.2	51.8	**58**	
6.9	11.9	16.9	21.9	26.9	32.0	37.2	42.5	47.9	53.4	**60**	
7.1	12.3	17.5	22.6	27.8	33.1	38.4	43.9	49.5	55.2	**62**	
7.3	12.6	17.9	23.3	28.7	54.2	39.8	45.4	51.1	57.0	**64**	

				400-Meter Intermediate Hurdles (Men)							
1	2	3	4	5	6	7	8	9	10	Finish	
5.9	10.0	14.1	18.2	22.3	26.5	30.8	35.2	39.7	44.3	**49.6**	
6.0	10.2	14.4	18.6	22.8	27.1	31.5	35.9	40.4	45.1	**50.5**	
6.1	10.4	14.7	19.0	23.3	27.7	32.2	36.8	41.6	46.5	**52.0**	
6.3	10.7	15.1	19.5	23.9	28.4	32.9	37.6	42.5	47.5	**53.0**	
6.4	10.9	15.4	19.9	24.4	29.0	33.7	38.5	43.4	48.4	**54.0**	

400-Meter Hurdles

This race is an altogether different race than the 300-meter hurdles because the hurdler is now starting on the curve. Good prospective athletes for this event would be 400-meter runners who demonstrate flexibility but may not be able to score in the 400 meters in your conference meet or qualify for your state or national championships. While the race is not easy, it usually attracts fewer quality athletes than the open 400 meters, which may provide the motivation for a solid yet not outstanding 400-meter runner to embrace the 400-meter hurdle race.

The first key for the 400-meter hurdler is to get the right number of strides to the first hurdle: 21 or 22 for males, 23 to 24 for females. This task is truly a challenge because the stride pattern may vary with the lane that the athlete draws to start from. The closer the athlete is to the first lane, the tighter the curve; the farther out, the more gradual the

effect of the turn is. The left leg lead is even more important in this race because runners need to establish themselves on a curve as opposed to the straight. A major factor in getting a quality start in this race is getting to the second hurdle under control, without effort, and having a good runoff from that hurdle. If this can be accomplished, the hurdles on the back straight should come easily without the athlete having to use a lot of energy.

Most problems begin as the hurdler enters the second turn. If the runner had a problem on the back straight and had to drop a stride or two, the second curve will be entered with less momentum. The hurdler will therefore need to make an adjustment to the stride pattern or to the running line within the lane.

The finish of the race is similar to the 300-meter hurdles, the difference being a longer run from the final hurdle to the finish line. This distance often allows for some small changes in the finish order.

It is easy for the athlete and coach to get

Table 8.4   Early-Season Workouts for Intermediate Hurdlers

Monday	3 × 5 to 6 hurdles focusing on lead, trail, and over the top (each leg) 3 starts through hurdle #1 2 starts through hurdle #2 10-minute jog with 5 hurdles randomly spaced on track
Tuesday	3 × 150-meter accelerations, 150-meter walk 1 × 200 meters in 28 seconds, 200-meter walk 2 × 450 meters at race pace plus 8 seconds, 15-minute walk 1 × 200 meters in 28 seconds 5 × short hill sprints
Wednesday	3 × walkovers (each leg) 2 × 10 trail-leg wall drill (each leg) 2 × lead leg over the top (each leg) 2 × starts through hurdle #1 2 × starts through hurdle #4
Thursday	3 × 150-meter accelerations, 150-meter walk 4 × 200 in 27 seconds, 200-meter walk
Friday	3 × 150-meter accelerations, 150-meter walk 3 × 200 in 30, 29, and 28 seconds; 3-minute walking rest
Saturday	Dual meet
Sunday	Rest day

Table 8.5 Late-Season Workouts for Intermediate Hurdlers

Monday	2 × lead leg, trail leg, and over the top (each leg); hurdles set at 39 inches 2 × 300 over last 4 hurdles in 42 and 43 seconds; 10-minute walking rest
Tuesday	3 × 150-meter accelerations, 150-meter walk 5 × 200 in 25 seconds, 3-minute walking rest
Wednesday	2 × lead leg, trail leg, and over the top (each leg); hurdles set at 39 inches 1 × start to hurdle #1 2 × start to hurdle #4
Thursday	3 × 150-meter accelerations, 150-meter walk 3 × 200 at race pace plus 4, 3, and 2 seconds; 3-minute walking rest
Friday	3 × 150-meter accelerations, 150-meter walk 3 × 200 in 29, 28, and 27 seconds; 3-minute walking rest
Saturday	Meet
Sunday	Rest day

caught up in the number of strides taken between intermediate hurdles, but it is important to establish a rhythm that can be maintained to the end of the race. Therefore, while fewer strides are always the goal, intermediate hurdlers shouldn't put so much effort into attaining an early stride pattern of fewer strides that they are fatigued and cannot finish the race strong. In some cases, more is better, and this just may be one of them. As a coach, you need to keep momentum on the side of the athlete in these races. The intermediate hurdlers must maintain an aggressive attacking lead leg and run with rhythm so that they do not lose horizontal momentum.

It is beneficial to use videotape in all events as a teaching tool, but videotaping the hurdle races along with touchdown times (the time when the lead foot strikes the ground after clearing the hurdle) can be an important tool for both the athlete and the coach.

Intermediate Hurdle Training

Tables 8.4 and 8.5 provide some sample training weeks for the early and late outdoor season for intermediate hurdlers. These workouts are especially good for 400-meter hurdlers but can be adapted for the 300-meter hurdlers as well. The drills used for the sprint hurdlers are also appropriate for intermediate hurdlers, the only modification being that the height of the hurdle changes the height the athlete's trail and lead legs.

Chapter 9

MIDDLE-DISTANCE AND DISTANCE EVENTS

Dr. Phil Esten

Retired Cross Country Coach, University of Wisconsin at La Crosse

© M. Messenger/Photo Network

As practitioners of coaching, we must analyze the demands of the specific competitive distance then determine the appropriate training to best prepare our student-athletes for championship competition. With this end in mind, coaches need to be concerned about what occurs between the stimulus we apply and the response of athletes to this stimulus. We need to continually remind ourselves that the athletes' genetic endowment and psychological approach have the greatest impact on optimal performance. Finally, as coaches, we must set our priorities after examining our value system.

How many of us have set up a seasonal program, administered many workouts, and seen the student-athlete experience early season success . . . only to become disgruntled at the end of the season because performances fell short of the predicted outcomes? This phenomenon happens much too often and can usually be attributed to either poor training values or unrealistic expectations. Most student-athletes join a team to meet new friends as well as to experience improvement in their skills and conditioning. A coach's role is to help them with this skill-development and learning process. By examining our coaching values closely, we can carefully plan a scheme that enables athletes to enjoy themselves and to achieve reasonable success in a team setting.

Training programs can have either beneficial effects for student-athletes or detrimental effects. As we design training programs and break them down into cycles and specific workouts, we should continually monitor our programs to determine which responses best indicate a beneficial effect. Too often we recognize detrimental effects when it is too late to change the program to ensure beneficial adaptations.

This chapter examines training programs for middle-distance and distance running for distances from 800 to 5000 meters. I present three different programs: one for 800-meter specialists, another for 1500- or 1600-meter specialists, and another for those student-athletes who run the 3000- to 5000-meter distances. Each of these three general distances makes different physiological demands. For example, the 800-meter event relies on more short-duration, high-intensity training for the development of the glycolytic energy system, whereas mile training requires more long-duration training for greater oxidative energy development. Effective training for the 3000- to 5000-meter events focuses much more on long-duration, low-intensity workouts. The value system I employ for training middle-distance and distance runners depends on specificity training; that is, training geared toward the respective physiological demands of a student-athlete's primary event.

Each middle-distance and long-distance training program is based on an understanding of the conditioning stimulus. The aspects of a training program that influence a training response include intensity, duration, frequency, type of training, and approach.

Intensity refers to how hard student-athletes work during an exercise bout (e.g., at 80 percent maximum heart rate or race pace). The intensity of a workout should be designed as a relative factor instead of an absolute factor. For example, let's say that we intend to design a workout that produces certain physiological results, such as a heart rate and a respiratory rate at 70 percent of the athletes' maximum workload. Such a workout would result in different heart and respiratory rates from your student-athletes. In other words, one athlete's 70 percent can be totally different from another athlete's 70 percent. What a coach can therefore do is calculate an intensity based on a percentage of each student-athlete's current best times in his or her event.

Three intensity terms that I use frequently throughout this chapter are *aerobic pace, anaerobic threshold pace,* and *race pace.*

Aerobic pace: 75 percent of fastest pace or percent maximum heart rate. If an 800-meter runner runs a 2:00 average pace per 800, then (120 seconds/.75) = 160 seconds = 2:40 per 800 pace.

Anaerobic threshold pace: 76 to 90 percent of fastest pace or percent maximum heart rate. For a 6-minute miler, the numbers would be (360 seconds/.90) = 400 seconds = 6:40 per mile.

Race pace: 100 percent of fastest pace for any specific running event.

Duration refers to the amount of time spent in a single workout. Three criteria govern how a coach decides the duration of a workout: depletions, accumulations, and imbalances of essential substances. Depletions include muscle glycogen, fluids, vitamins, ATP–PC, and other sources of muscle energy. Accumulations during a work bout consist of heat, H+ ions and hormones. Imbalances relate to fluids, minerals, and gases. Though

Individualizing Approach

One of our runners, Mike Junig, performed extremely well in practice but nowhere near his potential during competition. When we took him away from interval training with the team and had him individually run up-tempo distances on the hard days, he responded beautifully in competition. One runner may respond best to traditional distance training, whereas another may have a tendency to work beyond beneficial limits and thus need a modified program to achieve beneficial effects.

such criteria can only be measured in a lab, a coach needs to be aware that too much training may trigger these imbalances. Again, as a coach, you want to be sure the prescription for the duration of a student-athlete's workout relates to the individual, instead of being absolute.

Frequency refers to how often an athlete exercises between resting states (e.g., five times per week, or 4 × 600 meters with 1:00 between each). The frequency a coach prescribes for a workout or program should depend on the recovery process time of the athlete. In other words, frequency is, again, a relative factor instead of an absolute factor. Beneficial adaptation to training takes place only after complete recovery of the physiological mechanisms that were stressed. Recovery tiime varies. One-and-a-half minutes are required for respiratory normalization between intervals; 36 hours are needed for protein synthesis and protein renaturation in the muscles after an intense workout.

Type of training is simply the qualitative activity performed by the athlete. Obviously, for a middle-distance or distance runner the training generally involves running or a similar pattern of movement (such as water-running). *Type* implies specificity as well, meaning that the distances and paces should reflect appropriate competitive distances and times. Coaches should always encourage athletes to participate in alternative forms of training

that are specific to running; there are a variety of cross-training exercises and machines that can help athletes prevent boredom and possible injury.

The training *approach* refers to the particular environment in which training takes place for each athlete, and each athlete's approach may vary. For example, one runner may train too hard using traditional methods; therefore, the coach may write specific workouts for that athlete to train separately with a lighter workload.

800-METER TRAINING

During the early years of my coaching career training for the 800- and the 1600-meter runners was pretty much the same. This training consisted of the traditional hard-easy-hard-easy approach. That is, athletes would have a hard workout Monday, followed by an easy workout Tuesday, hard workout Wednesday, and easy workout Thursday. At Racine Horlick High School, where I coached, we had substantial success with the training of both the 400-meter and the 1600- to 3200-meter groups. We won the 1968 Wisconsin State High School meet for large schools with sprinters, jumpers, throwers, and relays, and in later years, we produced the individual state champion in cross country and the two-mile run in track. However, the one distance I had the most difficulty training successfully was the group that fell between these two—the 800-meter group.

The 400-meter runners were trained as sprinters so that each workout focused on specificity training, which met the physiological demands specific to their event: about 95 percent anaerobic and 5 percent aerobic. For boys, this training was based on a 50-second performance; for girls, a 60-second performance. For the 800-meter group, we stressed over 50 percent aerobic and less than 50 percent anaerobic work—training more similar to a 1600-meter runner's workout. It is no surprise that many of these 800-meter runners were actually better at the 1600-meter race because their training came closer to the physiological demands of a 4:30 to 5:00

performance than a 2:00 race. We had been training our 800-meter runners to be milers, not 800-meter runners. Training the 800-meter runners similarly to the 400-meter runners would have actually been more appropriate.

Having learned from this experience, in the early 1970s, at the University of Wisconsin (La Crosse), we completely changed the workout model for the 800-meter runner to better fit the physiological demands of this event. The following sections break down the revised training into five phases. The preseason phase, typically done in the fall for a spring season, is followed by the early indoor, championship indoor, early outdoor, and championship outdoor phases. Before we discuss each phase individually, let's establish the basis for specificity training for the 800-meter runner.

Specificity—Two-On, One-Off Principle

Two-on, one-off refers to the frequency of workouts. The 800-meter runner trains two consecutive days with specificity training and follows this with the third day off from running. This pattern is repeated as closely as a young runner can manage without interrupting his or her total life schedule. Given that some physiological mechanisms take up to 36 hours to recover from a strenuous workout and that adaptations from physical stress take place only during this recovery, it would be best for the athlete to work out every 36 hours. The most important adaptations are the changes that take place at the muscular and cellular levels—putting the structural proteins back into their proper order and shape.

Of course, allowing 36 hours between workouts isn't practical in our society, so we have found the next best schedule, which is to work out at the same time on two consecutive days, then take the third day off to allow a 48-hour recovery.

The most exact specificity training for the 800-meter runner is to run a timed 800 meters every 36 hours. This simulates exactly what the runner needs to do in a race and uses the same systems that a runner would use. This training, however, is impractical; it fails to train the athlete's body to tolerate higher loads of work and meet the speed demands of the event. Thus, it is wise to break the training demands down into specific segments or sets. The following is the model we use for many of the workouts for our 800-meter runners; it trains runners specifically for the 800-meter run. Each set is followed by a five-minute jog-walk recovery.

- **Warm-up**—The length of the warm-up varies from one to three miles of easy running, followed by one 600- to 1200-meter run at anaerobic threshold pace, which should be equal to 75 to 85 percent of the athlete's current personal best in the 800-meter race. For example, to find a 75 percent pace of an athlete whose personal best is 2:00, a coach would convert the 800-meter time to seconds (120) and divide by .75 (120/.75 = 160 seconds, or 2:40 pace). Having done the warm-up running and a few specific stretches and form drills, the runner will be safely prepared for a good workout.

- **Long set**—The first long set usually consists of one to two more repetitions than the last long set. The athlete does two to four repetitions of 400 to 1200 meters. The coach may use the longer intervals (800 to 1200) at the beginning of the season and the shorter intervals (400, 500, 600, or 700) toward the middle and later parts of the season. The rest interval is generous, two to five minutes, and it is in direct relationship with the length of the interval run. The idea with the rest interval is to allow the respiratory rate and the heart rate to recover to as close to a rested state as possible. The intensity of the repetitions in this set will vary depending on the phase of the season. This effort may be as low as 70 percent during the preseason phase to as high as 95 percent during the season.

- **Sprint set**—After a five-minute recovery from the long set, the runner begins the sprint set, which is a timed segment of generally three to five minutes. The repetition and recovery are both very short. The distance is generally 20 to 50 meters, and the rest interval is 20 to 40 seconds. For a team, the best way to organize this set is to run in a shuttle-relay style. The objective of this set is threefold. The runner should work on running form in a relaxed sprinting state. Because the rest interval is so short, this segment actually acts as an aerobic component. Finally, the sprinting action prepares the runner for the next set.

Kick set—After another five-minute recovery the runner is prepared for the kick set. This set simulates the kick at the end of the race. Because we never attempt to run at 100 percent effort in practice (to avoid the risk of injury and inhibited mechanics), the runner usually gives a 95 percent to 98 percent effort. The distance run during the kick set is between 100 to 200 meters. The number of repetitions is one to four, and the recovery is always walking the same distance back to the start. When on the track, we always run this over the last 100- to 200-meter segment of the 800-meter run. Because this set comes in the middle of the workout, the runner's muscles are usually well prepared for this speed but not so fatigued as to invite an injury. We always begin these repetitions from a slower, rolling start. This set really focuses on developing power or fast-twitch fibers.

Sprint set—The next sprint set begins the mirror image of the first two sets. Following a five-minute recovery from the kick set, we generally repeat the same protocol used that particular day for the first sprint set. Sometimes we adjust this set to accommodate runners who appear somewhat fatigued.

Long set—The last work set is the second long set. Again, this is followed by a three- to five-minute recovery. Often, this set is shorter than the first long set with only one to three repetitions. The

intensity and distance of the repetition remains constant with the first long set.

Cool-down—The cool-down doesn't need to be long; 5 to 10 minutes is enough. It should begin at 50 to 60 percent effort and finish at 20 to 30 percent effort.

The first few times your athletes do this workout, closely monitor them for signs of fatigue so that you can prevent them from deriving a detrimental effect from the workout. As the coach, you have the right to cut portions of the workout to ensure a beneficial effect, and you can insist that student-athletes proceed to the cool-down per your judgment.

Preseason Phase

For most high school and collegiate calendars, the preseason for the 800-meter runner is the fall season, from September through November. Most coaches encourage the 800-meter runners to work out with the cross country team, if possible. In fact, probably the best preseason training for the 800-meter runner is to run and actually compete in cross country, but if a student-athlete isn't suited to the longer distance, then other options are certainly available. If the student-athlete plays football, soccer, or volleyball, he or she should continue with these activities since running is fundamental in all three sports. If the student-athlete does not play a fall sport, then the coach should really try to include him or her in cross country using a modified program.

This modified program should include a variety of running activities to help strengthen and prepare the student-athlete for the track and field season. The two-on, one-off principle can even be used during this preseason phase. A mix of modified specificity training, hill running, traditional interval training on grass, varied fartlek runs, and medium-easy distance workouts can adequately prepare the athlete for the track and field season.

Along with this preseason running, the athletes should engage in a strength-training program with either a solid weight-training program

Preseason training is the time to prepare athletes for the in-season through strengthening exercises, group runs, and cross-training activities.

or body resistance program (or both). To keep the 800-meter runner motivated and interested in the program, include a variety of fun activities during the fall training—for example, scavenger hunts, ultimate Frisbee, running at different locations each week, and pool workouts.

Early-Indoor Phase

After the holiday break, the indoor track season begins in either January or early February. If there is a culminating championship (such as a state or national meet), then the coach will want to plan for this training phase by counting the number of weeks of the entire indoor season backward from the culminating meet. For example, if there are seven weeks to the indoor season, then the early-indoor phase should consist of five to six weeks. If the season is 10 weeks, the early-indoor phase should consist of 7 to 8 weeks.

Generally, the first two weeks of this phase consist of general strength and endurance activities that enable the student-athlete to continue building to endure the remainder of the season. Circuit training, combined with easy running and form sprints, allows the athlete to enter comfortably into a safe conditioning regimen. The first week should include only three to four workouts. For the second week, add one workout. A common mistake many coaches make is to work the athlete too hard during this phase. This often produces problems such as injuries instead of a gradual transition from the long holiday break.

After these initial two weeks, it is time to introduce the student-athlete to specificity training. Along with the specificity training, the coach should mix in some traditional interval training and an occasional long, easy run. The traditional interval training may include 4 to 6 × 400, 2 to 3 × 600, 8 to 10 × 200, or different combinations of distances and number of repetitions. The two-on, one-off approach—two days on and one day off during the weekly schedule—can be followed from this point until the end of the season. It is usually safe at this time to prescribe longer, slower segments in the long set with a bit shorter rest interval.

As the early-indoor phase progresses, the repetitions within the long set should shorten;

there should be an emphasis on higher intensity and longer rest intervals. The traditional interval training follows the same protocol.

An effective workout toward the end of this phase is the *simulator*. The intent of this workout is to simulate an actual competition in the 800-meter run. If your competition during this time of the season is Friday or Saturday, then a good day for this workout is Tuesday. After an extensive warm-up, including a 600-meter anaerobic threshold run, the student-athlete will break down the 800-meter distance into four segments. The idea is to add up the four times and see how far below the individual's personal record he or she can go. The first segment is a 400-meter dash, followed by a one- or two-minute rest interval. The second segment is a 200-meter dash, followed by a 30- to 60-second rest interval. The third and fourth segments are 100-meter dashes, separated by a rest interval of 20 to 30 seconds. This segmented 800-meter run should be followed by an effective cool-down, which can conclude the practice for this day.

Table 9.1 shows a sample of workouts during a typical early-season, indoor phase week.

Championship-Indoor Phase

Generally, the length of this phase is shorter than the championship-outdoor phase. If the entire indoor season is seven weeks, then this phase should be one to two weeks.

The most important concept during the championship indoor phase is to maintain the distance of the repetitions within the long sets while increasing the time allowed to run each set and increasing the rest intervals. Most physiological adaptations have taken place by this point in the season; now it is important that athletes do controlled runs with ample rest to allow for total body recovery so that they can compete at their highest level. We must remember that full adaptation to an exercise stimulus can only occur with proper rest.

Early-Outdoor Phase

Generally, there is a transition time between the indoor season and the outdoor season. If the entire outdoor season is seven weeks, then only one week is necessary for transition;

Table 9.1   Week of Early-Indoor Phase Workouts for 800-Meter Runners

Monday	1-mile striders Weight training
Tuesday	1-mile warm-up 600 meters at anaerobic threshold pace 4 laps striders 3 × 300 at race pace, 4-minute rest 3 minutes × 50 meters; 3 × 120 zooms (walk back); 3 minutes × 50 meters 300 meters at race pace 600 meters at anaerobic threshold pace 1-mile cool-down
Wednesday	20 minutes at aerobic pace Weight training
Thursday	Premeet practice of 30 to 40 minutes at aerobic pace
Friday	Meet
Saturday	4 miles at aerobic pace
Sunday	No running

if the outdoor season is ten weeks, then two weeks may be necessary for transition. This is a good time to move away from the track and focus once again on strength and endurance. A few ideas for transitional work include controlled fartlek runs, form drills, easy-long runs, and weight training.

The next three to four weeks of training will be a progression of quality specificity training that enables the athlete to attain the highest level of fitness (relatively speaking) for that particular season. Coaches must be cautious to prevent the athlete from over-training or getting injured. Table 9.2 provides a sample workout week for this phase.

For high school track and field, it is of utmost importance for the coach to monitor athletes' grade level and maturational state to ensure a safe developmental process. It takes a lot of time for a coach to personally talk with runners each day to see how they feel and to learn about their sleeping and eating habits. One way to work this type of communication in is to make it part of the lockerroom chatter.

Table 9.2 Week of Early-Outdoor Phase Workouts for 800-Meter Runners (Boys)

Monday	1.5-mile warm-up 4 × 70 meters 3 × (400, 200, 200)—run each set 2 to 3 seconds faster than the previous set; rest 1:30 between intervals; 6 to 7 minutes between sets 1-mile cool-down Weight training
Tuesday	1.5-mile warm-up 4 × 70 meters 600 meters at anaerobic threshold pace Ladder—100, 200, 300, 400, 600, 400, 300, 200, 100 (rest in minutes: .5, 1, 2, 3, 4, 3, 2, 1)—run everything at 800-meter race pace, plus or minus 2 seconds 600 meters at anaerobic threshold pace 1-mile cool-down
Wednesday	3 to 5 miles at aerobic pace Weight training
Thursday	1-mile warm-up 400 meters at anaerobic threshold pace Ladder—100, 110, 120, 130, 120, (walk back, rest)—run at 800-meter goal pace 400 at anaerobic threshold pace half-mile cool-down
Friday	Premeet run of 2 to 3 miles at aerobic pace; relay exchanges
Saturday	Meet
Sunday	4 to 5 miles at aerobic pace (or take the day off)

Championship-Outdoor Phase

At the beginning of the season, the coach plans each phase carefully to achieve the highest performance by each athlete during the championship phase, when the championship meets occur.

This phase shouldn't be much different from the championship-indoor phase except that it may be a week longer, which allows for a more gradual taper. Emphasize slower times of the repetitions with longer rest intervals. This shift in times and rest intervals should evolve gradually over the three-week taper.

Stride efficiency can only be maintained through continual training from the early-indoor to championship-outdoor phases. For the runners to feel that their running is effortless, balanced, strong, and rhythmical, they must stick with the five-phase program designed to enable them to perform at their best at the end of the season. The benefits of the previous four phases will be lost if the championship-outdoor phase isn't carefully

planned and followed. This is the science of coaching. You must continue to gain confidence in your ability to carefully plan the season so that your athletes trust the entire plan. Continually communicating with the student-athletes is the best way to check to see that your plan is working.

Table 9.3 shows a sample week of training for 800-meter runners during this phase of training.

800-Meter Racing

The following are tips that will benefit an 800-meter runner in competition:

✓ Run an even pace. Physiologically speaking, the most efficient pace for the 800-meter runner should be a perfectly even pace. Because of the competition and the adrenaline buildup most runners run the first 200 meters faster than the other three segments of 200 meters. If a coach helps each 800-meter runner break down the race into three parts (300, 300, and 200), it

Table 9.3 Week of Championship Phase Workouts for 800-Meter Runners

Monday	5 to 6 miles at aerobic pace
Tuesday	1.5-mile warm-up 600 meters at anaerobic threshold pace 600 meters in 1:45; 8 × 100, walk back, rest; 600 meters in 1:45 half-mile cool-down
Wednesday	2-mile warm-up 600 at anaerobic threshold pace 400 at race pace; 6 × 200 at race pace, rest 1 minute 600 at anaerobic threshold pace 1-mile cool-down
Thursday	3 to 4 miles at aerobic pace
Friday	Premeet of 3 to 4 miles at aerobic pace 1 mile of ins and outs
Saturday	Championship meet
Sunday	Championship meet

may help the runner to control the first 300 meters better and therefore to run a more even and faster 800 meters. In fact, most successful 800-meter runners begin fast and finish fast, with slower strides in the middle of the race. But generally speaking, the first half of the race will probably be 5 to 10 percent faster than the second half.

✓ Be strong during the last 50 meters. In many 800-meter races, victory comes down to the strength of the runner in the last 50 meters to either hold off or overtake a competitor.

✓ Have good race sense. Experienced 800-meter runners get the feeling or sense of a race, and whether to go out too fast or too slow. The experienced runner will either fall back or take the lead early; it depends on the early pace of the pack. The runner needs to be very attentive to the initial pace to pull off this effective strategy.

✓ Protect your space. A runner leading a race needs to be sure not to allow enough space on the inside to permit an opponent to pass. Also, if following a leader or lead pack, the runner needs to run off the outside shoulder of those in front and avoid getting boxed in by passing runners.

✓ Beware of the surge. Surging during an 800-meter race can deplete or tax the glycolytic process that provides the majority of energy for this event. A runner should try not to surge except toward the end of the race within the last 120 meters. A more experienced runner may be able to hold off a surging opponent but should be cautious in doing so.

✓ Know your opponents. Try to scout the strategies of your opponents and make a few strategic plans before race day. This race demands a sound plan that should be rehearsed mentally. One of the high school runners I coached, Rudy Alvarez of Horlick High School, was going to run against the defending state champ in the mile at a big meet late in the season. This opponent had run 4:09 in the mile, and I knew that Rudy couldn't run that fast. Because Rudy was going to be the next-best miler in that

field, we talked about his following the opponent from a distance of 10 to 15 meters, rather than within one meter. We thought this would slow the race down enough so that Rudy would be able to surprise him on the last lap. Going into the first turn of the last lap, Rudy closed the gap on his opponent's outside shoulder, then passed him at 100 percent effort on the backstretch and carried it all the way to the finish. The plan worked; Rudy held his fast-approaching opponent off by less than 0.5 seconds at the tape. Rudy ran a personal best 4:17 and was overjoyed at the success of the plan in which he shared ownership.

✓ Learn to take out the first three to five steps. The first steps of an 800-meter race may be the most important. An initial fast start won't deplete runners if they adjust within the first 10 to 15 seconds. A runner who gets out too fast can always shut down enough to get into the proper flow of the race. This takes a lot of discipline and experience.

✓ Keep elbows wide for the indoor 800-meter races. Because of the tight turns and narrow lanes in the indoor meets, it is often necessary for 800-meter runners to run with wider elbows to protect their self-space.

✓ Break in a straight line. During most 800-meter race starts, the runners either run in lanes or alleys around the first turn until a break line at the beginning of the backstretch. From this point until the end of the backstretch, the runner should run a straight line. It is the most efficient path since the shortest distance between two points is always a straight line.

1500- TO 1600-METER TRAINING

When planning a training program for a 1500- to 1600-meter runner, the coach must first find out the physiological demands for a performance of 4:00 to 7:30 (i.e., the time depends on sex, age, and fitness level of the athlete). Although the demands of the 1500- to 1600-meter race are similar to those of the 800-meter events, the biggest difference is that the longer events demand more energy from the oxidative energy system than the anaerobic energy system. Most exercise physiologists feel that 65 percent of the energy needed for the 1500- to 1600-meter run comes from the oxidative (aerobic) energy system, 30 percent from the glycolytic (anaerobic) energy system, and 5 percent from the creatine-phosphate ATP source. Corresponding training to these systems includes medium- to slow-distance running for the oxidative energy system; medium- to fast-repetition running for the glycolytic energy system; and shorter, faster sprinting for the creatine-phosphate energy system.

Many of the principles used in training the 800-meter event are also the same for the

Successful training for milers includes the right mix of speed repetition running, sprint training, and endurance work.

1500- to 1600-meter event. As I did with the 800-meter training discussion, I will list each component, but I will focus on the differences in the training of these two events rather than repeating each aspect. The components of specificity training are the same for the 1500- to 1600-runner as they are for the 800-meter runner, and again, each set is followed by a five-minute jog-walk recovery.

Warm-up—The length of the warm-up can be greater than that for the 800-meter training to help satisfy the increased oxidative energy demand of this longer event. If time permits, this distance can be from one to four miles, followed by one 800- to 1600-meter run at anaerobic threshold pace. Again, this warm-up, along with a few specific stretches and form drills, should safely prepare the runner for a good workout.

Long set—The first long set is the same as it is for the 800-meter training, although the distance of the repetitions may vary from 400 to 2000 meters. The number of repetitions stays the same, but the rest interval may be longer for the longer segments.

Sprint set—The first sprint set is exactly the same as it is for 800-meter training. Again, emphasize good running form and a relaxed sprinting state.

Kick set—The kick set is also the same as the 800-meter training, except that the length of the repetitions may be longer, from 150 to 300 meters. The purpose of this set is to develop running power by innervating the fast-twitch fibers.

Sprint set—The second sprint set is the same as it is for the 800-meter training. Often, the coach will shorten this set from the first sprint set. This is final preparation for the final set of the workout, the second long set.

Long set—The second long set is often adapted from the first long set. Adjustments may include fewer repetitions and a shorter distance of the segment. It is extremely important for the coach to monitor this final phase to ensure that the runner does not reach an unnecessary state of fatigue.

Cool-down—The cool-down should again be regressive in effort. The distance may be longer than that for the 800-meter training, sometimes 10 to 20 minutes. This increased distance encourages oxidative development and stride efficiency.

Preseason Phase

For most 1500- to 1600-meter runners, the preseason is cross country training in the fall. There really isn't a better format for effective preseason conditioning than cross country because it has all the components directly related to setting a firm base, developing the oxidative energy system, and providing strength training for the muscles supporting the joints. If cross country isn't available for preseason conditioning, the coach should provide a diversity of training for the 1500- to 1600-meter runner similar to the preseason schedule presented for 800-meter runners but with 15 to 30 percent more mileage. For the high school student, this may be the most important time during the maturational process. With proper preseason or off-season training, gains in performance can be quite impressive. Of course, if the athlete is participating in a fall sport other than cross country, he or she should focus 100 percent on that activity for that time of year. Activity in other sports is better than not doing anything.

Early-Indoor Phase

Generally, the first two weeks of this phase consist of general strength and endurance-building activities, much like this phase of training for the 800-meter runner. The 800-meter runners and milers can even train together during the early-indoor phase. Moderately long-distance runs combined with some circuit training and form drills allow athletes safe entry into a conditioning regimen.

Following the first two weeks of the indoor season, introduce specificity training, traditional interval training, anaerobic threshold runs, and selective distance running. The training for the 1500- to 1600-meters may be accomplished two different ways. If the runner is a 800- to 1600-meter runner, the training leans more toward specificity training. If the runner is a 1600- to 3200-meter runner, the training includes some specificity training but there is more emphasis on distance running. The 800- to 1600-meter runner's training should consist of 60 to 70 percent specificity training and 30 to 40 percent distance training. The 1600- to 3200-meter runner's training should consist of 60 to 70 percent distance training and 30 to 40 percent specificity training.

The coach may have to write separate workouts for student-athletes who run the 1500- to 1600-meter distance to fit their needs. For the pure 1500- to 1600-meter runner, the two-on, one-off principle is the best method of training. While using specificity training, these runners should run long sets that are longer than the 800-meter runners' long sets. The interval distances should extend from 300 to 1600 meters. The specificity training should be used one to two times per week during this phase.

As for the 800-meter runner, an effective workout toward the end of this phase for the miler is the simulator. The intent of this workout is to simulate an actual competition in the 1500- to 1600-meter run. If your competition during this time of the season is on Friday or Saturday, then a good day for this workout is Tuesday. After an extensive warm-up, including an 800-meter anaerobic threshold run, the athlete breaks down the 1600-meter distance into four segments. The idea is to add up the four times and see by how much the athlete can beat his or her personal record. The first segment is a 800-meter run, followed by a two-minute rest interval. The second segment is a 400-meter dash, followed by a one-minute rest interval. The third and fourth segments are 200-meter dashes, separated by a rest interval of 30 seconds. This segmented 1600-meter run should be followed by an effective cool-down, which can conclude the practice for this day.

Table 9.4 provides a sample week for milers during this early-indoor phase.

Table 9.4 Week of Early-Indoor Phase Workouts for 1500- to 1600-Meter Runners

Monday	3.5-mile warm-up 1, 2, 3, 4, 3, 2, 1 minutes at anaerobic threshold pace, 1.5-minute jogging-rest 1-mile cool-down Weights
Tuesday	4-mile warm-up 800 at anaerobic threshold pace 4 laps striders 2 × 600 at race pace; rest 5 minutes 3 minutes × 50 meters, 3 × 120 zooms (walk back), 3 minutes × 50 meters 600 meters at race pace 800 meters at anaerobic threshold pace 1-mile cool-down
Wednesday	40 minutes at aerobic pace Weights
Thursday	Premeet of 30 to 40 minutes at aerobic pace 2 × 200 at race pace, rest 1 minute
Friday	Invitational meet
Saturday	6 to 7 miles at aerobic pace
Sunday	60 minutes at aerobic pace

Championship-Indoor Phase

This phase follows the same format as for the 800-meter training group. If the entire indoor season is seven weeks, this phase should be two or three weeks. The idea is to maintain the distance of the repetitions within the long sets but to increase the time allowed to run each and to increase the rest intervals by 30 seconds to one minute. Because most physiological adaptations have taken place during earlier phases of training, it is now important to run controlled paces with ample rest so that the athlete is well rested for the upcoming competitions.

Early-Outdoor Phase

Generally, a one-week transition time is necessary to adapt to being outdoors and to begin training on the big 400-meter oval. Focus on long, easy runs and controlled fartleks that can be done away from the track.

The next three to four weeks should be a progression of quality specificity training preparing the 1500- to 1600-meter runner for the championship outdoor phase. Table 9.5 on page 114 shows a sample week in this phase. This may be the most intense training of the entire season. The coach must be careful to monitor all student-athletes to protect them from overtraining.

Championship-Outdoor Phase

This is the final phase of the five-phase season. To prepare for the championship meets during this phase, the runners will focus on the most important training—the progressive tapering throughout this three-week phase (see table 9.6 on page 115 for a sample week). Again, emphasize slower times for the repetitions with longer rest intervals. Remember that this is the time to allow physiological adaptations to take place. Stride efficiency is

Table 9.5   Week of Early Season Outdoor Workouts for 1500- to 1600-Meter Runners (Boys)

Monday	3-mile warm-up 4 × 70 meters 800 at anaerobic threshold 4 × (400, 200, 200) at progressive pace through sets (:66 to :60) (:34 to :30); rest 1 minute after 400, 30 seconds after 200s, and 6 to 7 minutes between sets; half-lap retro-walk 2-mile cool-down Weights
Tuesday	3-mile warm-up 800 meters at anaerobic threshold pace 4 × 1200 at race pace plus 2 seconds; surge alternate 100s on 3rd 400; rest 5 minutes 800 meters anaerobic threshold 2-mile cool-down
Wednesday	6 to 8 miles at aerobic pace Weights
Thursday	4-mile warm-up 4 × 70 meters 600 meters at anaerobic threshold pace 1 mile ins and outs 600 meters at anaerobic threshold pace 2-mile cool-down
Friday	Premeet of 5 to 6 miles at aerobic pace
Saturday	Dual meet
Sunday	60 to 90 minutes at aerobic pace

very important; therefore, training continues during this phase but at a moderate intensity. To the runner trained for this event, at the end of the season the 1500- to 1600-meter run should feel effortless, balanced, strong, and rhythmical.

1500- to 1600-Meter Racing

Most of the tips suggested for the 800-meter runner also apply for runners of this distance. The 1500 meters can be broken into five segments, with the coach setting up a "pace plan" for the marks at 300, 600, 900, and 1200 meters. This accomplishes more than reading splits at the traditional marks of 400, 800,

and 1200 meters. With shorter distances between splits, the runner isn't as likely to get off-pace. Also, the 300-, 600-, and 900-meter locations are at places on the track where few if any other people will be reading splits.

If you have a 1600-meter runner who generally loses during the kick yet is a very strong runner, consider having that runner surprise the opponents with a strong surge with 500 meters remaining in the race. This only works if the pace has been relatively slow and if the event has been set up as a tactical race (as many championship races are).

The part of the race race between 800 and 1200 meters is usually the most difficult segment for the 1500- to 1600-meter runner to maintain his or her focus. Therefore, it is usually important for the middle-distance run-

Table 9.6   Week of Championship Phase Workouts for 1500 to 1600 Meters

Monday	5 to 6 miles at aerobic pace
Tuesday	7 miles with the following midrun pickups (:30, 1:00, 1:30, 2:00, 1:30, 1:00, :30); double the rest between each segment
Wednesday	3-mile warm-up 800 meters at anaerobic threshold pace 6 × 400 at race pace; rest 90 seconds between; 10 minutes rest 6 × 200 at race pace, walk back 600 at anaerobic threshold pace 1 mile cool-down
Thursday	5 to 6 miles at aerobic pace (or take the day off)
Friday	5 to 6 miles at aerobic pace
Saturday	Championship Meet
Sunday	Championship Meet

ner not to go out too fast in the first segment. It helps if the coach and student-athlete discuss this concept before each race. Generally, the 1500- to 1600-meter event is best run with even splits so that energy is expended evenly throughout the race.

3000- TO 5000-METER TRAINING

Physiologically speaking, the 3000-, 3200-, and 5000-meter events pull up to 80 percent of their performance energy from the oxidative energy system. Most of us know this system as the aerobic energy system. Therefore, 70 to 80 percent of training should be actual distance or aerobic running, which activates the oxidative energy system.

The ways in which 3000- to 5000-meter runners use the different pace intensities are similar to those highlighted earlier in this chapter, but they are based on each runner's average speed for five miles. (Intensities shown here were provided by Tom Schwartz, a former University of Wisconsin-La Crosse runner and assistant coach.)

Aerobic pace: 75 percent of five-mile pace. If your runner runs a 6:00 average pace per mile, then (360 seconds/.75) = 480 seconds = 8:00 per mile.

Anaerobic threshold pace: 90 percent of five-mile pace or 85 percent maximum heart rate. For the same 6:00 per mile five-miler, the numbers would be (360 seconds/.90) = 400 seconds = 6:40 per mile.

Race pace: 100 percent of fastest pace for any specific running event.

When training young distance runners (ages 14 to 20), it is important for coaches to modify training to the maturation level of the individual student-athletes. Coaches must be very careful not to overtrain and overcompete the immature distance runner. Aerobic development is often a slower process for younger athletes. Some studies show the oxidative energy system doesn't fully mature until the late 20s or early 30s. Girls respond best to strength training during the year in which they have their greatest growth spurt, whereas boys respond best to strength training the year after their greatest growth spurt. Girls sometimes finish their growth as early as 11 to 13 years, and boys may not finish their growth until 17 to 19 years. Overuse of joints and bones while the athlete is maturing can lead to injuries that delay development.

Because much of a distance runner's training is off the track, it helps to find a softer running surface than concrete or blacktop. We have our student-athletes run on soft trails or dirt roads whenever possible. We know that younger runners, before the growth plates in their bones are complete, are more susceptible to shinsplints and stress fractures. If the time spent running or the number of miles run is closely monitored by a coach, such injuries can usually be avoided.

Throughout the distance runner's season, it makes sense to have a recovery week every three to four weeks. Beginning during the preseason and continuing through the midseason, the distance runner anatomically, physiologically, and psychologically needs a break from progressive training. We like to cut back the duration and intensity of training by 5 to 10 percent every four weeks to allow

full adaptation of the physiological mechanisms to take place.

Preseason Phase

Cross country is typically the preseason conditioning phase for the distance runner. In fact, most distance runners prefer cross country to running on the track. Although the two sports are different—primarily because of the differences in the location of the competition and the different team tactics used— the training philosophy is quite similar for both. The specificity of training principle applies to cross country; the goal is to train the systems that are directly related to the time demanded by the event.

The transition from cross country to track occurs over a two- to three-month period (November to January). Coaches should encourage the distance runner to engage in cross- or alternate-training activities. Swimming, biking, or using aerobic exercise machines can help the athletes by preventing

© Human Kinetics

Ideally, 3000- to 5000-meter specialists should race every two weeks during the early season to allow proper recovery between races.

them from having to log all their training miles on hard surfaces. This break from running is also important for psychological, physiological, and anthropometrical reasons. Coming off an intense season of cross country, the runner needs time to recover but also to maintain a moderate level of fitness.

We usually have our distance runners train progressively from one year to the next during their preseason phase. For example, a freshman may run 20 miles per week in the preseason but may log 30 miles per week as a sophomore. This training is 95 percent aerobic pace running and about 5 percent up-tempo running. The up-tempo work can vary range from doing "strides" twice a week to doing one or two 800-meter runs once a week at anaerobic threshold pace. The striders can be 4 to 8 × 60 to 80 meters at a sprint speed, no higher than 95 percent of maximal heart rate.

For the 3000- to 5000-meter group, I divide the in-season training into just three phases: the early-season phase, the midseason phase and the championship phase. It is more difficult for a distance runner to peak for both an indoor and outdoor track season because of the distance involved in the training. Distance runners often also peak for their cross country season. Taking these factors into consideration, I divide the season into just three phases instead of four; it just seems to make more sense for distance runners.

Early-Season Phase

This training phase takes place during the indoor season, or for the first 6 or 7 weeks of an 18-week complete season. After months of training outdoors during the fall and having done cross-training since November, the distance runner is anxious to run fast and to compete. The beginning of the indoor season includes a transition period to introduce the distance runner to running on a different surface with drier air and sharp corners (if an indoor track is available). During the first week of training on an indoor track, the runners shouldn't run anything fast on the cor-

ners. Every other day, toward the end of their workout, they should run "striders" on the straightaways to gradually adjust to running faster on the indoor surface.

Beginning the second week, the runners should do only one full workout on the indoor track per week. Actually, it is best to run a warm-up outdoors and then come in for the remainder of the workout. Tuesday is the one day per week that athletes should do this up-tempo workout throughout the season.

If you choose to have your distance runners run two up-tempo workouts per week, the second one should be less intense and should be on Friday except during the week of a Saturday meet. In this case, the second up-tempo workout is on Thursday. Ideally the distance runner follows a 14-day cycle, with a race every 14 days and five up-tempo workouts or meets in this same time period. One of the biggest mistakes in coaching distance runners is to run too many up-tempo workouts and too many races during a season.

Because the duration of work is so important to the distance runner, we spread the workouts throughout the week by having our more mature, experienced runners train twice a day from two to four times a week. Research has taught us that it is the total time of training that is most important, not the length of a particular workout. If the work is split up as suggested, the coach must make sure that the student-athlete doesn't take advantage of fresh legs to run at higher intensities. This could negate the benefits of splitting up the workout sessions. Instead of running 8 to 10 miles in one workout on a Monday, the athlete should run 3 to 5 miles in the morning and 5 to 7 miles in the afternoon. Coaches should monitor their student-athletes to ensure that the athletes don't become overly fatigued over time. This second workout does not always have to be running. Many runners respond best to doing an alternate form of training for one of the workouts, such as swimming, biking, or using an aerobic machine. Most runners who do so respond with fresher legs for the running workout and have a safeguard to help prevent injuries.

A typical week during the indoor season is

Table 9.7   Week of Early-Season Phase Workouts for for 3000- to 5000-Meter Runners

Monday—A.M. **Monday**—P.M.	3 miles at aerobic pace 5 miles at aerobic pace 800 meters of striders Weight training
Tuesday	3-mile warm-up at aerobic pace 800 meters of striders 800 meters at anaerobic threshold pace 1 1/8 mile at race pace (2 seconds faster than race pace for last lap) 4 × 400 at race pace; rest 1 minute 800 meters at anaerobic threshold 15 minutes at aerobic pace cool-down
Wednesday—A.M. **Wednesday**—P.M.	3 miles at aerobic pace 5 miles at aerobic pace Weight training
Thursday—A.M. **Thursday**—P.M.	3 miles at aerobic pace 8 miles at aerobic pace
Friday	9 miles fartlek (2 miles at aerobic pace plus 5 miles, alternating 800 meters of 93% race pace and 800 meters at aerobic pace, plus 2 miles at aerobic pace)
Saturday	7 miles at aerobic pace
Sunday	12 miles at aerobic pace

to follow aerobic-paced mileage on Monday and Wednesday with a hard up-tempo workout on Tuesday (anaerobic threshold and race pace), a softer up-tempo workout on Thursday, a premeet practice of 20 to 40 minutes of easy running on Friday, and a race on Saturday. The more experienced runners can run a long, easy run on Sunday, but the inexperienced runners should take Sunday off. Table 9.7 shows a sample week from this phase.

During the early-season phase the runners should have one very long run every 14 days. This run should be 20 to 50 percent longer than their next-longest run of the week. Thus, if their longest run is generally 8 miles, then once every 14 days they should run 9 1/2 to 12 miles. Sunday is a good time to perform this long run because of the amount of time required for the run and for recovery.

This distance should be run at an aerobic pace.

One of our favorite Tuesday workouts is a progression done each Tuesday for four to five consecutive weeks. We begin with a warm-up outdoors of 15 to 30 minutes followed by two to four laps of striders indoors and an 800-meter anaerobic threshold run. The meat of the workout is the *race* pace work, which is next.

The first week of this progression, the runners run 1 1/8 miles (nine laps) on a 200-meter track. The first mile, the athletes are to run at their goal race pace for the two miles; on the ninth lap, the runner strives to run two seconds faster than that original pace. This part of the workout is repeated for the next three weeks, but it is extended by one lap each week. For example, the second week, the runners run 1 1/4 miles, with the first mile on goal pace for the two-mile and the ninth and tenth laps at the faster pace. The third week the runner runs 1 3/8 miles at goal pace and the fourth week 1 1/2 miles. The goal of this workout is to have the distance runner run a negative split for the third 800 meters of this segment. We have had many runners at the University of Wisconsin at La Crosse successfully complete this phase and go on to set huge personal best times and become all-Americans. Generally, if runners can accomplish this task, they can run the entire second mile on pace and accomplish their goals.

The next part of the workout is a rest phase of a five-minute jog. This is followed by 4 × 400 meters at the student-athletes' goal race pace for the mile, with a 90-second rest between each. After another five-minute jog, the runner does another anaerobic threshold run of between 800 and 1600 meters. Finally, the runners finish the workout with a 10- to 25-minute cool-down. The 400s can be exchanged with 200s, 300s, or 600s on subsequent weeks. The pace for the 200s, 300s, or 600s should vary according to the length of the repetition.

The workouts during the early-season phase should progress in duration or intensity. Most injuries, if they occur, happen toward the end of this phase; therefore, it is vital that workouts be planned and based on the athlete's individual needs.

Midseason Phase

For an 18-week season, the midseason phase should begin at week 7 or 8 (after indoor season) and should continue through week 14, before the final phase of the season. Many times, we refer to this time of the season as the "grunt and groan" phase, meaning that this is the time when the distance runner works very hard and sustains top-level conditioning into the championship phase.

The recommendation presented in the early-season phase of having 5 up-tempo days over a 14-day cycle also applies during this phase. This means that whenever the schedule allows, a maximum of two (lower intensity) rest days should be allowed between up-tempo days. A big difference with this phase as compared with the early-season phase is

that both the duration and intensity of the work bouts should be at a higher level.

During this phase, the runners should again have one very long, aerobic-paced run every 14 days (20 to 50 percent longer than their next-longest run of the week). Sunday is a good time to run this so that the athletes have time for both the run and the recovery. See table 9.8 on page 120 for a sample week of training for this phase.

During this phase, the Tuesday workouts are more traditional than those sampled during the early-season phase. The repetitions should vary from 100 meters to 1200 meters. The pace can be progressive from 115 percent race pace for the shorter repetitions to normal race pace as the repetition becomes longer. The rest interval should last until the runner's heart rate is back down to 120 beats per minute. A combination of repetition distances can be used within the same workout to stress different aspects of the race distance. Intensity should always be derived from a percentage of the race distances: one mile, two mile, or 5000 meters. In other words, the greater the race distance, the lesser the intensity; that is, anaerobic threshold pace instead of race pace. The intensity should never be 100 percent or greater if the repetition distance is 50 percent or greater than the race distance. So for a runner training for the 3200-meter run, a set of mile intervals would need to be at an intensity slower than the pace of the runner's best 3200-meter time. That is, if the runner is an 11-minute, 3200-meter runner, that runner's mile repeats should be slower than 5:30 per mile.

We have found that some runners race best by training at aerobic pace, and others do better with anaerobic threshold runs with no repetitions at a faster rate. Again, the coach must take the time to get to know each runner and what works best for him or her. Also, some runners simply need several rest days throughout a season to be more effective. When runners appear to be stagnating during the season (showing no improvement), give them three to five consecutive days rest from all training. You will be surprised how well they will bounce back.

Table 9.8   Week of Midseason Phase Workouts for 3000- to 5000-Meter Runners

Monday—A.M.	4 miles at aerobic pace
Monday—P.M.	6 miles at aerobic pace Weight training
Tuesday	4-mile warm-up at aerobic pace 800 meters (alternate 50 hard, 50 easy) 1 mile at anaerobic threshold pace 6 × 1000 at race pace; rest 2 minutes 6 × 100 at 1500-meter race pace; rest 1 minute 1 mile at anaerobic threshold pace 2-mile cool-down
Wednesday—A.M.	4 miles at aerobic pace
Wednesday—P.M.	6 miles at aerobic pace Weight training
Thursday	Premeet 4 miles at aerobic pace
Friday	Dual meet
Saturday	8 miles at aerobic pace
Sunday	10 miles at aerobic pace

Championship Phase

This phase covers the last 3 to 4 weeks of an 18-week season. The goal of this phase is to prepare the runner to perform at the highest level of the entire season. If the athlete didn't overtrain or overrace throughout the season, then he or she should find this phase the most enjoyable and rewarding segment of the season.

During this phase, we decrease the duration progressively but not by more than 5 percent per week. If you decrease by more than 5 percent per week, you risk losing much of what has been gained throughout the season of carefully planned workouts. We also decrease the intensity somewhat, yet we put more emphasis on longer rest intervals between repetitions. We maintain the distance of repetitions from the midseason phase to avoid shocking the physiological system late in the season. Table 9.9 shows a sample week during this phase.

It is important to continue with sufficient aerobic-paced runs to ensure stride efficiency.

A common mistake made by some programs is to cut the mileage way back in the final three weeks; consequently, the distance runner loses the all-important stride efficiency. By maintaining duration (minus the 5 percent cutback per week), increasing the rest interval, and slightly decreasing the intensity of the repetitions, the runner effectively recovers from the midseason work and is able to perform at optimal levels.

Morning or two-per-day workouts become less important during this phase of training. It is more important for the student-athletes to get plenty of rest during this final phase so that their bodies can continue to fully recover from the hard training of the midseason phase. Because of the way the competition schedule is set during the championship phase, it may be impossible to remain on the 14-day cycle of racing. If this is true, the coach must still be sure to allow only 5 up-tempo days within a 14-day cycle, including meets. When in doubt, always lean toward a softer training schedule during the championship phase.

Table 9.9   Week of Championship Phase Workouts for 3000- to 5000-Meter Runners

Monday	8 miles at aerobic pace
Tuesday	3-mile warm-up at aerobic pace 800 meters at anaerobic threshold pace 4 × 600 at race pace; rest 2 minutes Walk 5 minutes. 4 × 200 at 1500-meter race pace; walk back, rest 800 at anaerobic threshold pace 1-mile cool-down
Wednesday	Optional: 5 to 6 miles at aerobic pace (or no running)
Thursday	Premeet: 4 miles at aerobic pace
Friday	Championship meet
Saturday	Championship meet
Sunday	13 miles at aerobic pace

3000- TO 5000-METER RACING

There are several ways to run a successful distance event on the track. Here are some tips for racers:

✓ Run the first two minutes of the race conservatively. The early splits are the most important ones. Adrenaline can negatively affect the athletes' ability to properly pace in the early stages of a distance race. Energy stores will be used up rapidly without the runners realizing it, making the second half of the race more difficult.

✓ It helps if the coach can use a code to help the runners stay on pace by giving them splits at locations other than the normal 400-meter intervals; the 300- or 500-meter intervals work just as well. We've used the following numbers for the coach to communicate to the athlete: (1) too fast, (2) too slow, (3) on pace.

✓ Negative pace tactics, in which the first half of the race is run more slowly than the second, can be quite efficient. Surges are also more successful in the second half of the race if the runner employs a negative pace tactic.

✓ Avoid becoming boxed-in. Toward the end of the race, if the runner is following another runner, he or she should run off the outside shoulder of the lead runner or runners. This allows the runner to escape from being boxed-in and puts him or her in an offensive position to pass late in the race.

✓ Race with the "end in mind." The race plan and its execution should be focused on the end of the race.

✓ Take the lead of the race only once. Runners who have the ability to win a race should be careful not to take the lead until they are convinced that they will not have to relinquish the top spot.

✓ Race in contact with teammates. This can help runners to conserve energy. The confidence that comes from running within one arm's length of a teammate can help relax a runner to relax.

✓ Cool-down. Long, slow cool-downs are necessary after racing and quality training to regain aerobic efficiency and balance.

Chapter 10

HIGH JUMP

© Human Kinetics

Over time, the high jump has evolved from a jump, to a roll, to a flop. The third style, the flop, is the most widely used technique today. Dick Fosbury, using his knowledge of physics, first developed and implemented the flop because he discovered that the technique, when properly executed, allows one's center of mass to actually pass beneath the bar. His theory and his now widely accepted technique changed everything about the jump, making it necessary for jumpers to start from scratch—from the approach to the landing. This chapter details each aspect of the high jump, beginning with the approach, or run-up.

APPROACH

With its curved approach (or J-approach), the flop poses one of the more difficult problems in all jumping events in track and field as far as achieving run-up accuracy. Most floppers approach the bar at a 90-degree angle, which is the ideal angle. The best way to ensure an approach at this angle is to use the near standard as a measuring point and apply the Pythagorean theorem (figure 10.1). This method will always place the athlete on a 90-degree angle to the pit, no matter how the pit is placed on the jumping surface.

The approach to the bar must be exact and consistent; otherwise, the athlete will have to compensate for any miscalculations by traveling down the bar, changing the angle of approach, or taking a long last step. These compensations result in suboptimal jumps.

Using the J-approach offers several advantages over other approaches, including

1. better speed development during the straight line portion of the run,

2. better control of the speed, and

3. improved accuracy to and at the take-off point.

I recommend to my athletes that they take a 10-step approach, regardless of which side of the pit they are running from. The side of the approach is determined by the foot an athlete leaves the ground with; that is, a left-footed jumper approaches from the right side of the pit and vice versa. During the straight portion (or the initial five steps), the athlete should concentrate on developing controllable velocity and a smooth rhythmical stride pattern.

Consistency, control, and confidence are crucial parts of the first five steps of the approach. The run should be quick and the center of mass should be over each foot as it lands, with each step being faster than the previous. There should be a quick acceleration during the initial steps followed by a slight acceleration into a short last step (figure 10.2, a and b).

The final portion of the approach—the last five steps—involves the turn-and-plant and the curve of the J up to the bar. The inside foot is the first to move inward from the straight

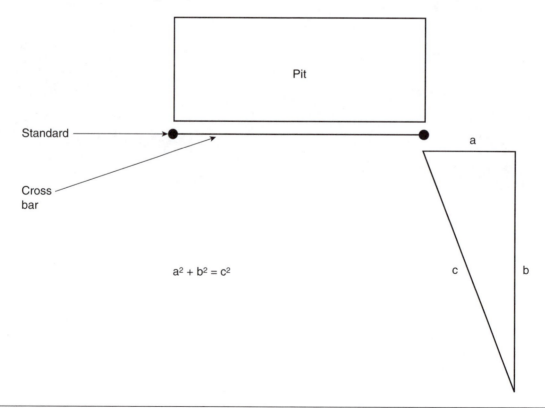

Figure 10.1 Using the Pythagorean theorem to find the starting point ensures the proper angle of approach.

Figure 10.2, a-e The athlete accelerates with each of the first five steps of the 10-step approach. Rounding the curve with the last of the 10-step approach, she leans inward to maintain speed.

line, thereby initiating the turn (figure 10.2c). The jumper, by running this curve, generates centripetal force and will have to develop an inward lean to maintain the accelerated speed prior to takeoff (figure 10.2d). A jumper can increase this force by shortening the turn radius, and increasing the velocity.

The penultimate step of the approach (in the case of a ten-step approach, the ninth) is slightly longer than any of the other steps. This longer step allows the athlete to lower the hips to place them in a more powerful position. The tenth and final step (figure 10.2e)

should be almost the shortest, up to one foot shorter than the longest step, for the following actions to take place:

1. To allow for a hip rise from the penultimate step to the last step
2. To bring the trail leg through faster, since it is a shorter lever
3. To place the jumper's center of mass directly over the takeoff foot sooner
4. To create "quickness" off the ground

Table 10.1 provides a ten-step approach checklist.

Table 10.1   Ten-Step Approach Checklist

Step 1	Focus eyes on the first step marker. Use a waterfall start (leaning forward until movement is initiated). Some athletes may use a walk-in approach; however, this type of approach can vary by a couple of inches and change the takeoff point.
Steps 2-4	Most of all run-up problems occur during the first three steps. Focus on the straight line marker extending out from the near standard. Start your curve run on step 4. *Do not* step out with step 4—keep it in a straight line. Begin your inward lean with your head and shoulders and bring your right hand to your left shoulder.
Steps 5-7	Focus on the top of the far standard while you lean inward and achieve horizontal speed.
Step 8	Your hips begin to settle; you lean backward while still maintaining a slight inward lean.
Steps 9-10	Your center of mass is directly over your plant foot; your hinge moment is completed, both of the arms and free leg block. The plant foot is parallel with the crossbar, and the body is tall over the plant foot.

PLANT

Once the athlete has arrived at the takeoff point, the actual plant is the most important part of the jump. It is critical that the athlete's center of mass is directly over the plant foot and leg at the moment the athlete initiates the lift off the ground. The takeoff leg must be perpendicular to the surface as the lead leg and both arms drive upward and block at a 90-degree angle (figure 10.3a). The center of mass then shifts from the vertical position to over the takeoff point toward the bar (figure 10.3b). If the jumper goes beyond the vertical position and starts to lean inward toward the bar during the transition from horizontal to vertical velocity, the body will crash into the bar on the way up. On the other hand, if the jumper does not maintain the horizontal momentum that has been developed over the previous nine steps, the athlete will not clear the crossbar.

The plant angle is important to the quickness of the takeoff. The greater the angle, the greater the time it takes for the center of mass to move over the takeoff foot. Severe plant angles keep the jumper on the takeoff foot for a longer period of time and require a long-radius, free-leg swing.

Severe plant angles are caused by a long last step or by improper arm action. If both arms are brought back together prior to the jump, the end result will be a plant angle that places the center of mass behind the takeoff foot. Arm action should be continuous throughout the approach with the outside arm moving through. The inside arm should "hold" only on the conclusive penultimate step. At no time should both arms be brought back together.

The free-leg swing and the arm drive must occur simultaneously to achieve a 90-degree angle at the moment of takeoff. Coordinating these exact positions and stopping them at the exact time that the plant foot leaves the ground results in the unweighting of the free leg and arms. This upward drive provides a downward force that creates an eccentric contraction, resulting in a greater force and velocity. Quickness off the ground is very important; the jumper who can apply the greatest force in the shortest period of time will achieve success.

TAKEOFF

One of the most important benefits of the curved run is that it causes the jumper to lean away from the bar. This allows the jumper to maintain horizontal velocity into the takeoff, but it also allows time to move into a vertical takeoff position. Leaning away from the bar creates a "hinge moment," which in turn creates horizontal rotation over the bar, accomplished by stopping the foot while the upper body accelerates (figure 10.3c).

As the bar moves higher, some jumpers change their velocity or shorten the radius of their curve to enhance their vertical lift. The basic rule for heights under 72 inches is that the takeoff will occur about an arm's length from the near standard. The distance of the foot plant from the standard or the cross bar is approximately 45 to 50 inches for heights of 72 inches or higher. This same general rule applies to women attempting to clear a cross bar over 69 inches.

The takeoff point should be directly out from the closest standard. Jumpers who take off too close to the bar will not be able to maintain momentum during bar clearance. Consider the following advantages of taking off just off the standard:

1. The jumper will clear the bar at the lowest point of the cross bar, where the measurement to determine jumping height is made.

2. The jumper will land directly on the pit; that is, it is very unlikely that the jumper will miss the pit.

3. The bar has a better chance of staying on if it is hit near the center.

FLIGHT AND CLEARANCE

Once the takeoff has been completed, the most important principle to keep in mind during the airborne portion of the flight is that the movement of the center of mass will not change from the moment of takeoff until landing in the pit. The flight path that ensures this physical law is known as the parabolic curve, which means that any movements made while not grounded—that is, movements made only in the air—will not alter the speed of rotation or the position of the body in relation to the center of mass. The ideal bar clearance is where the center of mass rises the least while the body clears the crossbar (figure 10.3d).

Figure 10.3, a-c   During the plant phase the objective is to apply the greatest force in the shortest period of time, springing off the foot into the takeoff.

Also, having both arms as close to the body and legs as short as possible will allow for faster rotational speed over the crossbar. The following two points are important to remember during this phase:

- The jumper must avoid lifting the legs up after takeoff and instead allow the legs to relax and hang once clearance has been achieved.
- If the jumper's seat is down and the head and feet are in an up-position, it becomes impossible for the jumper to attain the appropriate layout position.

During the flight or layout position, I like to have the jumper's head to drop straight back for greater hip height when on top of the crossbar (figure 10.3d). If the head is not in this position and assumes a position that is sometimes taught (the head looking down the bar to the far standard), it will act as a blocking movement and not allow for the hips to rise to their maximum height.

The arms that were used to block at the moment of takeoff never travel beyond the eyes and ultimately float to the hips at the apex of the flight. During the arch position, the head should go back and the eyes should focus beyond the pit. The legs are bent at the knees to decrease their length by rotating outward while the heels are pulled in, thus increasing the speed of rotation over the crossbar. The wider or shorter the legs can become, the shorter the lever, and thus, the faster the rotation over the bar.

LANDING

The jumper has achieved the best possible bar clearance when the hips have cleared, when the head is as low as possible, and when the layout position is completed. At that time, a simple bend of the hips will bring the legs

Figure 10.3, d-f Once the athlete is airborne and has cleared the bar with her hips, she should bend the hips to form a V, bringing her legs clear of the bar.

and feet up, and by bringing the chin to the chest, the body will form into a V (figure 10.3e) and assist in the clearance of the legs. The jumper should land in the pit on the lower-to-middle back with arms and legs extended to the front (figure 10.3f). The athlete does not want to land on the base of the neck for obvious reasons.

HIGH JUMP TRAINING

Most technique-specific high jump training involves drilling various aspects of the approach and takeoff. Table 10.2 features some sample early-season workouts that use these techniques and provides ideas for additional conditioning work for high jumpers.

Table 10.2 Early-Season Workouts for High Jumpers

Day	Workout
Monday	Back drops, from 3 steps and 5 steps; start with bar 16 inches below best height and take 3 jumps at each height, moving up by 1-inch increments Plyometrics Lower body weights
Tuesday	Curved runs, run-throughs 3 × 300 meters at 46 seconds; 5 minutes rest 3 × 200 meters at 30 seconds; 3 minutes rest 3 × 100 meters at 15 seconds; 2 minutes rest Mirror drills Upper body weights
Wednesday	Run-throughs, back-drops, curved runs 3-step knee drills 5 × 5-step jumps, starting 4 inches below best 5-step height Plyometrics Lower body weights
Thursday	Curved runs, run-throughs (check marks) 6 × 200 meters at 30 seconds Mirror drills Plyometrics Upper body weights
Friday	Mirror drills 4 × 100-meter accelerations Pick up meet itinerary
Saturday	Meet
Sunday	Rest day

Adapting to the Situation

Good athletes have a way of making you reevaluate how you do things. As a high school coach, I had a young man who qualified for the state meet all four years; he won the state title once and lost the title on misses another year, clearing seven feet. Throughout his high school career, he continued to improve, was never injured, and continued to make physical and mental progress in this event, as well as his other sport, football.

When he departed for college, he signed with an NCAA Division I school and headed off to conquer more heights. It was a year after he left high school that I also left for the college ranks as a coach. One year later he contacted me regarding a possible transfer to my school because of a change in his major. That transfer did in fact take place the following year; however, in the meantime he had suffered compartments syndrome in both of his legs.

Because of his injury and subsequent surgery, he had to complete a rehabilitation period before resuming regular training. As we moved into the season, it became evident that the way I had trained him during his four years in high school was unrealistic now; he couldn't handle the training load we would have liked.

As a result, we both sat down and put together a plan. The plan allowed him to rest more while shifting the work load to focus on quality efforts as opposed to a second jumping session per week. That second session is when we did strength work and increased volumes. The end result of adapting our training approach was his recovery from the injury and taking the national title while tying the NCAA Division III indoor high jump record. This experience showed me the need for compromise, alternative training, and continual communication with the athlete.

Chapter 11

POLE VAULT

Joshua Buchholtz

Pole Vault Coach, University of Wisconsin at La Crosse

© Human Kinetics

The pole vault is perhaps the most dynamic and exciting event in track and field, one that you have to make fun and safe for your athletes. Every pole vault coach and athlete must become a student of the event in order to be successful.

Inch by inch, it's a cinch . . . yard by yard, it gets very hard describes how to become a successful pole-vaulter as well as how to become a successful coach. The pole vault is an event that requires the mastery of the basic skills before progressing to the next level. There is no easy way to the top in vaulting.

WHAT TO LOOK FOR IN A VAULTER

Vaulters just don't often fall into a coach's lap, and most often, the good ones go undiscovered. So it's important to be able to know what to look for when keeping an eye out for potential recruits. This was very apparent when I stumbled upon a college athlete on her third year of competition. She was a high jumper and sprinter by trade. With her speed, body awareness, gymnastic background, and a whole lot of tenacity, she became in just two years of competition a vaulter who could pole-vault 12 feet, 4 inches.

A good pole-vaulter tends to be a good all-around athlete. A potential pole-vaulter has no set body type that you can look for. Though it may seem advantageous for a vaulter to be tall and have long levers, this is not always the case. When looking for an aspiring vaulter, consider the following important factors:

• Speed. This is key! In general, the velocity with which the vaulter leaves the ground directly relates to the size of the pole, which in turn transfers into the height attained; that is, horizontal energy transfers into vertical energy. It should not surprise you to find a good vault candidate already on your team in the sprints, hurdles, or even the long and triple jump events.

• Kinesthetic, or body awareness. Coordination and body control play a large role in vaulting. It is important for vaulters to be able to sense what their body is doing and have the ability to make corrections in fractions of a second. As a vaulter progresses, this awareness can be developed and refined. An athlete with good kinesthetic awareness will have more success than a vaulter without it; a good vaulter may often even have a background in gymnastics. This was especially true in the early stages of the women's pole vault during which top vaulters usually had an extensive background in gymnastics.

• Strength. Strength is the next factor in the success of a vaulter. Strength also affects the principle of speed: the faster vaulters can become, the more readily they move to longer and bigger poles, resulting in the potential for higher marks. Strength also plays a role in maintaining health throughout training during the track season. By preparing athletes through a sound weightlifting and strengthening program, you can reduce the chance that they will injure themselves.

• Coachability. A vaulter has to understand first that the pole vault is an event that requires commitment and that often he or she will need to put in more time than athletes who do other events on the track. Time spent working out, practicing both mentally and physically, competing, and being a student of the event, takes dedication. For the coach, determining what makes vaulters tick is part of the job. Knowing how they prepare to compete, what their likes and dislikes are, and what their strengths and weaknesses are constitutes being a good coach. Using these characteristics to motivate and teach the vault will help you get the most out of an athlete without having a negative experience. For example, if you know that an athlete has a tendency to run a little harder on the third attempt and thus "blow through" the pole, you have the athlete move the standards back accordingly. A coach learns over time, through observation in practice and meet settings, how to get the best from each athlete.

• Attitude and strength of mind. This may be the most important part of vaulting. Many have said that pole vaulting is 90 percent mental and 10 percent physical. If you have been around pole vaulters before, you know it seems that some of them are a little strange or crazy. This is how some vaulters deal with the idea that they must hang upside down on a long piece of fiberglass that bends in half, and hope that it throws them in the right direction as they fly in most cases 10-plus feet off the ground. It is inevitable that at some point in a vaulting career, a vaulter will crash, no height in a meet, or just simply have a bad meet. The good vaulters are those who can shake it off, learn from their mistakes, and move on. This mental toughness, while inherent in many vaulters, is also a trainable characteristic.

Many times, the coach will need to serve as a mediator between the vaulters and their minds. By recognizing how they best cope with situations and by setting them up for success early in their career, the coach can facilitate the vaulters' development and encourage their mental toughness, which will help them to overcome tough times. Many times, this toughness is apparent in those with less natural ability. They overcome their deficiencies by becoming mentally stronger and more mentally prepared than their opponents. I was told a story by a former coach that I now pass down frequently. It's a story of an athlete who was never the stand-out vaulter—never the fastest, never the strongest. But he was mentally tough and always prepared. One rainy day at the NCAA National Championships, he became a national champion because he was mentally tougher in the inclement weather when his competitors faltered.

Vaulting Technique

One key training activity is form running to establish or correct any inefficient running patterns. I like to break down the vault event into segments that help a coach and athlete pinpoint and correct any errors in technique.

Pole Grip

You may think that the pole grip and carry are quite basic and don't need to be worked on in practice. On the contrary, the grip and carry can be a vital components in squeezing out inches over the bar.

First you need to establish whether your vaulter has a preference of takeoff foot. From this, you can determine the best grip and pole carry. Normally, right-hand dominant vaulters place their right hand at the top of the pole and the left hand lower on the pole, which makes the takeoff foot the left foot (figure 11.1).

Once you have established top and bottom hands, consider the grip distance or distance between the hands. The most efficient way to gauge proper grip distance is to begin with the

length of the vaulter's arm from palm to armpit. Have the vaulter grip the pole with the top hand as if preparing to throw it like a javelin then extend the pole back behind the body so that it comes to rest under the armpit. The vaulter should grip the pole by placing the thumb of the lower hand in the armpit and grasping the pole at the point of contact. Increasing the distance between the hands can make it easier to plant the pole, but it may interfere with the inversion of the vault or getting upside down. Narrowing the grip will make it easier for a vaulter to get inverted.

I've found that the best method for finding the right grip distance is to have the athlete

Figure 11.1   Proper form for a right-handed vaulted is shown here. A left-handed vaulter would place the left hand at the top and would take off from the right foot.

establish the plant with a slightly wider grip, then begin narrowing it by small increments. This method assists the vaulter in finding a happy medium.

Pole Carry

With the grip established, it's time to turn to the proper pole carry. To achieve proper form for the carry, the vaulter should put an imaginary gun in an imaginary holster with one hand while checking an imaginary watch with the other. The hand at the top of the pole should rest along the hip like a gun in a holster, and the other hand should be positioned as if the vaulter were checking a wristwatch at about chest height (figure 11.2a). The pole then naturally angles across the front of the vaulter.

As the vaulters carry the pole down the runway, they must keep their shoulders square. Most important is that the vaulters have a comfortable and efficient approach run, with the pole tip being raised to a nearly vertical position, then gradually lowered

throughout the approach (figure 11.2b). I often stress that a vaulter is a sprinter who happens to carry a pole and that running form and body position should be similar to sprinting form and position.

Approach

As I mentioned, a pole vaulter is really a sprinter carrying a pole! The mechanics are nearly the same: An athlete carrying a pole simulates the arm positions of a sprinter, with the major difference being that the upper body movement is limited by the carry. The upper body should stay relaxed and the vaulter should stay in control of the pole.

It is not important for a beginning vaulter to establish a full run until the basic pole carry, approach, and simple pop-ups can be done efficiently. The vaulter should become comfortable handling the pole before shifting attention to consistent runs or approaches. Rules and regulations regarding when athletes can begin to use facilities and equipment vary from school to school and state to state,

Figure 11.2, a and b   The hand at the top of the pole rests along the hip; the other hand is placed at chest height.

but generally, the sooner the vaulters begin practicing, the better off they are. If poles are not available, athletes can use anything that simulates a pole—broken poles cut into shorter sticks or old broom sticks are adequate substitutes for preseason training.

Once the fundamentals of carrying and running with a pole become efficient, it is important to start establishing a consistent run. The length of the approach and the type of run-up will vary depending on the characteristics of each individual athlete. In general, when determing the length of the approach, consider the vaulter's ability, body type, speed, and comfort or experience with vaulting. New vaulters should use a shorter approach than that used by the more advanced athletes. An athlete who takes more time to reach peak speed will benefit from a longer run; however, an athlete who attains peak speeds quickly may be comfortable with a short or long approach.

Approach work is important to all levels of vaulting. There will be times when more advanced vaulters who are struggling with their run need to return to working on their approach for consistency. As a coach, it is important for you to recognize this and to get the struggling vaulters off the runway and on the side to work on their run.

The approach can be started various ways. I recommend the four-step, walk-in approach that consists of a rock-back step, with the takeoff foot being forward, followed by four steps. I recommend this start because it allows for more consistency by adding a checkpoint after the four starting steps. Another approach start is the simple run with little or no buildup. Some athletes prefer the shuffle or skip start, in which they shuffle or skip into the run and check their step as they pass their starting mark.

I also recommend using checkpoints on the runway to mark the starting point, the four-step mark, and the takeoff point. If the athlete's run is inconsistent, a coach may want to add a midmark halfway into the approach and a four-step check mark for those using a four-step walk-in. The vaulter can develop a more consistent run, and you, as coach, can see

more clearly the discrepancies in each section of the approach and communicate them to the vaulter. (Remember to use the term *step* to refer to every time the takeoff foot hits the runway and the term *stride* to refer to every time any foot hits the runway.) Generally, a beginner would use an 8- to 10-step approach plus a 4-step walk-in. This would mean that the athlete's takeoff foot would hit the runway four or five times, not including the walk-in.

Once the vaulter has established a start, the rest of the approach should be identical no matter what the length of approach. With the pole nearly vertical, the approach should be a consistent acceleration through the plant. The pole should then be lowered gradually throughout the run. Remember that a vaulter is a sprinter who carries a pole; the lower

Developing a Consistent Approach

Consistency is key in developing an approach, and repetition is at the heart of consistency. When I was in high school, our track season started in early spring. Living in northern Wisconsin and not having an indoor facility, we were often forced by the snow to conduct many of our practices in the gym. This is where I developed my approach run. I would measure out my run diagonally in the gymnasium, lay down tape for my start and takeoff points, then do 15 to 20 runs each day. Going into my freshman season, we had an indoor meet before I ever had a chance to leave the ground and actually vault. I had been doing my runs religiously for two weeks prior to the meet, but I had never bent a pole before, and my personal best in middle school was nine feet. In my inaugural high school indoor meet, however, I bent the pole in warm-up from a full run the first time down the runway. What a rush! It was addictive, and I wanted more. I ended up clearing 10 feet, 6 inches in the first meet of the year without one day of full vaulting—I had only spent time on the run.

body mechanics of a vaulter should be the same as those of a sprinter.

During the early season, it is important that athletes establish a good run before actually vaulting in practice or competition. Vaulters should do this by running and recording the takeoff step. A slide box made from two-by-fours can be used to simulate a plant box during approach practice. Use a line or tape on the floor to give vaulters a visual mark for the appropriate plant point. When vaulters run approaches for consistency, record each approach to determine any adjustments the athlete needs to make from the previous run and the takeoff point. To determine a takeoff point, place tape or chalk marks on the floor to indicate the distance in feet from the back of the plant box. Once the individual becomes consistent, you may need to put only three or four marks down (e.g., at 10 feet, 10.5, 11, 11.5).

Pole Plant

The plant begins four steps out from the plant box when the vaulter's right foot hits the runway (figure 11.3a). With the pole parallel to the ground from the approach and the upper body still in the "gun in the holster, check your watch" position, the pole should begin to pivot on the hand that is lowest on the pole as the top hand runs the pole directly up and along the side of the ribcage (figure 11.3b). Both arms should be extended one step from the plant box (or as the dominant foot hits the ground). The top hand should be directly over the takeoff foot as that arm extends fully (figure 11.3c). I tell the athletes to make sure they put the biceps of their top arm in their ear. It is also important to push the plant up and away from the body and to keep the head and eyes following the forward hand. Body position at this point should be tall and aggressive.

Takeoff

This is where the vaulter takes on the characteristics of a long jumper, since the movement of takeoff is similar in each event. The takeoff, or plant, foot should be directly under the

Figure 11.3, a-c   The plant begins four steps from the plant box as the athlete pivots the pole. The arms extend forcefully to complete the plant.

Figure 11.4, a and b The pole is pushed up and away from the body as the knee drives the lift of the body.

body as the pole hits the back of the plant box (see figure 11.4a). The center of gravity then rotates forward and is projected slightly upward, with the knee driving the lift (figure 11.4b). The athlete should drive the thigh up so it is parallel to the ground, and the takeoff leg should be allowed to trail as it pushes off the ground through the toes, creating a hang or dragging motion with the trailing leg. As the athlete leaves the ground, the pole should be pushed away from the body and separation between body and pole should be maintained. As the vaulter is traveling forward and upward, the pole is moving forward and bending but not swinging.

The drive now becomes important, as this is where the horizontal energy from the run is "loaded" into the pole. This also dictates how far a vaulter gets into the mats. If vaulters use the proper pole—one that is rated for body weight and of the appropriate length for their ability—they may still come up short by not getting into a proper drive position. By holding this "drive" position a split second longer, the vaulter gives the pole more time to travel to near-vertical position before it unbends,

taking the athlete deeper onto the landing mats.

Swing and Inversion

Now the vaulters are in a position in which they are literally hanging from the pole with their takeoff leg dragging behind and their lead leg driving off the ground. It is important that they keep separation between the pole and the body. The swing should start with a long but vigorous movement of the trail leg and hips. The athlete should continue holding the drive position of the lead leg and not let it drop to a double-leg swing position, which could cause a loss of forward momentum. Another key as the vaulter goes through this swing motion is to keep the top hand moving. Use the analogy of paddling a canoe to represent what "moving" means. Have the vaulters imagine pushing their top hand from above their head in a big half-circle out in front of their body and continuing back to their opposite thigh. With this upper body action, the lower body should swing through while the entire body swings as a whole.

Figure 11.5, a and b　The athlete continues to drive forward, tucking the drive leg to create greater rotation and speed.

Think of a clock as you observe a vaulter from the side. The vaulter's head should be at 12 o'clock, with drive leg leaving the ground at 6 o'clock (figure 11.5a). As the vaulter drives forward, the trail leg should trail behind close to 8 o'clock, then swing through long and hard until the upward swing at about 5 o'clock, where it should start to be tucked inward to created a quicker rock-back motion into a vertical position (figure 11.5b). This is similar to the principle that figure skaters use during a spin. When skaters begin to spin they start out with arms extended, similar to the long leg-swing of a vaulter; this causes slower action. To spin faster, they bring their arms in, or tuck them in, just as vaulters do with their leg to create greater rotation and speed to achieve an upside-down position.

Extension and Clearance

As the swing leg is tucked in, the top hand continues to move to its position near the opposite thigh. This is when the vaulter must work with the pole to time an extension that will create the most vertical position possible. As the pole starts to unbend, the vaulter must pull and extend, bringing the hips close to the pole and laying the head back (figure 11.6a). As the vaulters start the turn while

moving upward, they should try to put their right foot over their left foot (if the vaulter is right-handed; it's vice versa for a lefty). When the pull and turn are completed, it is important to continue the vault with a solid push off the top of the pole as the bottom hand leaves the pole, with the top hand pushing off vertically (figure 11.6b).

The objective is to literally fly off the top of the pole and continue to gain height. As the feet clear the bar, the vaulter should imagine another bar about a foot above the actual bar; the vaulter should then imagine clearing that mental bar before bringing his feet down by folding at the hips. A vaulter clearing the bar should look a lot like a slinky. Be sure that the parabolic pathway, through which the vaulter travels over the bar, is a tall and narrow one. To be sure, a coach may want to watch a vault from the side.

SELECTING THE RIGHT POLE

An important question for vaulters and coaches is what pole an athlete should choose. Pole selection is determined by many factors. First, consider the weight of the athlete. A vaulter should not exceed the factory weight limit of the pole he or she is using. In fact, to

Figure 11.6, a and b Once the athlete is upside down and the pole unbends, the legs extend upward and over.

get more snap out of the pole, a vaulter should strive to use a pole with a higher weight rating than the vaulter's actual body weight would dictate.

How do you know when it is a good time to go to a stiffer pole? One indicator is when the athletes are consistently going deep into the landing mats. Another sign is when they are getting inverted well, but still knocking off the crossbar on the way up. When moving up in weight, use five-pound increments, if possible, so that adjustments are minimal.

The length of the pole is another factor in proper pole selection. As with the weight of the pole, the length of a pole that a vaulter uses will increase progressively as the vaulter improves. Beginner vaulters, male or female, should start vaulting by "straight-sticking" (pole vaulting without bending the pole). Therefore, beginners can use any pole length because they are not running fast and are usually not gripping to height. I recommend that beginners use a 10- or 11-foot pole because of the simple fact

that these poles are easier to handle.

A sign that it is time to move up to the next longer pole length is when a vaulter starts to clear heights that are the same height as the pole. When moving up to a longer pole, the athlete may need to grip further down on the pole while becoming accustomed to that pole. Another aspect to consider when increasing pole length is the weight rating. If you increase the length of a pole, it may be necessary to go back down to the next lower weight because gripping down on a longer pole makes the pole stiffer.

There is no formula for when to go up a pole in length as opposed to weight. As a coach, you will need to work that out with your athlete; it is a game of trial and error. Generally, if the vaulters are blowing through at relatively low heights, then they will need to go up in weight. If it seems that the athlete is achieving an apex in the right spot over the bar but is just not getting enough height for clearance, then a longer pole may be needed.

TRAINING SEASON

The vault is an all-around event that uses the whole body, and because of that, the whole body needs to be developed. Training needs to address all aspects of preparation including technique work, lifting for strength, speed training for technique, cross-training for endur-ance and all-around fitness, and mental training for competitions.

We break the season into three general phases: preseason, in-season, and off-season. If enough time and effort is put in during the preseason, the actual season can be much more productive, as the body will be fit and able to adjust quickly to new techniques.

Table 11.1   Pole Vault: Event-Specific Lifts

Body area focus	Recommended lifts
Chest	Incline press Bench press Incline dumbbells/press
Shoulders	Upright row Straight-arm fly Bent-over fly Push press Push jerk
Back	Seated row Hyperextension
Lats	Pull-up (front and behind) Chin-up Lat pull (front, behind, and reverse; and regular grips) Pull-over (regular and reverse grip)
Biceps	Biceps curl and reverse curl Hammer curl
Triceps	Triceps extension (straight bar, v-bar, and rope) French curl Close-grip bench press Medicine ball "throw-up"
Quads	Squat (front and back) Lunge (regular and step backs) Step-up
Hamstrings	Leg curl (one- and two-legged) Straight-leg deadlift Glut-ham machine
Core (Olympic lifts)	Hang clean Power clean Split jerk Jerk Snatch Shrug
Combo lifts	Full clean, to front squat, to split jerk, to front squat, and down

Table 11.2 Typical Weekly Schedule During the In-Season

Monday	Vault day. It is important that the vaulter be relatively fresh, which is why Mondays seem to be the best for vaulting, after a day of rest Sunday.
Tuesday	Relatively hard workout day of nonvaulting; gymnastics.
Wednesday	Active recovery day, mild workout, and underwater vaulting.
Thursday	Vault day.
Friday	Premeet day or cross-training day. Premeet involves 6 to 8 × 100-meter builds, working running form, taping pole, preparing for meet, and any small drills done without mats (i.e., box plants, pole runs). Limited activity allows body to be prepared for meet.
Saturday	Meet day. Premeet warm-up follows abbreviated vault warm-up, same as practice.
Sunday	Active rest day; light jogging, anything but sitting and doing nothing.

Table 11.3a Typical Nonvaulting Practice Day

Warm-up and stretch. Laps, stretching, functional stretch, and form drills

Workout #1	One or more of the following:		
	cadence hurdles	55-meter form sprints	
	100- to 150-meter builds	200-meter pace	
	300-meter pace	cardio run	
Workout #2	One or more of the following:		
	plyometrics	sled pulls	hills
	stairs	overspeed	

Cool-down

Pool or gymnastics

Lift and ab work

Table 11.3b Typical Vaulting Practice Day

Warm-up and stretch; laps, stretching, functional stretch, and form drills.
Pole runs off runway
Pole runs on runway (with catch step and takeoff)
Pop-ups (one-arm plants, long to long, long to short)
Chase the bend
Full vaults (with no bar)
Individual work (plant-chase bend, not back-kick off bar, run short with soft pole)
Bar work when comfortable (bungee and bar work)
Form work (little)
Cool-down
Ab work and lift
Treatment (if needed, massage, stretching, ice)
Video

The preseason is when the foundation is laid for the whole year. This is the time to build strength and speed without worrying about being fresh to vault. Coaches can alter the schedule for the preseason to work around any camps or clinics the vaulter needs to attend. Camps and clinics are absolutely great preseason training. Not only do your athletes get a chance to vault, but they also learn new techniques and see other vaulters of varying abilities. Many areas also have track and field clubs that have meets throughout the summer, giving athletes a great opportunity to vault through the summer months. Generally, though, lifting two to three times a week is most important for the vaulters. Table 11.1 provides a list of lifts that are especially beneficial for vaulters, including some of the best lifts for the vault—the power clean and jerk, and the snatch. Coaches should implement aerobic conditioning and form running as well.

Once this basis of training has been established, the in-season training phase is the time for vaulters to continue honing technique while maintaining strength and fitness. Table 11.2 provides a sample training week for vaulters during the in-season. Table 11.3 (a and b) shows examples of a typical nonvaulting practice day and a vaulting practice day. These workouts all depend on the time of the season and the shape the athletes are in. Coaches may wish to give extra days of rest if productivity is lacking. Remember, too, that a vaulter is a sprinter carrying a pole, so it is good to train vaulters as such. Have them work out with the sprinters and horizontal jumpers, if possible.

Don't forget that an athlete also needs a recovery period after a season. This should be a period of three to five weeks that includes nothing more than light running and activity before the athletes get back into full training. I call the off-season the time for active rest; athletes stay physically active without focusing on anything vault-specific. Hiking, biking, and canoeing are perfect active-rest activities to do two to three times a week during the off-season. An athlete may want to continue doing some sort of running two times a week as well. This period is important to give the body, as well as the brain, time to recuperate from the previous season and to get hungry for vaulting again.

Vault Drills

Numerous drills and activities can be done to supplement vaulting workouts, either on vault days or on nonvault days. Here are some of my favorite drills.

Two-Pole Sand Drill

1. Tape together two poles. The tape should form an X a couple feet from the top of the poles.

2. Place the bottoms of the poles in the sand so that they are somewhat buried and standing upright on their own.

3. The vaulter grasps the poles about 6 to 12 inches above reach when the poles are vertical.

4. The vaulter takes one step and jumps off the ground, simulating the takeoff of a vault. A coach may help beginners by physically pulling the pole through the motion.

5. The vaulter takes off and maintains the lead thigh position parallel to the ground with a 90-degree separation between thigh and calf. The trail leg is extended behind the body. The vaulter holds this position and lands in the sand in that takeoff position.

As the athletes become more comfortable, allow them to grip higher and higher, taking a couple walking steps into the takeoff. Keys to this drill include the athletes' hanging lengthwise from the poles and maintaining the separation between their legs from the takeoff point. This drill is great for beginning vaulters because it allows them to get the feeling of taking off the ground and hanging from the pole—all in a safe environment, over a sand pit.

Beginners can also try the drill with one pole. This drill can be less intimidating than the athletes' having to rely on the pole vault pads and plant box while they are still being introduced to basic pole vault concepts. Again, the vaulter grips the pole with the top hand about 6 to 12 inches higher than can be reached with the pole standing vertical (right-handed vaulters use their right hand, and vice versa).

Pole Runs

This is a must-do drill for all vaulters, it and involves simple full-approach work, away from the pole-vault area (e.g., on a track straightaway). Experiment with different takeoff positions and techniques. Practicing these approach runs on a track gives athletes unhindered repetitions of running with the pole, thereby helping them to develop a routine and some consistency. Remember that the vault is a chain of events that starts with the approach; therefore, it is critical that athletes first develop a consistent approach.

Jog Plants

This drill emphasizes the last five steps of the approach and the plant.

Carrying a pole, the athlete starts the approach at a jog and focusses on accelerating the last five steps as well as hitting the correct hand positions when lowering and planting the pole. In other words, the sequence is as follows: gun in the holster, check your watch; gradually lower the pole (it should be parallel to the ground); move top hand up the side of the body; and extend top hand straight over head (biceps in the ear). As the vaulter maintains focus on the correct positions, it is important that he or she also build a progression of five aggressive steps.

Plant Drill

This drill reinforces building strength and maintaining the plant and drive positions. It creates and maintains body positions similar to the plant and takeoff of vaulting. This coach-assisted drill can be done against the wall in the gym, in the plant box, or just about anywhere you can plant a pole against an object that won't move.

1. Using a pole rated 10 or more pounds over the vaulter's body weight, the vaulter simulates a plant with the butt-end of the pole against a plant box or wall.

2. The vaulter then takes three steps away from the plant area. From this point, with the pole tip sliding on the ground, the vaulter simulates the last three steps of the approach into the plant.

3. With the coach standing on the side of the athlete and following closely, the vaulter takes the three approach steps; the coach then places his or her hands in the mid-to-upper back of the vaulter.

4. The coach gradually pushes the vaulter upward and inward, simulating the takeoff. Additional assistance may be useful to help the vaulter reach the correct positions. Often the knee may drop during the drive phase and may therefore require another person to physically assist the thigh and lead leg into the correct drive position. Another focus of this drill is for the vaulter to keep the trail leg dragging behind. This can be assisted by having another person block the trail leg from swinging under the body, by stopping it with a hand from the side.

Warm-Up Series

Also called pop-up drills, the following series of drills are an effective way for beginning vaulters to start vaulting as well as a good set of drills for the more advanced vaulters to use to warm up. These drills highlight on the main vaulting positions.

One-Armed Hangs. This drill emphasizes the tall takeoff by the vaulter's hanging from the pole and holding the takeoff and drive positions.

1. The vaulter grips the pole with one hand, no more than a foot higher than can be reached with the pole vertical. This is important. The more comfortable and capable the vaulter becomes, the higher up the pole the vaulter can hold, as long as he or she is making it into the pit without stalling out.

2. Holding the pole with the top hand in the "gun in the holster position," the vaulter slides the pole's butt-end along the runway, starting about 20 to 30 feet from the box.

3. The vaulter slides the pole along the runway and into the plant box. The plant should simulate the whole motion of the top hand. Make sure the acceleration during the run is aggressive at the plant.

4. Once the pole plants, the athlete projects off the ground, holding this drive position all the way until landing on the mat. Make sure the vaulter's body is traveling between the top hand and the pole. A right-handed vaulter (whose right hand is top hand) will take off with the left foot on top, the right hand above the head, and the left shoulder rubbing the pole as it passes by.

Other variations that work as part of the warm-up series include the following:

Long-to-long. The focus of this drill is on the takeoff and leg swing. Attacking the plant box, the vaulter should have a tall, high plant and solid takeoff from the ground. The trail leg should trail behind momentarily as the knee drives and the thigh stays parallel to the ground. Then using a vigorous, long, trail-leg swing, the whole body moves as one piece without bending at the waist.

Long-to-short. Working on the same principles as the long-to-long drill, the long-to-short drill adds the tucking action of the trail leg. With a solid plant and takeoff, the long leg swing is tucked in as the trail leg starts its upward swing. This creates a quicker rock-back action so that it may seem as if the only thing stopping the vaulter from doing a complete back flip in this position is the contact with the pole.

Long-to-short and extend. Continuing the long-to-short action, add an extension of the legs and hips from the tuck position. Coaches can add a turn to this as a vaulter progresses. With the turn, the vaulters land on their belly, looking back down the runway.

Kick Off the Bar

This drill is for a vaulter who has established a solid plant and swing, but may not be getting fully inverted or upside down. Set a bar or bungee cord approximately two feet above the vaulter's personal best height. The goal is for the vaulter to knock off the bar or get both feet over the bungee. Make sure the vaulter is holding a good drive off the ground; make sure that there is a big swing, that the shoulders drop back, and that the vaulter is able to look directly back down the runway. You can turn this drill into a mini-meet by providing an opening height, then raising the bar up, giving the athlete three attempts to knock off the bar.

Window Vaulting

Similar to the kick-off-the-bar drill, this drill allows the vaulter to work not only on getting back into an inverted position, but continuing the vault to extension, hip height, and bar clearance. With one bar or bungee placed at a high but maintainable height and another bar or bungee two feet higher, the vaulter strives to get inverted, kicks off the top bar, and clears the bottom bar.

Gymnastics Work

Gymnastics is one of the best cross-training tools for a pole-vaulter. Everything from tumbling to working with parallel bars stresses the concepts of vaulting by developing the muscles used in vaulting and by training kinesthetic development.

Tumbling. I recommend focusing on tumbling for beginners. In particular, two basic skills that are helpful for pole vaulters to master are walking on the hands and being able to roll out of a fall and roll backward into a handstand. By repeating these skills, the vaulter develops strength and kinesthetic awareness, and prepares the body for more advanced training techniques related to gymnastics.

Parallel Bars Takeoff Swings. Swings off the parallel bars focus on the swing phase of the vault while strengthening the vaulter's upper body. Have your vaulters prop themselves up on the parallel bars—both hands on the bars, with their arms straight and their legs hanging down. From this position, the athlete should be able to assume a good takeoff position by swinging freely with the arms and driving the knee up, allowing the trail leg to follow. To propel the vaulter into takeoff, it is key to allow the trail leg to swing back and get a full-forward swing-through.

Stationary Swings. Divided into three separate drills, stationary swings are excellent for honing the full swing and extension. On a set of stationary rings, have the vaulter assume a good takeoff position with the drive knee and trail leg in proper position. The vaulters should swing from their shoulders, keeping their body in line without breaking at the waist (a common fault). Have them swing all the way to a vertical position while keeping the body in line and maintaining the separation of the drive knee and trail leg. Abdominals and shoulders should be the main propellants for this drill. This first basic ring drill is called the *long-to-long* and is identical to the long-to-longs done in the warm-up series (with the exception that these are done on the rings).

Long-to-short. Working on the same principles as the long-to-long drill, the long-to-short ring drill adds the tucking action of the trail leg. With a good plant and takeoff, the long swing is tucked in as the trail leg starts its upward swing at approximately the five o'clock position (using the clock analogy), thus creating a quicker rock-back action.

Long-to-short and extend. Continue the long-to-short action and add an extension of the legs and hips from their tuck position. Instruct the vaulter to lay the shoulders back and allow the head to stay neutral. If you want to stress the extension off the top, have the athletes (once upside down) tuck back into a ball and slowly lower their body back until their back is parallel to the ground; then have them extend and shoot their legs back to a vertical position.

Underwater Vaulting

If you have a swimming pool, use this activity to keep the interest of the vaulters. It is an excellent simulation of the body positions in a full vault.

1. Find an old, long pole to use in the pool, one that you will never use again.
2. Have one person sit on the end of the diving board, holding the pole in a vertical position

so that it is resting on the bottom of the pool. (Be sure the pole is long enough to extend out of the water.)

3. The vaulters start by holding the sides of the diving board near the wall of the pool. They then drop straight down the side of the wall to the near-bottom of the pool. With arms extended (to reach for the pole), they push off the wall.

4. They grasp the pole and maintain a drive position until they are pulled nearly parallel to the pole.

5. When the top arm is in line with the body, they should initiate the swing, continue through the tuck, rock back, pull, turn, push, and by using the surface of the water as a crossbar, finish with a hip clearance and a fly-away. The resistance of the water slows the whole process down and allows the vaulters to concentrate on the positions they must maintain.

Swimming is a great strength workout for the shoulders but is also an excellent conditioning workout. Try to incorporate a swimming workout along with the underwater vaulting.

Videotaping and Reviewing

Videotaping and reviewing the results could be the most beneficial part of each day's practice. Videotape everything—form running, underwater vaulting, gymnastics, and most important, practice vaults and vaults at meets. If possible, watch these tapes as soon as possible with your athletes, and view them repeatedly thereafter. This gives vaulters a visual image to go along with their impression of what they did and felt during a particular drill or vault. It is important for them to see themselves making mistakes as well as correcting mistakes and being successful. Besides viewing tapes of themselves, vaulters should observe vaulters of their own caliber as well as elite vaulters. Tell your athletes to immerse themselves in vaulting videos whenever possible. If they can see vaulting done correctly and can recognize common vaulting mistakes in themselves and others, they will have a better chance of vaulting correctly.

Mental Imagery

Probably one of the most underrated and underused drills in vaulting is mental imagery. If the vault is 90 percent mental and 10 percent physical, as many say, vaulters need to strengthen the mind as well as the body. Mental practice is one way to do so. When vaulters can see themselves vaulting correctly and performing well in their mind, they are more likely to do so on the track. From drills to competition, mental success breeds physical success.

Develop a routine of mental imagery practice that your athletes can do repeatedly throughout the day. Have them get to a point where they can view every motion of the vault not only as if they were actually vaulting but as if they were watching themselves from outside their body. By incorporating other senses, such as sounds, with the motions of the vault, vaulters can bring a heightened realism to the mental vaulting. For example, instruct them to have that big trail leg make a "swoooosh" sound as it swings through. It may also be beneficial for the vaulters to imagine themselves being successful in different kinds of situations, such as on a windy day, in the rain, or on a cold day. Mental imagery does work, but like other practice drills, it must be done regularly.

Mental imagery is essential to a vaulter's training; if you can picture yourself clearing the bar, you are more likely to do so.

Vaulting Safety

As a coach, it is your responsibility to maintain a safe and effective vaulting facility. From training to competition areas, you must see that the activity is safe for athletes.

Your governing body has established recommended guidelines for the size of the landing pad, the surrounding padding, standard covers, and box protection. I recommend exceeding these regulations whenever possible.

It is a fact that vault mats are an expensive investment for your facility, so it is important that you and your athletes take good care of them. After practice, have athletes place covers over the mats to protect them from the elements when not in use. Use pallets (without nails), tires, or professional risers to keep the mats off the ground.

Track programs often have small budgets, and poles are not the cheapest track and field equipment; therefore, it is important to take care of your vault equipment. Store and transport poles in the factory tube or in a reinforced case. A plastic-drain tile inside a pole-vault carry bag is a one of the best ways to transport and store each pole; anything that keeps the pole from direct contact or damage is ideal. When the poles are not going to be used for an extended period of time (i.e., over the summer), take the tape off the poles and store them in an area that is room temperature. Keep the poles in a place where they are not liable to be damaged.

There are also a couple things you can do to extend the life of your poles. By keeping them out of the sun, you decrease the wear on the resins in the structure of the poles. Most poles have an outer layer of protective wrap, but it is a good policy to have athletes put any poles not in use in the case. When a vaulter bends a pole, many times the bend will rub on the side of the plant box and create scarring on the side of the pole. This weak spot in a pole is a potential spot for a break. To prevent this, you can either buy a specially designed protection strip from a track and field catalog or you can tape tongue depressors or Popsicle sticks over the wear area.

The pole vault is a dynamic event, and the athletes who participate in the event are dynamic athletes. With each unique individual comes a particular set of abilities, characteristics, and vaulting styles. Because there is no one correct way to vault, the strategies presented here are basic concepts of vaulting and can be adated for each athlete. With the basic concepts in mind, vaulters can explore what works for them and find personal success.

Chapter 12

LONG JUMP AND TRIPLE JUMP

Evan Perkins, MS, CSCS

Marinette High School (Marinette, Wisconsin)

© Human Kinetics

The horizontal jumps—the long jump and triple jump—both require good sprinting mechanics as well as optimal speed at takeoff. We present them both in this chapter as a result of their several similarities in approach technique, takeoff, flight, and landing, as well as similarities in the way coaches train both types of jumpers.

LONG JUMP

The long jump is one track and field event that often receives little attention. Coaches and athletes generally assume that the fastest athlete is the best candidate for the long jump, but the event cannot be oversimplified. Careful attention to the technical details of the event give any athlete an advantage over his or her competition. It takes time and hours of practice for athletes to master the phases of the long jump; they must perfect an effective approach run, proper body positions during takeoff, the flight, and the landing phase.

Approach

The goal of the approach is to develop a consistent run-up while achieving maximum speed at the takeoff. Speed at takeoff is crucial because the two factors that determine the distance of flight for any object are the speed and the angle of takeoff. It is important to understand how to establish the proper approach distance to consistently achieve maximum speed at takeoff.

An aspect of the long jump that often gets overlooked and undercoached is developing a consistent approach. In the event, there is a distinct line to which each jump is measured—the edge of the takeoff board closest to the landing pit. During a jump attempt, if the athlete's foot contacts beyond this line, the jump is deemed a foul and is not measured. Also, if the athlete jumps several inches or more in front of the foul line, the jump is considered legal but the jumper loses that distance from the actual jump because the jump is measured to the foul line, not to where the athlete foot makes contact. Many big jumps have been fouled or reduced because of the foot position relative to the takeoff board. For the best jumps to happen, it is crucial that the jumper be consistent and accurate in getting the takeoff foot as close to the foul line as possible without going over.

Establishing the Approach

The length of the approach run depends on the strength, skill, and ability of the athlete. Generally, a high school athlete will have an approach run of 13 to 19 strides to the takeoff. Keep in mind, though, that a longer approach run doesn't necessarily mean a longer jump because athletes differ in acceleration patterns, strength, and skill.

The best approach for coaches is to start younger athletes at 13 to 15 strides and have them increase the distance as they mature and are able to hold their acceleration further down the runway (or reach top speed after more strides). Remember, the key is getting the athlete up to his or her maximum speed at takeoff.

When establishing an athlete's approach, start with each athlete at the foul line of the takeoff board in front of the landing pit, facing the runway. Take a tape measure and place it next to the runway with the zero end at the foul line. Stretch the tape measure down the runway. Have additional athletes stand along the runway so that they can read the tape measure. As the athlete sprints down the runway, count out loud the stride number. You will be counting only the odd numbered strides. "One, three, five, seven, nine . . . " The first step is taken with the athlete's takeoff

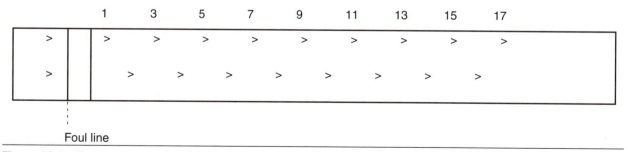

Figure 12.1   To measure an athlete's ideal approach, have him or her start at the foul line and sprint down the runway counting each odd step.

foot, which is why you are counting the odd-numbered strides (see figure 12.1).

For each athlete, record the measurement of the competition starting distance. This distance depends on how many strides (that you have determined) each athlete should do to achieve optimal speed in competition. In the early season, athletes may be jumping from a shorter starting distance. As the season progresses and athletes get stronger, they may increase the distance of their approach run. Also, record the stride distance (e.g., "steps 5, 7, and 9") for short-approach jumping drills, practice runs, and pop-ups that the athletes can perform in practices. Warming up for competition, athletes will measure their starting distance. Have them leave the tape measure along the runway during warm-ups so that they can locate their specific measured distances for pop-ups and short approach jumps (e.g., steps 5, 7, and 9).

Individualizing Practice Jumps

I have seen coaches have athletes perform a short approach jump from an arbitrary distance, like 40 or 50 feet, instead of using the distance based on a specific number of strides individualized to each athlete's stride length. The problem with using an arbitrary distance is that athletes are going to alter stride lengths by "chopping" steps or over-extending steps in an attempt to hit the takeoff board. This hesitation leads to bigger problems later in a competition. By working with a set number of strides that are measured out, athletes can work on the start of the approach without guessing the location of the board. Practicing this, athletes can establish consistency and develop a rhythm to their approach.

So how do you know if your athlete's approach needs to be adjusted, and if so, how to do it? Assess your athletes' jumps for the following problems, common to long jumpers, and ways to troubleshoot them (see table 12.1).

Practicing the Approach

To develop consistency in practice and therefore in competition, the jumper must perform each approach run the same way, every time. You see many athletes who initiate their run with skips, hops, and or some type of rocking motion. The problem with starting an approach this way is that all the extra movement can cause inconsistency with the first steps on the runway. To be consistent, athletes should keep it simple and practice it the same way, every time. Compare the long jump approach to shooting a free throw in basketball. Basketball coaches tell their players to establish a rhythm; for example, *Dribble three times, exhale, and shoot.* Developing a rhythm is crucial for performing a consistent approach run.

There are many styles and philosophies about how an athlete should initiate the approach run. Some coaches use check marks or coaches' marks with chalk or tape alongside the runway. Use whatever you and your athletes feel most comfortable with. The system that I have athletes use has been developed by trial and error. It is basic, simple, and we practice it everyday, with every sprint, drill, and jump. The technique is called the "waterfall" start, in which the athlete stands on the runway with feet shoulder-width apart. The jumper then rolls onto the balls of the feet, leans forward, and immediately sprints down the runway. No rocking, no extra steps; the athlete sprints as if hearing the gun fire in a sprint race.

The athlete's first step is with the takeoff foot. We teach jumpers to do this for two reasons. First, I have had athletes in competition forget which foot they start with on the runway; if they start with their takeoff foot, they shouldn't have this problem. The other reason I have them start with their takeoff foot is to simplify my coaching. As a coach, if you are standing by the takeoff board watching several athletes perform their approach runs, it is easy to get confused, trying to remember which foot each athlete jumps with. Watch each athlete start the approach run; whichever foot he or she starts with is the foot you should be looking for at the board.

Table 12.1   Troubleshooting the Long Jump Approach

Problem	Probable cause	Solution
The athlete achieves top speed prior to reaching the takeoff board. This results in a slowdown with additional strides.	The approach run is too long.	Shorten the approach run.
The athlete doesn't achieve top speed before reaching the takeoff.	The approach run is too short.	Lengthen the approach run.
Stride length is not consistent; the athlete does not achieve top speed or develop the rhythm necessary to consistently hit the takeoff board.	Improper warm-up. The warm-up prepares the athlete for jumping. Stride length and stride frequency can be affected by the athlete's lack of flexibility and slow neuro-muscular activation.	Structure a warm-up that includes 5 minutes of aerobic effort to warm the muscles, followed by flexibility exercises and approach drills to prepare the athletes for their best jumps.
The athlete does not consistently hit the takeoff board.	Lack of awareness of the takeoff board's location.	Have athletes practice the approach run until they are comfortable and confident in knowing where the board is located. This sounds like an easy skill, but running at top speed and consistently hitting the takeoff board can be very difficult for young jumpers.
The athlete is shortening or chopping steps before the takeoff board.	Lack of awareness of the takeoff board's location. Commonly this is caused by improperly moving the starting mark for the approach run to be too close to the takeoff board.	Lengthen the position of the start mark from the takeoff board.
The athlete is lengthening steps before the takeoff board.	The start mark is too far away from the takeoff board.	Move the start mark closer to the takeoff board.

Takeoff

For the athletes to jump from the sprint-tall position, they must lower their hips to cause the takeoff leg to bend at the knee and hip; in other words, they cannot jump from a straight leg. A slight lowering of the athlete's hips takes place one stride before contact with the board (figure 12.2a). This is called the penultimate step. The jumper should not be settling down with this step, but instead should be bouncing down and accelerating up from the takeoff foot. A common error is for the jumper to block with this step, put the brakes on, and lose speed while dropping the hips. However, this penultimate step must be a very active and explosive maneuver. The athlete should think of accelerating through the entire takeoff. Cue the athlete by focusing on the last five steps of the approach, *toe-toe-toe-flat-quick*. The *flat* stride is where the athlete is dropping the hips, preparing to jump by bouncing down. The final stride (*quick*) is the takeoff. The athlete should try to rapidly accelerate the hips up and over the takeoff foot.

Remind the athlete that the last two strides (*flat* and *quick*) are the quickest in the approach. As the athletes are toeing-off the board, they should use an *active foot,* clawing the toes through the takeoff board (figure 12.2b). They should *not* slam the takeoff foot down flat since this will cause a loss of horizontal speed. The athlete's hips should be positioned in front of the takeoff foot as they toe-off the board. The body should be tall, eyes focused forward, while driving the lead knee and opposite arm upward into a block position.

Figure 12.2, a-e Mastering the long jump means focusing on proper body positions during the takeoff, flight, and landing phases.

Flight

Once the athlete leaves the ground, he or she has already established a projected path. The speed at takeoff and the angle of takeoff determine this distance. Nothing an athlete does in the air will add to this distance, though there are things the athlete can do in the air to diminish this distance.

The goal is to get into a position that maximizes total jumping distance. In the takeoff position, the athlete has his or her hips (center of gravity) ahead of the takeoff foot. This causes a forward rotational effect, which means that the athlete's head and shoulders naturally move forward and down, causing the feet to move down and back. Prematurely dropping the legs causes the jumper to lose valuable distance.

The goal of the flight-phase technique is to slow down the forward rotation. Several styles have been developed to accomplish this. Most commonly, athletes perform the "hitch kick" style (figure 12.2c) or the "hang" style (figure 12.2d). In both styles, the athlete's trunk is in an upright position. He or she extends the arms and the legs, using long levers from their center of gravity so that forward rotation is minimized. In springboard diving, an athlete performs a tight tuck position while doing a somersault. The closer the athlete tucks around the center of gravity, the faster the rotation of the somersault. When the athlete opens up and extends the arms and legs, rotation is greatly reduced. The hang style and the hitch kick accomplish the same effect for the long jump.

The hitch kick looks as if the athlete is running through the air. Some jumpers feel that the hitch kick is a more natural transition from the run-up. The legs continue to cycle as in running while the arms rotate overhead and down in a clockwise movement. Performing the hang style, the athlete extends arms overhead and slightly back. The hips are pushed forward, with an arch in the back. The legs are down, with the feet positioned behind the hips. The athlete holds this position until ready to prepare for landing.

Landing

The athlete needs to remain patient while in the air. If the jumper starts the landing too early, the feet will drop, causing the jumper to lose valuable distance. The position of the hips indicates the efficiency of the landing. When the athlete's heels contact the sand, look at the height of the hips relative to the ground. Ideally, the hips should be low to the ground. If the athlete is in a half-squat or appears to be sitting in a chair, he or she initiated the landing phase too soon and lost distance on the jump. Performing the landing, the athlete needs to flex at the waist, causing the head, shoulders, and arms to move forward (figure 12.2e). This action causes a reaction with the lower body—the legs and feet extend forward in front of the athlete. The athlete's heels contact the sand, and the athlete should bend the knees to allow the hips to pass forward, while both arms sweep down and back.

Long Jump Drills

Take the following considerations when working with younger athletes as they perfect their long jump skills.

- Emphasize proper sprint mechanics in every practice. Tall posture, positive foot-to-ground contacts, and consistent stride frequency are components of a successful jump.
- It may be necessary to break down the learning process. Focus on specific parts of the jump before having them attempt the entire action.
- Have athletes master drills at slower speeds and lower intensities by having them use short approach jumps. If the athletes cannot perform drills correctly at slower speeds, they will not be able to perform them with a full run-up.
- Emphasize from the beginning correct takeoff position and a smooth, fast transition from the run-up to the toe-off.

- Do not get caught up teaching an elaborate flight phase. Slow down an athlete's overrotation by having him or her lengthen the levers (arms and legs) and prepare for landing.

Takeoff Drills

Stationary pop-up. Have athletes drive off their takeoff leg, emphasizing knee drive, arm block, and tall-body position. Progress to dynamic pop-ups in which athletes hold this takeoff position into the landing pit.

Suspended object. These are short approach pop-ups. Have athletes try to touch a basketball net or suspended object with the top of their head on these pop-ups to give them a goal to shoot for.

Short approach drill. Short approach work allows the athlete to focus on takeoff mechanics at a slower speed than they would with a full run-up. Use a five-step, seven-step, and nine-step approach. Start by drilling the takeoff with this short approach, and progress to the entire jump sequence.

Skip for height. Have athletes do a series of skips down the runway, emphasizing the sprint-tall position and the active foot-to-ground contact at takeoff.

Single-leg hop. Have athletes practice their takeoff by doing a series of single-leg hops down the runway. Athletes should focus on the speed of the hopping action. Athletes should minimize contact time by coordinating the takeoff leg, knee drive, and arm block. This drill helps build power for the takeoff position.

Alternate-leg bound. Athletes place one foot slightly ahead of the other and push off with their back leg driving the lead knee up to the chest, trying to gain as much height and distance as possible. Have them continue down the runway by immediately driving with the other leg upon landing. They should strive to attain a tall body position and drive the lead knee parallel with the ground. Athletes should focus on the distance and height of the bounding action. This drill builds leg power in both legs.

Flight and Landing Drills

Half-hitch. From a short approach, athletes perform a hitch kick, coordinating arms and legs with tall posture.

Standing long jump. Athletes jump from a standing position into the sand pit, emphasizing leg extension through the flight and landing.

Box standing long jump. Athletes jump from a standing position on a sturdy box (6 to 12 inches high by 2 feet by 2 feet) into the high jump pit, emphasizing flight positions and leg extension on landing.

TRIPLE JUMP

The triple jump is uniquely different from the other jumping events in track and field. It can best be compared to a floor routine in gymnastics. Both are a series of movements flowing one after another. A gymnast may perform a run-up with a round-off and a series of back handsprings or flips. If the gymnast loses momentum or control, it negatively affects the action that follows. In the triple jump, if the athlete struggles with the hop phase of the jump, the subsequent step phase is negatively affected as well. The end result is the loss of total distance for the entire jump.

To be proficient in the triple jump, an athlete not only needs to possess speed and explosiveness, but body awareness and balance to

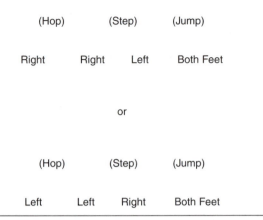

Figure 12.3 After generating speed in the approach run, the athlete follows one of these foot patterns to complete the triple jump.

perform a rhythmical and controlled effort. Because of this, a coach must look at the event from the big-picture perspective. A coach can more easily notice a breakdown in technique (the effect) than find the cause of that breakdown. In other words, a coach needs to analyze the technical actions preceding the breakdown to find the cause.

Just like the long jump, the triple jump is performed on a runway with a sand pit. Unlike the long jump, however, the takeoff board is located farther away from the sand pit so that the athlete can perform the hop, step, and jump takeoff phases on the runway while still landing in the sand pit. The National Federation of State High School Associations recommends a 24-foot distance from the sand pit to the takeoff board for girls and 32 feet for boys. As the jumping ability of the athlete increases, the takeoff board needs to be farther away from the sand pit. At the collegiate level, the distance to the boards may vary from facility to facility. Generally, the women's boards are in the 32 to 36-foot range, and the men's boards are up to 40 feet away from the pit.

There are six phases to the triple jump, from the approach to landing in the pit. The athlete performs an *approach* run to generate speed to transfer into the jumping phases of the triple jump. At the takeoff board, the athlete performs the *hop* phase by taking off from the ground on one foot and landing on the same foot. Immediately afterward, the athlete performs the *step* phase by taking off from the ground on one foot and landing on

the opposite foot. The *jump* phase is the point from which the athlete takes off from one foot and lands on both feet in the sand pit. The triple jump pattern is shown in figure 12.3.

Finally, there is the *flight* phase and the *landing*.

The key points for an athlete to perform a well-executed triple jump include the following:

- Maintain horizontal velocity, created by the approach run, throughout the entire jump.
- Keep an erect body position or posture.
- Have an *active* takeoff position.
- The summation of movements (arm block, knee drive, and takeoff foot) should create an explosive impulse.
- Be aware of takeoff angles for each phase.

Approach

Remember that the two factors that determine flight distance of an object are the speed at takeoff and the takeoff angle. Developing horizontal velocity in the approach run is crucial to performing an effective triple jump. Many young jumpers fail in their attempt to make a big jump before they even reach the take-off board because they slow down or do not reach top speed at the board. Table 12.1 on page 152 highlights common long jump approach problems and solutions. This table can also be used to troubleshoot the triple jump approach.

To help the athlete remain focused and confident, try to keep things as simple as possible. A standard warm-up routine helps the athlete stay focused on the event. Script out a specific warm-up including flexibility work, technique drills, and short approach jumps. Many younger athletes, when faced with too many decisions or outside distractions, can lose their composure or mental focus on their event (paralysis by analysis). I have seen coaches break an athlete's confidence by giving them too much advice or changing the normal routine before a competition. Be specific and consistent with your athlete's warm-up before competition. Weekly practice sessions are a more appropriate time to make major technique changes.

Routine Consistency

When your athlete takes a practice run on the runway, make a mental note of where the takeoff foot is located in relationship to the takeoff board. Do not have him or her change the starting mark after every approach run. I have seen coaches move an athlete's starting marks after every run-through. They might move it four, five, or even more times before the competition begins. This change and inconsistency can make an athlete have self-doubt and lose valuable confidence. The athlete then becomes hesitant and is not able to attack the takeoff board.

Let an athlete take two or three run-throughs to see if he or she is consistent in hitting the same spot in relationship to the takeoff board. If the run-throughs are consistent, you can then make a simple adjustment to the starting mark. If they are not consistent, then you can look at the other common approach problems (see table 12.1 on page 152) and troubleshoot from there. Additional considerations about the approach run that apply to triple jump approaches are discussed in greater detail in the long jump section of this chapter.

Table 12.2   Horizontal Jumper Training Phases

Early-season training	
Focus	Strength and conditioning
Running	Tempo training; longer intervals and fartlek runs at 75% max speed
	Hill and bleacher sprints
Sprint drills	Technique drills focusing on posture, arm carry, knee lift
Strength training	Circuit training (alternate legs, back, biceps with chest, triceps)
	Abdominals
	Clean progressions (light weight with focus on technique)
Power	Low-intensity plyometrics

Midseason training	
Focus	Power and speed development
Running	Shorter interval training (50-200 m at 75-90% max speed)
Sprint drills	Technique drills focusing on stride frequency, posture, arm carry, knee lift
Strength training	Power lifts (cleans, lunge press, and push press)
	Abdominals
Power	Low-intensity plyometrics
	Skill-specific bounding

Late-season training	
Focus	Skill and technique
Running	Shorter interval training (25-100 m at 80-100% max speed)
Sprint drills	Technique drills focusing on stride frequency
Strength training	Power lifts (cleans, lunge press, and push press)
	Abdominals
Power	Skill-specific bounding

Takeoff: Hop, Step, and Jump

We've discussed that distance is determined by the speed at takeoff and the angle of takeoff. In the triple jump, we have three different takeoffs for the three different phases: hop, step, and jump. If an athlete has too high of a takeoff angle, the next phase will not be performed effectively. For example, you see this with inexperienced jumpers when they have a very high hop phase and short step phase, because the force generated at the landing of the hop is greater than what the athlete can handle. The ground contact time will be too great, which will cause a dramatic loss of horizontal velocity. You may even see the supporting leg buckle upon the landing. If an athlete loses substantial horizontal velocity, he or she will also lose substantial distance in the total jump.

Each phase of the triple jump should be approached with a different takeoff goal. First, the takeoff for the hop uses a greater amount of horizontal velocity. Because a high takeoff angle can be detrimental to the total distance of the triple jump, emphasize that the takeoff for the hop phase be *low and long*. Cue the athletes by telling them to sprint or drive off the takeoff board—not jump up from the board. When looking at an effective hop, you see that the athlete doesn't gain substantial vertical lift (figure 12.4a).

After the drive knee and foot cycles back under the body of the athlete, notice that the foot is only 12 to 18 inches from the ground (figure 12.4b). Compare this to a person skipping rocks on the water. If you throw a rock and it bounces high into the air, the force of the rock coming down is too great for it to rebound again. Consequently, the rock sinks. If you throw a rock with a lower takeoff angle, it continues to bounce off the water for several skips.

Figure 12.4, a-c   The takeoff for the hop phase uses horizontal rather than vertical velocity.

Figure 12.4, d and e   Flight is higher in the step phase than in the hop phase and highest during the jump phase.

The landing of the hop phase causes the athlete to lose horizontal speed. Because of the decrease in horizontal velocity in the takeoff of the step phase, the athlete needs to compensate by increasing the takeoff angle of the step phase (figure 12.4c). In other words, if athletes lose speed at takeoff, they must increase the angle of takeoff.

Now the flight pattern moves from *low and long* in the hop phase to *higher* in the step phase (figure 12.4d). This same process continues into the jump phase. When the athlete's foot makes contact on the landing of the step phase, it loses more horizontal velocity. When a jumper loses speed at the takeoff, the takeoff angle must be increased to compensate (figure 12.4e). So the overall takeoff pattern should look like this:

Hop phase—low and long

Step phase—higher

Jump phase—highest

Flight and Landing

The flight and landing phases (figure 12.4, f and g) of the triple jump are executed the same as for the long jump. During the flight phase, the head and shoulders move forward and down, causing the feet to move down and back. It is important not to drop the feet too early; doing so will mean a loss of distance on the jump. During the landing, the athlete flexes at the waist; brings the head, shoulders, and arms forward; and extends the legs and feet. See page 154 for a complete discussion of proper flight and landing techniques.

Figure 12.4, f and g   The landing of the triple jump is similar to that of the long jump.

Triple Jump Drills

Standing triple jump. Have athletes perform the hop-step-jump-flight-landing sequence from a standing position. This drill allows the athlete to get the feel of the whole movement without adding speed from the approach.

Short approach jump. Have athletes drill their jumps from a five-step and then seven-step approach run, adding a controlled amount of sprint-up speed before performing the jumping action.

Single-leg hop. Have athletes practice their takeoff by doing a series of single-leg hops down the runway. Athletes should focus on bouncing down and up with the foot to achieve height, and they should also focus on driving the lead knee up and out. Instruct them to land on the same foot and continue jumping. This drill helps build power for the takeoff leg.

Alternate-leg bound. Have the athletes place one foot slightly ahead of the other, and instruct them to push off with the back leg, driving the lead knee up to the chest while trying to gain as much height and distance as possible. Have them continue down the runway by immediately driving with the other leg upon landing. This drill builds leg power in both legs and helps coordinate transitions from the right to the left leg.

Combination bound. Have the athletes alternate triple jump hops and steps with this bounding drill (hop, step, step, hop). This power-bounding drill coordinates transitions from the right leg to the left leg. Athletes should focus on body posture and arm swing.

Multiple box drill. Using five sturdy plyometric boxes that are 6- to 12-inches high by 2 feet by 2 feet, place boxes 3 to 5 feet apart in a row in the grass. Athletes should stand on the first box with feet slightly over the edge. They step off the first box and upon landing on the ground, jump upward and outward to land on the second box. Repeat the action for the remaining boxes. This can be performed with double-leg and single-leg bounding.

TRAINING THE LONG AND TRIPLE JUMPS

Both the long and triple jumps are an extension of proper sprint mechanics; therefore, emphasizing sprint mechanics throughout the training season is crucial in developing a strong horizontal jumper. Focus your training plan based on the demands of the specific activity that you're training. The long and triple jumps are explosive, single-leg jumping events. Your workouts must reflect these types of physical demands.

When developing a training plan for horizontal jumpers, realize that your conditioning program will need to change throughout the year and from one year to the next to account for the athletes' progressing in training age, strength, and skill level. In other words, as athletes progress, they need to be continually challenged by their conditioning program. Periodized training (periodization) is one way to continually keep your athletes evolving and improving.

Periodization is simply an organized blueprint of the year's training, broken into different phases or cycles throughout the season. Your plan should provide a progression from the beginning of the training season until the final track and field meet (i.e., early season, midseason, and late season, as shown in table 12.2 on page 157). While the focus of early-season training is in building strength and improving overall conditioning, it is important to emphasize specific techniques of movement early in the training season as well. Learning proper technique and skill early reduces the risk of injury and facilitates performance improvements later in the season. The midseason is the time to focus training on power and speed development while the late season's training focus is on honing and polishing skill and technique in the event.

Any training program for long and triple jumpers needs to include an adequate strength and conditioning base for athletes. Focus on developing joint integrity, allowing tendons and ligaments to strengthen so that they can increase their ability to work against resistance without injury. An important part of strengthening involves developing the body's "core," the structural foundation that supports all movement. The athlete's core includes the abdominal and back muscles that are crucial in transferring force during bounding. This can be accomplished through progressive buildups of strength training and plyometric exercises, from low-intensity to medium-intensity and finally to high-intensity exercises once the athlete has worked up to this.

Plyometric exercises—such as bounding and box jumps—are particularly important for horizontal jumpers to help train the stretch-reflex mechanisms of the muscle. In plyometric exercises, the muscle is stretched (lengthened) and then contracted (shortened) very rapidly. The focus of such exercises is on the speed and explosiveness of the movement. Low-intensity plyometric drills include skips (for height or distance), jumping rope, alternate bounding, and single-leg hops. As the athlete matures in age, increasing the training stimulus by adding box jumps and hurdle hops may be necessary. But be very careful not push the athlete too fast into plyometrics. Athletes under the age of 16 should focus on the lower-intensity plyometrics, such as skips, rope jumping, alternate bounds, and hops. Be patient when helping an athlete progress! If the training intensity is too great, injury is often the result.

Chapter 13

THROWING EVENTS

Dennis E. Kline

Assistant Track & Field Coach, University of Wisconsin at La Crosse

© Human Kinetics

The throwing events—shot put, discus throw, hammer throw, and javelin—while different and unique in technique and implement thrown, all start from a solid base of rhythm, strength, and perhaps most important, skill and technique.

The rhythm of the throw is both seen and heard by the coach. In all the throws, you see the acceleration of the athlete and the implement, and you hear acceleration of the feet. The accelerating rhythm of the feet during the throw highly correlates to the acceleration of the implement, yielding a high velocity at the release—a long throw.

Both strength and power are very necessary for optimum throwing performance, but having too much strength will impair a thrower's natural movement patterns. For example, if a shot putter spends too much time increasing upper body strength and power, the upper body will become the major means of power generation in propelling the shot during the throw. Such an athlete will then have a very difficult time acquiring the appropriate throwing skill of leading with the hip girdle and not the shoulder girdle.

Another drawback of becoming too strong is that it often compromises the recovery time needed between strength training sessions. If an athlete is spending too much energy trying to become stronger, that athlete will have significant muscle soreness that will decrease the technical development at subsequent practices. The longer an athlete puts off learning a high level of technique as a result of spending too much time acquiring strength, the more difficult the obstacles to learning the optimal technique become. With this in mind, the best advice for strengthening throwers is to take a stair-step approach. This means that the farther athletes throw, the stronger they need to become—strength should be built gradually, without sacrificing appropriate technique work.

Throughout this chapter, I use the following location terminology in reference to the ring, the implement, and the athlete's body position. This terminology applies to all throws, and throughout this chapter, I provide all examples in reference to a right-handed thrower.

Some coaches refer to positions around the ring or runway as times on a clock (e.g., 12 o'clock), but I prefer to use the degrees of a circle (e.g., 360 degrees), starting with the back of the ring as zero degrees. The direction of the throw, therefore, is 180 degrees. Other positions of the ring that are critical are 90 degrees and 270 degrees (figure 13.1). These positions are used as reference points for the position of the implement and the athlete. Other degrees within the ring are integral to event-specific technique, but for general referencing, I will not discuss these yet.

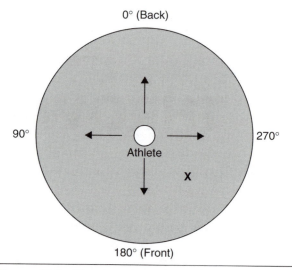

Figure 13.1 The throwing ring is a 360-degree circle; the implement is thrown in the direction of the 180-degree mark.

The interrelated position of the athlete, the implement, and the ring provide a means of describing a technique to an athlete from the coach's viewpoint that leads to optimal results. As seen in figure 13.1, the implement in relation to the athlete is at approximately 225 degrees as is the implement in relation to the ring, giving a complete snapshot of proper positioning throughout the throw to the athlete.

The shot put, discus throw, and hammer throw all start at the back of the ring facing 15 degrees to –15 degrees (or 345 degrees). A coach or athlete may choose a starting position that varies slightly from this per individual preference, but doing so may not necessarily have any correlation to performance, specifically torque development. However, using a starting position at –15 degrees in the ring allows a longer path for acceleration to occur. For the javelin throw, the optimal starting position is with the tip of the javelin pointing to 180 degrees while the thrower's shoulder girdle faces 270 degrees. But just as the other throwing events reflect individuality, so does the javelin. An individual thrower may find more success with a banana-shaped approach (rather than a straight approach) in which the tip points to 160 degrees and the shoulder girdle faces 240 degrees.

Now that I have covered some similarities of throws, let's discuss some of the specific techniques of each.

DISCUS

The discus is similar to the rotational shot, but the rhythm is quicker, the levers are longer, and the event has a slightly lower angle of attack.

The discus is held by the hand with the fingers spread comfortably (figures 13.2a and b). The feet split the 0-degree position of the circle with the majority of the weight on the left ball of the foot (for a right handed thrower). This position is created by dorsiflexing the

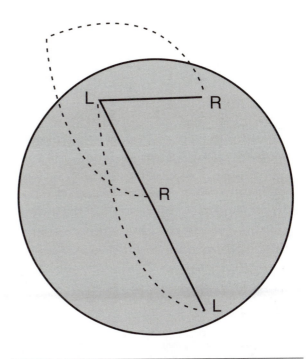

Figure 13.3   The movements of the feet within the ring form a backward seven.

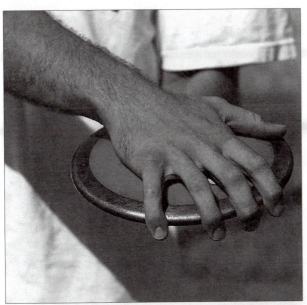

Figure 13.2, a and b   Spread the fingers comfortably across and over the discus.

ankle until the soleus is taut, bringing the heel off the ground, rather than plantar flexing the ankle. The arms are held out wide, but natural. The pattern the feet make through the ring make a backward seven (figure 13.3).

To begin, the thrower rotates clockwise on both feet, but the pivot point is on the ball of the left foot (figure 13.4a). More torque is not necessarily important at this point in the throw. The most important thing is that the thrower is on balance and has started the rhythm of the throw. The left palm of the hand is held upward, and the thrower looks through the left hand. Both feet stay on the ground a long time. The body position is vertical and the left arm is still parallel to the ground (figure 13.4b).

At this point, the (right-handed) thrower directs the throw from the left side of the body. The left arm and left leg rotate synchronously (figure 13.4c). The next series of events starts by driving the right knee up and toward the left sector line along with right ankle dorsiflexing, toe up, and knee up. The left shoulder and arm position do not change, however the right arm is pointed upward toward 220 degrees or the left sector line and

Figure 13.4, a-c Proper balance and a quick rhythm initiate a strong throw.

Figure 13.4, g and h The movement of the discuss throughout the sequence features a lower angle of attack than the shot put.

166

Figure 13.4, d-f The shoulder girdle stays torqued as the lower body moves across the ring.

the left arm points downward (figure 13.4d). The upper body travels minimally across the ring as the lower body travels aggressively across the ring, creating a body angle of around 75 degrees.

The left leg action is simpler than most coaches make it out to be. The athlete does not extend the left hip out of the back of the ring for two reasons. First, the athlete's sprint will carry the center of gravity and upper body too far across the ring. Second, the athlete's left leg now has a greater distance to cover to land at the front of the ring, which causes a slower end rhythm rather than a slow-to-fast rhythm. Instead the left leg is adducted with the heel as the leading edge while the right foot is over the center of the ring and extended into the posting position. During the left leg motion, the right foot and leg rotate counterclockwise over the center of the ring. From the 90-degree view, the left

leg should block the view of the right leg when the right foot is grounded, and the left elbow should be directly above the left knee. During this lower body action, the shoulder girdle with arms extended stays as torqued as comfortably possible with the right arm pointing at about 270 degrees (figure 13.4e). Throughout the throw, the timing of each foot contact with the ring is quick and rhythmic. I compare the timing of each foot contact to the movement of the eyes by someone reading from right to left. When the left foot is posted, the left elbow continues to be directly above the left knee (figure 13.4f). The right hip rotates inward and upward, and the left elbow is driven toward the center of the ring (figure 13.4g). The hips precede the shoulder girdle and right arm. The final effort and the flight of the discus are a result of correct sequential movements (figure 13.4h).

It often helps beginning throwers to compare the upper body's rotation to that of the lower body throughout the throw. As the right-handed thrower gains rotational speed in the ring, the left arm and leg rotate together as the left hand and knee point down the left sector line of the ring at 40 degrees (figure 13.5a). The left hand continues rotating with the left leg until the left foot is posted (figure 1.5b). Once the left foot is posted, the left elbow is driven toward the center of the ring as the thrower releases the discus (figure 13.5c).

Consistently working on correct throwing technique with every practice throw is the best way to improve discus performance. Coaches should help athletes combine such technique work with the right mix of strength training, plyometric exercises, and sprinting (to build speed and power) throughout the training season. Pages 181 to 187 provide guidelines for developing a solid yearly training program for throwers.

Figure 13.5 a-c Notice the movement of the arms in relation to the knees during the discus throw.

HAMMER

The hammer throw is different than the other throws in that the implement and thrower develop a relationship—the hammer-thrower system—to enable great distances to be thrown. Modern technique of the hammer is still under scrutiny. My version of how to throw the hammer has been developed from years of contact with former American record-holder Jud Logan and with Al Shoterman, from personal experience, and from attending various clinics of Stewart Togher, the U.S. national coach, and Yuriy Sedych, the current world-record holder.

The starting position for the hammer throw begins with the athlete's gripping the hammer handle with the left hand first and the right hand over the top of the left hand's fingers (figure 13.6). Unlike the discus or rotational shot, the left foot is placed at 0 degrees, rather than the feet splitting 0 degrees. This position allows for maximum use of the ring diameter as the left foot never leaves the ground. The thrower's shoulder girdle turns about 15 degrees to the right. The feet are placed between 18 and 32 inches apart.

The preliminary rotations are a means to obtain optimum ball speed with a positive postural position into the first turn. The motion includes movement from the arms, trunk, and legs. The movement of the hammer is in a fixed elliptical shape. As the hands, with straight arms, go from the right to the left so does the shifting of the weight. The path of the hammer is leftward and upward. The elbows bend as the hammer approaches 75 degrees. The thumbs then come across the forehead to just outside the right shoulder. At this point, the hammer is picked up visually and tracked (figure 13.7a). This is continued for a total of two to three preliminary rotations. Remember that the hammer must be in a path of continuous acceleration.

The last preliminary rotation is extended to 90 degrees where both feet are on the ground. This becomes the start of the first turn (figure 13.7b). From this point on, the thrower has the hammer in vision the entire time. The left ankle is dorsiflexed, and the heel is in contact

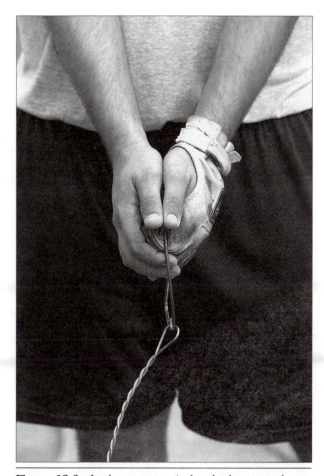

Figure 13.6 In the proper grip for the hammer throw, the dominant hand is the top hand.

with the concrete. The right foot is in a parallel position to the left foot, and the center of pressure is on the ball of the right foot. The position of the hammer at 90 degrees is at shoulder height, with the arms parallel to the ground and the knees bent approximately 15 degrees. The hammer, hands, head, left knee, and left foot create a single plane (figure 13.7c). This is the concluding position of the double-support phase and the beginning of the single-support phase. The hammer accelerates through 90 degrees in an upward plane (figure 13.7d).

The thrower has two objectives during the single-support phase:

1. Keep deceleration to a minimum.
2. Maintain radius.

Success is determined by the timing of the thrower's body (and the hammer) as it relates to the acceleration path of the hammer.

During the single-support phase the speed of the pelvic girdle must exceed the speed of the shoulder girdle and the hammer. In doing so, the right foot steps forward toward the throwing direction. The left foot is on the ground with pressure on the lateral edge until it reaches the ball of the foot. This curvilinear action continues until the catch position. The right foot never steps over the left. This is where the double-support position begins and the hammer, hands, right knee, and right foot make a single plane (figure 13.7e).

From the 90-degree view you should notice the right foot slightly behind the left; this is called under-turning; this is ideal. The feet can be even, too, but the worst-case scenario is when the right foot is in front of left, this is called overturning (figure 13.8). Incidentally, the turns are counted by the contacts made by the right foot. The high point of the hammer is at 180 degrees. The total number of turns can be three or four. When doing a fourth turn, the initial turn is done on the toe (a toe turn). In each turn, the angle of delivery increases slightly as the amount of space that each turn requires decreases. The final effort is no different than any other turn, except for full extension of the knees at 90 degrees.

Figure 13.7, a-c The hammer continuously accelerates throughout the throw.

What is the advantage of doing four turns rather three you may ask? The answer is that doing a correct toe turn to initialize the hammer-thrower system at a slower rate can more easily be accomplished. The opposite argument is that when a thrower does three turns, the entry must be aggressive and also be technically and rhythmically correct. Most coaches think that the fourth turn is about creating more speed. In my opinion, it does not do so.

Figure 13.7, d and e During the single support phase, the pelvic girdle moves faster than the shoulders.

Figure 13.8 Before the release, the dominant foot should be even with or behind the nondominant foot rather than in front as shown here.

Figure 13.9   Hold the shot comfortably against the neck, with the fingers spread and the thumb pointing toward the ground.

SHOT PUT

Although there are two techniques for throwing the shot put—the glide and rotation—neither technique is necessarily better for certain ages or experience levels. Rather, shot throwers often choose a style that suits their body type and strength levels (the choice also depends on the coaching they received when they were first learning). Generally, stronger athletes tend to do well with the glide technique, and more powerful athletes tend to do well with the rotation.

Glide

For the right-handed thrower, the shot is properly held in the right hand at the base of the fingers with the fingers comfortably spread and the thumb pointing to the ground the entire throw. The shot is against the neck in a comfortable position (figure 13.9). The humerus is perpendicular to the spine the entire time. The foot placement starts in the middle of the ring. The athlete becomes stationary, then approaches 0 degrees with the right foot. The right foot slides up against the ring

Figure 13.10, a and b   The body moves continuously throughout the glide technique.

for a dynamic start rather than a static one. A dynamic start promotes a positive attitude as well as less loss of balance.

The put now begins. It is important that the motion be dynamic and the athlete always be moving. The torso goes into flexion, and the left hip goes into extension, bringing the foot off the ground (figure 13.10a). The spine and femur are linear at this point. The shoulder girdle is closed, perpendicular to 0 degrees. The left arm is straight and hangs with gravity. As a visual cue, the putter may watch the left thumb. The left hip and knee are brought into flexion as the right knee is slightly flexed; be sure the right heel stays on the ground.

At this point, the left leg extends forcefully toward 210 degrees, opening the hips, perpendicular to 45 degrees. The right leg also extends, but not as forcefully, with the heel leaving the ground last (figure 13.10b). As the heel leaves the ground, the hips approach the center of the ring. The right hip and knee flex,

and the ankle dorsiflexes underneath the center of gravity (figure 13.10c). This position is called toe up, knee up. The thrower "pre-turns" the right foot as much as comfortably possible, hopefully less than 45 degrees. The goal is for the thrower to land the right foot and then the left in a very close rhythm (figure 13.10d). The left foot should point to the throwing sector as it is grounded and it is a "hard" position. This means the left leg and foot extend into the ground with some authority. As this happens with the lower body, the shoulder girdle stays perpendicular to 0 degrees. But the left shoulder goes under horizontal extension, and the elbow is flexed to 90 degrees until the humerus is pointing to 90 degrees and parallel to the ground. A body angle of around 75 degrees is created (figure 13.10e). The right hip rotates towards the direction of the throw, and the left elbow is driven back toward the center of the ring, causing the body to come over the left leg in

Figure 13.10, c-e   When the sequence of movements is performed correctly, the shot looks as though it is being flicked off the hand.

Figure 13.11 Notice the 75-degree angle between the upper and lower body just before the throw.

Figure 13.12 Holding the shot at the top of the palm with the fingers spread and the thumb pointing downward, the athlete presses it inward against the neck.

Figure 13.13, a-c The rotation shot put technique is similar to the movement throw, but the heavier shot means the rhythm of the put is slower than that of the discus throw.

a catapult fashion. The hips precede the shoulder girdle and right arm (figure 13.11). The final effort is a result of correct sequential movements. When done correctly, the shot looks as though it is flicked off the hand, however this itself is not a coaching point, it is an accumulation of correct sequential movements.

Rotation

The rotation shot is similar to the discus throw, except the shot itself pauses in the middle due to the shorter levers, and its rhythm is different because of that. Along with that, the angle of attack of the shot is a little more vertical. However the most important factor is the speed of the shot; angle of release is a far second!

The shot is held at the top of the palm of the hand with the fingers spread comfortably. The thumb points downward—in fact, the thumb points downward, in relation to the athlete, during the entire throw. Slight pressure is applied to the shot in an inward motion against the neck (figure 13.12). As in the

glide method, the feet split 0 degrees, with the majority of the weight on the left ball of the foot. The thrower lets the ankle dorsiflex until the soleus is taut, bringing the heel off the ground (figure 13.13a). This raising of the heel is unstable. The arms are held out wide, but natural. The pattern of the feet through the ring resembles a backward seven.

To begin the throw, the thrower rotates clockwise on both feet, but the pivot point is on the ball of the left foot. More "torque" is not necessarily important at this point in the throw. The thrower must be on balance and start the rhythm of the throw. The left palm of the hand is held upward, and the thrower looks through the left hand (figure 13.13b). Both feet stay on the ground a long time. The body position is vertical, and the left arm is still parallel to the ground (figure 13.13c).

At this point, the throw is directed from the left side of the body (for right-handers). The left arm and left leg move synchronously in rotation until the left knee and hand point down the left sector line in a 40-degree sector (figure 13.13d). The next series of events starts with the athlete driving the right knee up and

Figure 13.13, d-f As with the glide method, the body's angle during the rotation approaches 75 degrees.

toward the left sector line along with right ankle dorsiflexion; toe up, knee up. The left shoulder and arm position do not change, however the right elbow is pointed upward toward 220 degrees, or the left sector line, and the left arm points downward (figure 13.13e). The upper body travels minimally across the ring as the lower body travels aggressively across the ring, creating a body angle of around 75 degrees.

The left leg action has been misunderstood and is simpler than most coaches make it out to be. The athlete does not extend the left hip out of the back of the ring for two reasons. First, the athlete's sprint carries the center of gravity and upper body too far across the ring. Second, the athlete's left leg now has a greater distance to cover to land at the front of the ring, creating a slower end rhythm rather than a slow-to-fast rhythm. Instead the left leg is adducted with the heel as the leading edge while the right foot is over the center of the ring and extended into the posting posi-

tion. During the left leg motion, the right foot and leg rotate counterclockwise over the center of the ring (see figure 13.13f).

From the 90-degree view, the left leg should block the view of the right leg when the right foot is grounded, and the left elbow should be directly above the left knee. During this lower body action, the shoulder girdle (with arms extended) stays as torqued as comfortably possible, with the right arm pointing at about 270 degrees (figure 13.13g). The rhythm of the feet at the front of the ring should be as easy for the thrower as reading from right to left (this refers to the amount of time between each contact made by foot to the ring). When the left foot is posted, the left elbow continues to be directly above the left knee (figure 13.13h). The right hip rotates inward and upward, and the left elbow is driven toward the center of the ring (figure 13.14). The hips precede the shoulder girdle and right arm. The final effort is a result of correct sequential movements.

Figure 13.13, g and h Throughout the final rotation of the throw, the hips precede the upper body.

Figure 13.14 The right leg moves counterclockwise over the center of the ring.

JAVELIN

Of all the throws, the javelin is the one most dependent on an athlete's natural ability to throw the implement. In most coaches' terminology, it is the event that is most "technically critical." Perhaps the easiest way to find a javelin thrower is to line up your entire team on the infield and have all the athletes throw the javelin. Then keep the top two or three prospects, based on distance thrown and ease of motion exhibited. Using this method of selecting throwers tends to produce more success than spending time trying to turn athletes with little natural talent for the event into javelin throwers. The javelin doesn't have to go a great distance, but the throw should not hurt or (from the coach's viewpoint) look like it hurts. This approach may seem unfair, but it may the easiest way to find out which athletes have the appropriate anatomical and biomechanical qualities of the shoulder that can lead to good throws.

The javelin can be effectively gripped in a number of ways. None of the three grips shown in figure 13.15, a through c is better than another. Athletes should choose the grip that is most comfortable, after experimenting with each to determine which feels best.

The javelin is held with the arm drawn back in a straight and relaxed position. The longer the lever, the better. The body faces 90 degrees to the right of the direction in which the javelin is being thrown. The point of the javelin is next to the thrower's face. The angle of the javelin is 0 degrees; in other words, the javelin is perpendicular to the body, with the throwing angle created at the plant. The left hand is in front of the javelin

point, with the elbow bent and as high as the hand (figure 13.16a).

The advance, which can be the most frustrating part of the throw, is the number of steps before the three-step approach or the seven-step approach. The key to success is to

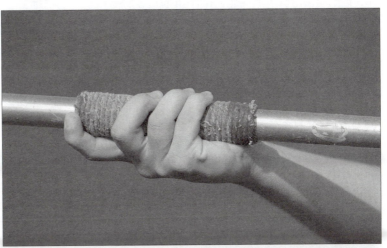

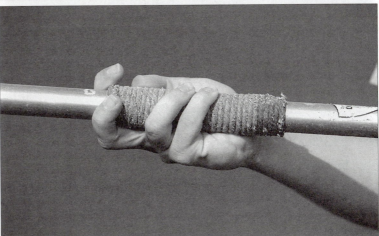

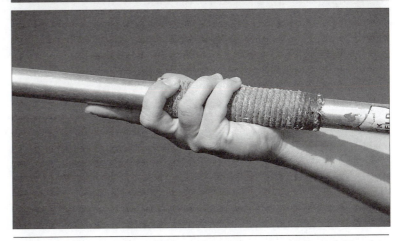

Figure 13.15, a-c   These three javelin grips are correct and effective; athletes should use the grip that feels most comfortable.

have constant acceleration throughout. In other words, the javelin must get faster throughout the entire throw. If you stick by this rule, choosing the number of steps or distance that is best for you becomes a simple task. During this phase, the upper body should have minimum movement (figure 13.16b)

The athlete should have a mark to begin the three- or seven-step approach. At this point the hips are perpendicular to the throw, and a definite rhythm is established (figure 13.16c). For the right-handed thrower, the first step is with the left leg, as is the last step as the athlete enters the crossover. The crossover is a transition phase from the approach to the power position. It is initiated by the last step in the approach with the left leg (figure 13.16d). At this time, a series of events are executed.

- The body performs a pendulum movement in which the upper body moves minimally and the lower body moves greatly.

- The center of gravity does not rise a great amount; however, the goal of the lower limbs is to cover the greatest amount area as possible in a controlled manner, right leg and then left (figure 13.16e). To enable the left leg to carry as much ground as possible, the right hip and knee are "soft." This means that extension and flexion occur in the right leg passively until the left leg is planted.

Upon the landing, the thrower lands with a body angle of approximately 75 degrees. In this position, the left leg is straight, with the foot landing on the heel and rolling to a flat position and pointing to the middle of the sector (figure 13.16f). The right leg is bent. The right ankle is dorsiflexed to allow the foot to land flat and point at about −45 degrees from the middle of the sector.

The left elbow is drawn in and down. The hips rotate by the driving force of the right leg. The javelin is thrown through the point, and the body comes up and over the left side (figure 13.16g). The followthrough is indicated by the right hand on the right thigh (figure 13.16h).

THROWING PRACTICE METHODOLOGY

Coaches can use a variety of instructional techniques to enhance the effectiveness of a practice session. These include guidance techniques, partial-task strategies, attentional cueing, and whole practice.

Guidance Techniques

Guidance techniques may range from the coach's providing intermittent performance cues during throwing, to manual guidance, to the athlete's using mechanical performance aids (e.g., a harness).

Physical guidance of the athlete by the coach during the throw is a common technique used to guide early skill development and provide psychological support to a young learner. Despite its many positive effects, physical guidance (or manual guidance), if overused, can have negative consequences for the athlete. These can include the athlete's becoming increasingly dependent on the coach to throw and the athlete's failure to use his or her own intrinsic sources of sensory feedback.

It takes most athletes two or more years of throwing the hammer before they are able to get a natural, adequate release height. Beginning hammer throwers tend to throw the ball at a lower than optimal release angle. Therefore, I find that the best use of this tool is during the first and second years of training to help the young athlete understand his or her body positioning as it relates to the implement and the surroundings, such as the ring and the throwing cage. I work with these beginning athletes by physically running around them while holding the hammer in my hands at the proper height so that they can learn to feel the appropriate position of the hammer in the air. As each athlete matures, I rely less and less on this method and use it only when an athlete is not achieving a needed position during the throw. I've had wonderful results with using this method for hammer throwers.

Figure 13.16, a-d During the advance and approach of the javelin throw, the key to success is constant acceleration.

Figure 13.16, e-h From the approach to the power position (the crossover), the objective is to cover the greatest amount of area possible. Upon release of the javelin, the throwing arm must follow through with the motion.

Partial-Task Strategies

There are two types of part-practice methods—segmentation and simplification.

Segmentation involves the athlete's partitioning the event to work on specific parts. The focus is for the thrower to master small portions of the event and then put them together. When the small parts are then executed in proper sequence, the athletes have a high level of skill acquisition and thus improve their performance. Often the contraindications to a high level of performance in the throws include a lack of experience with a competitive skill as well as a total disregard for natural movement patterns.

Simplification is best used when the athlete has a poor assimilation of a skill involved in a complex portion of an event—for example, if the arm needs to perform a movement simultaneously with the leg, but the movements of each are poor. The simplification technique would dictate that the athlete acquire the one limb skill first, then once it is mastered, acquire the other limb skill. Using this technique can be very helpful in initially understanding a movement and moving toward the mastering of the skill. However, it is best if athletes use this strategy in the very short term, just a few minutes for a few sessions. Once the athlete masters each component, there is no need to practice them individually; they just need to be integrated in sequence.

Attentional Cueing and Whole Practice

This type of practice method represents a compromise between part- and whole-practice methods. The learner's attention is directed to one component of the skill while the skill is practiced in its entirety. This technique conserves the spatial and temporal characteristics of the skill. In other words, the natural rhythm of the movement and location in the ring will be true to those of a competitive throw, but the athlete will simply be concentrating one aspect.

Learning From a World-Record Holder

At the end of a clinic I attended in the fall of 1994, I had a conversation with Yuri Sedych, the current world-record holder in the hammer throw. With a group of others, I posed the following question: "I have a 13-year-old athlete who wants to learn how to throw the hammer. Today is her first day of practice; what would you have her do?" His response was quick and without hesitation: "I would have her take two windups and three turns." This is a whole-practice competitive technique in which the athlete starts from the very first day. I was astounded that his methodology did not have the technique broken down into parts, where all the separate components add up to make the whole. As a former competitive athlete, I concluded that this strategy made good sense. It has since produced success for me as both an athlete and as a coach. I now suggest this methodology of attentional cueing and whole practice as the most effective way to teach the throws.

DESIGNING A YEARLY PROGRAM

Your athletes look to you, the coach, for the answers to all their training questions. Unfortunately, the questions they ask never seem to be the ones that you can easily answer. If you cannot answer a training question quickly and precisely, athletes may start to lose faith in your abilities to coach.

My favorite question that athletes ask is "How many throws today?" To answer with a number of throws, however, is useless. There are other questions that each athlete needs to have answered to determine the number of throws they should complete on any given day. For example: What time of year is it? How long before the first competition? How hard should the athlete throw? How many throws will be done as drills? What are the athlete's individual goals, strengths, and weaknesses?

One athlete may need to focus on speed and therefore need to throw lighter implements; another may need technical correction with a self-attentional cueing format at a lower level of intensity and distance.

Other common questions that pertain to all the events include the following.

How many days a week do I practice throwing? Pick at least three days a week, with a maximum of five days a week. Be as consistent from week to week as possible, as this will yield the best performances. Three times a week is adequate until the athletes approach the elite level, where five is needed. The key here though is to be consistent within the year that the athletes are training. The number of throws and the goals of each practice should differ within the week.

How long should I practice each day? After a proper warm-up, the practice session should last no longer than an hour. If the athlete is throwing and lifting on the same day, it is advisable to throw first and then lift—one hour each session—with (optimally) four-plus hours between each session. This guideline becomes more evident to the athletes as their performance levels increase.

The following yearly program is one that can be adapted by any coach. By having a yearly program, a coach earns the confidence of his or her athletes and thus strengthens the coach-athlete relationship. Moreover, developing a yearly training program provides a systematic approach to periodization for the throws (periodization is a detailed plan, broken up into phases over a long period of time for optimal results).

The best way to start a yearly training design is to determine the competitions for that year. First, get a calendar and note the date of the championship meet for the year (i.e., the state meet or the national championships) for which your athletes are striving to peak. Then note how much time your athletes have to train between now and then. For the purposes of my example, I use the USATF National Meet, which is usually held the third or fourth week in June. Working backward from that meet, we have the following five phases of training in the yearly plan:

- the competition-season phase (8 to 12 weeks)
- the power phase (4 weeks)
- the maximum-strength phase (12 weeks)
- the hypertrophy phase (25 to 28 weeks)
- the preparation phase (4 to 8 weeks)

Once you have determined how each phase fits into your training plan, you next need to determine how much work and time to dedicate toward training parameters. For example, in figure 13.17, I divide the throwing event's training parameters into two distinct areas.

1. The first is *skill,* where time and effort are dedicated toward the technique mastery of the throw, with the best determinant of technique improvement being distance thrown.

2. The second is *athletic,* where time and effort is dedicated toward improving the at-

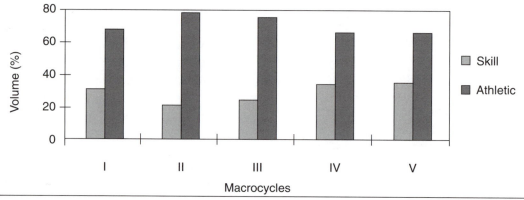

Figure 13.17 When designing a training program for throwers, divide the total time into skill training and athletic training.

tributes that an athlete needs to perform well. In the case of the hammer throw, the athletic goal is increased power output through resistance and assistance exercises.

Through each macrocycle, I alter the focus based on the athletes' intermediate goals. For instance, to effectively practice a few days in a row with a high volume (heavy weight) of training, the athlete needs to be able to handle the workload such that technical improvement is not compromised. So the previous macrocycle's goal is solely to improve the work capacity of the athlete. If it is not done, the athlete will fail halfway through the first day and will not be able to recover for the second and third days.

At the end of the training year, the percentages of concentration should ideally average out to be evenly split between skill and athletic abilities. Realistically, a changing climate and physical well-being are additional factors in the equation, and training focus can be altered to best suit optimum performance. For example, I believe that skill mastery of the hammer throw in a cold climate is more difficult for a thrower to achieve and that the athlete may have greater competitive results if some of that time is put toward athletic improvement. So, during the coldest part of the year here in Wisconsin (during our hypertrophy and maximum strength phases), we decrease the percentage of skill training and increase in athletic improvement. The result of this is fewer training throws. Consequently, an increase in skill work will need to be applied to the preparation, power, and competition macrocycles.

Preparation Macrocycle

Before any high volume training is done, athletes must go through a preparation macrocycle to prepare their bodies for the future demands of training. The preparation macrocycle varies in length from four to eight weeks, depending on training age. The younger the athlete, the longer the preparatory cycle. In the example in table 13.1, I picked six weeks because the beginning (the start of September) coincides with the start of a new month

along with the start of a new training year. The intent of training during this phase is to push the lactate threshold (for future recovery), to increase flexibility, and to prepare the joint stability of the body for the upcoming volume. The methods of training for these goals include circuit training, 50- to 500-meter runs, and nonspecific throwing.

Hypertrophy Macrocycle

The hypertrophy phase is the foundation of the training year in which throwers attain every major physical adaptation and technical mastery per event. To optimize phosphagen levels at rest in the muscle, athletes must participate in 180 to 200 days of specific training. Optimizing phosphagen levels at rest early in the year is important for two reasons. The first is that once the optimal levels of phosphagen are reached, a natural peaking will occur for the rest of the year, so the athletes must ensure that they start early enough to allow this to happen. The second reason this optimizing needs to happen during this time frame is that it allows athletes to practice day to day while picking up the technique where they left off the day before.

We can break the hypertrophy macrocycle into three microcycles, with the middle microcycle being the most demanding and constituting the highest volume of work per year. For the example in table 13.1, the start date of this phase would be around the second week in October. The objective of this microcycle is for the throwers to handle as much volume (tonnage) as possible while still improving or maintaining their training distance. Do *not* overtrain athletes by asking them to handle too much volume and thus destroy their motor learning patterns! Performing simple field tests throughout this phase of training, such as body weight and standing long jump tests, can uncover indicators of overtraining: significant losses or reduced scores in either of these tests indicate that an athlete is overtrained. If you find that an athlete is overtraining, reduce tonnage immediately and (if necessary) give the athlete two to three days of full rest before returning to practice.

Table 13.1 Strength Training Phases

Macrocycle	Weeks in macrocycle: total weeks in training year (% of training year)		Volume of training year	Difference of macrocycle length and volume
Preparation	6:44	(14%)	12%	-2%
Hypertrophy	12:44	(27%)	34%	+7%
Maximum strength	12:44	(27%)	31%	+4%
Power conversion	4:44	(9%)	8%	-1%
Competition	10:44	(23%)	15%	-8%

Maximum-Strength Macrocycle

The maximum-strength macrocycle generally lasts 12 weeks. Tonnage should be the same here as in the preceding macrocycle, but the overall volume is slightly less and the intensity greater. The goal of the practices during this phase is to get the athletes' muscles to recruit the high-threshold motor units not previously recruitable. Three microcycles fall within this phase, each four weeks in length, with the second one being the most demanding.

Power Macrocycle

Four weeks before the competitive season, the athletes enter into a macrocycle that emphasizes power. In this macrocycle, volume is reduced, and near-maximum weights are used to increase the rate of force development. Tonnage drops severely, but throwers will experience personal records with light balls.

Competition Macrocycle

The first week of your team's outdoor competition season may vary, depending upon your geographic location and the availability of meets. (For this section, I'll use the first week in April as the start of the competition season.) The competition season is designated as a training macrocycle, or phase in which the sole goal is to improve performance of one specific training parameter. For example, the goal during this phase for a hammer thrower is to improve the distance of the 16-pound

hammer throws. Prospective improvements in distance from the end of the hypertrophy macrocycle to the competitive macrocycle could be as much as 7 percent (or more).

Volume of Each Macrocycle

I have adapted the volume of each macrocycle from the United States Weightlifting Federation (USWF) guidelines. I break down training volume percentages according to the length and intent of each of the five macrocycles (table 13.1).

The training volume number for the year is alterable and depends on the length of the athlete's season and competition level. For example, if the athlete is competing in the national or state meet, a longer training year is needed along with a greater volume of work than that of an athlete whose last meet is the conference meet.

The volume of work reflects the number of event throws, plus resistance, plus assistance. Or, in other words the formula is as follows: repetitions + repetitions in the weight room + (number of plyometrics + sprinting + pud throws) = volume of work. Throws include any throw with any weight implement using any technique, as long as there is a release. The hammer can vary in weight from 4 to 15 kilograms with various lengths from 1 to 1.215 meters. The discus can vary in weight from 1.6 to 2.25 kilograms, the javelin from 600 grams to 1 kilogram, and the shot from 5 to 9 kilograms.

The intensity of most throws should be between 85 to 92 percent of the thrower's

Table 13.2   A Sample of Weight Training Exercises for Throwers

		Neural		Hypertrophy	
	Intensity	90 to 100%		60 to 100% (max isometric strength)	
	Reps	1 to 5		5 to 20	
	Sets	1 to 5		3 to 5	
	Rest	2 to 3 min		3 to 5 min	
Exercise	**% volume**	**Neural #1**	**Tempo**	**Hypertrophy #1**	**Tempo**
Snatch related	15%	Close grip snatch	X	Power clean	X
Clean related	15%	Close grip snatch	X	Power snatch	X
Squat related	30%	Paused back squat	2E:2I:2C	Back squat	2E:2C
Overhead	10%	Push press	2E:X	Bench press	2E:2C
Individual need	10%	Straight leg deadlift	2E:2C	Romanian deadlift	3E:3C
Specific	20%	Erect bends	2E:2C	Pull-a-round	2E:2C
Exercise	**% volume**	**Neural #2**	**Tempo**	**Hypertrophy #2**	**Tempo**
Snatch related	15%	Prog. range clean	X	Power hang clean	X
Clean related	15%	Prog. range snatch	X	Power hang snatch	X
Squat related	30%	Leg press	2E:2C	Front squat	2E:2C
Overhead	10%	Push press	2E:X	Bench press	2E:2C
Individual need	10%	Pull-ups	2E:2C	Row-to-neck	3E:3C
Specific	20%	Crunches	2E:2C	Nino	2E:2C
Exercise	**% volume**	**Neural #3**	**Tempo**	**Hypertrophy #3**	**Tempo**
Snatch related	15%	Jump squats	X	Progressive range clean	X
Clean related	15%	Split jumps	X	Progressive range snatch	X
Squat related	30%	Telemark squat	3E:X	Lunge	2E:2C
Overhead	10%	Hyperextensions	2E:2C	Push press	2E:2C
Individual need	10%	Pull-ups	2E:2C	Row-to-neck	3E:3C
Specific	20%	Russian twists	1E:1C	Crunches	2E:2C

E = eccentric, C = concentric, I = isometric, X = explosive
Adapted from United States Weightlifting Federation and Charles Poliquin

maximum effort, as technique can suffer on throws attempted outside of this range. However, an athlete can attempt to throw one out of six throws in practice further than 92 percent of the maximum. A thrower with 30 throws planned for the practice is allowed 5 attempts at greater than 92 percent of his or her maximum. Again, a throw that an athlete *intends* to be beyond 92 percent of the maximum that ends up between 85 and 92 percent of the maximum does not qualify as a throw within the range.

The volume of weight lifted is assigned as *repetitions* and not *tons*. Tonnage reflects how intensely the repetitions are executed by an athlete. This way, the coach can assign intensity, sets, and reps based on individual need and availability. The selection of exercises should not be limited to those provided in table 13.2, which were used for a year of

Table 13.3 Example of a Week of Training for a Hammer Thrower (Week 20)

Throwing Work (% max) 43%		Mon.	Tues.	Wed.	Thurs.	Fri.	Sat.
Hammer throw	69	10	19	0	10	21	9
		6 kg for 70m+ 16 lb for 61m+	20 lb for 49m+ 16 lb for 61m+ 6 throws of 35 lb. on a hammer wire		If you can throw 6 kg-70m+, then try 14 lb—65 m	Focus on 16 lb. throws	If throws < 92% of PR, repeat Friday's workout
Puds/ kettlebells				42 throws			
Plyometrics				83 contacts			
Sprinting				12 × 30m			

Weight lifting (Hypertrophy #3)							
Exercise	Tempo	Mon.	Tues.	Wed.	Thurs.	Fri.	Sat.
Progressive range snatch	X	17 reps					
85% of best power clean		100 kg × 6 105 kg × 6 120 kg × 3 130 kg × 3		100 kg × 6 105 kg × 6 120 kg × 3 130 kg × 3			
Progressive	X	17 reps				range cleans	
Barbell lunge	2E:2I:2C	20 reps				15 reps	
45% of best back squat		55 kg × 10 60 kg × 10				65 kg × 8 70 kg × 7	
Push press	2E:X					11 reps	
85% of best bench						100 kg × 4 100 kg × 4 100 kg × 3	
Row-to-neck	2E:2C			11 reps			
15% of best bench				55 lb × 11			
Crunches	2E:2C			23 reps			
Add weight as needed				23 reps			

The weightlifting does NOT include warm-up sets, just work sets. Sunday is a day off.

E = eccentric, C = concentric, I = isometric, X = explosive

training in 1996 (and which led to two athletes' qualifying for the Olympic Trials). Alter these exercises to fit your own facilities, beliefs, and knowledge. These exercises are safe and effective, and they are appropriate for training athletes 14 years old and older.

Speed-assisting exercises include plyometrics and sprinting. The volume of plyometrics should be counted by the number of contacts made, and the intensity of the plyometrics is determined by the coach. These exercises must reflect the macro- and microcycle standards as well as the abilities of the athlete. Sprinting repetitions are counted by the repeats, with the maximum amount of total distance per week being 300 meters. The work:rest ratio for any speed assisting or sprinting should be 1:3.

Pud throws include any throw, with any weight, with any technique—as long as there is a release. Puds are used to create general throwing power. Athletes' throws should be distributed evenly between their left and right sides to avoid developing any muscle imbalance.

Table 13.3 provides a sample weekly program for week 20 (early in the maximum strength microcycle).

Figure 13.18 provides a graph of a year's volume over five macrocycles. Each week is broken down into its respective components.

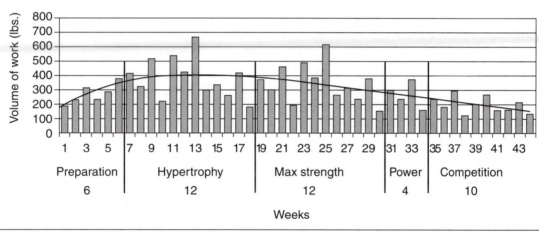

Figure 13.18 In this sample graph showing annual volumes of training, the year has been divided into five macrocycles.

Part 4

COACHING MEETS

Chapter 14

MENTAL TRAINING FOR TEAMS

© Empics

The road to success is always under construction. Just the fact that you're reading this book indicates that you are interested in improving the performance of your athletes and paving the road for their future successes.

Most athletes and coaches focus their efforts on developing the physiological and biomechanical aspects of an athlete's event through new physical training methods, practice procedures, drills, and event techniques. So much information is available to coaches and athletes on technique, drill training, and physiological and biomechanical aspects of conditioning that many athletes are probably doing a training program that is similar to that of other athletes.

One specific, often-overlooked variable, however, can negate the biological aspects and scientific preparation of a solid physical training program. This variable is within athletes: It is their desire, their will to win, their mental toughness. In other words, an athlete's psychological makeup and mental preparation can separate one performance from another.

The training development of this important variable—the mind—is often overlooked in athletic conditioning. Most athletes spend tremendous amounts of time developing their routines, muscles, and technique only to forget that peak performance requires consistent mental preparation as well.

This chapter not only discusses mental preparation, but it also suggests some simple techniques you as a coach can use within practices to improve your athletes' performances. Most of the techniques I highlight here are addressed in more detail in *The Mindset for Winning: A Four-Step Approach to Improving Athletic Performance* by John D. Curtis (1991, Coulee Press).

WHY MENTAL PREPARATION

Mental preparation is important because it is impossible to separate the mind from the body. Whether they are aware of it or not, all athletes create images in their minds that have an effect on their performances. An athlete may be subconsciously thinking thoughts such as "I'm really good in the shot put" or "I can't do well in the discus." These thoughts create images in the minds of the athletes, whether they are true or not.

All too often the images an athlete carries are negative, and this can create problems and blocks in performance. Negative images lead to negative feelings, which in turn often cause increased anxiety, negative attitudes, and poor expectations. When this occurs, an athlete's self-esteem is affected, and his or her chance of performing up to potential is diminished.

However, if an athlete's images are positive, they help the athlete feel more confident of a successful performance. Such athletes can enter a competition with a completely different mind-set, focusing on the positive and visualizing what they want to have happen rather than what they want to avoid. If athletes think thoughts such as "I like to compete" and "I do better under pressure," they will enter the competition *expecting* to do well, rather than just *hoping* to do well. This is the mind-set of a competitor rather than a participant, and it helps champions see that the only limits they have are the ones they set themselves. You can reinforce this maxim during workouts or meets, but the actual teaching and practice should be done in a separate session away from the track.

An athlete can achieve many benefits from mental training that can help not only in competition, but in other areas of life as well. For the purposes of this chapter, we'll focus on the following four main benefits:

1. First, mental training can help your athletes' self-image. If athletes are not performing to the level of their abilities, it is quite probable that they are experiencing some doubt and that their self-image is not as strong as it could be. Since we all generally tend to perform consistently with our self-image, it benefits us to turn negative thoughts into positive ones. An athlete must remove all doubt to improve performance. By following a daily mental training program and repeatedly using positive-affirmation statements, mental recall, and mental rehearsal techniques (discussed in the following section), an athlete can picture a perfect performance. When this practice is done on a regular basis, it helps strengthen self-image and enhance performance.

2. Mental training can improve skill level. When an athlete visualizes a performance, physical training is supplemented with neuromuscular practice. In other words, when an athlete repeatedly visualizes a skill being properly performed, he or she

lays down a blueprint in the nervous system and muscular system that helps him or her perform that movement properly at the next opportunity. Athletes can actually improve their physical performance by improving their mental performance.

3. Mental training also allows athletes to practice handling different competition situations successfully. Not only can they visualize what they want to have happen, but they can anticipate almost every conceivable situation that might arise during a competition and prepare to respond more effectively to these situations should they occur.

4. The fourth benefit of mental training is enhanced concentration. The ability to concentrate is a prerequisite for consistently high performances, and mental training helps athletes learn to concentrate more intensely, for longer periods of time. Athletes can attain these benefits with the coach's help. Coaches can encourage mental training in practice by using some of the ideas outlined in the following sections.

Calm in the Storm

Mental training is invaluable in staying calm in the heat of the moment. At the 1984 National Association of Intercollegiate Athletics (NAIA) Indoor Championship, Tori Neubauer from University of Wisconsin–La Crosse lost her shoe in the early stages of the two-mile race—but she stepped to the inside of the track, replaced her shoe, and gradually began to work her way back into the race. Since she had rehearsed this possibility, she maintained her composure and followed her plan, which resulted in her winning the national championship in this race.

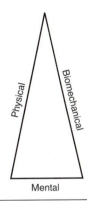

Figure 14.1   Most athletes build their training foundation on only physical and biomechanical development.

ESTABLISHING THE FOUNDATION FOR MENTAL TRAINING

Most athletes' training programs are represented in figure 14.1. Most time and effort is devoted to physical and biomechanical development while a very small portion of time is spent developing the mental toughness needed to achieve peak performance. When this imbalance occurs, the athlete has a very narrow foundation, the result of which is often a shaky and inconsistent performance.

Figure 14.2, on the other hand, represents a well-rounded training program that covers all three aspects of training: physical, biochemical, and mental. Notice how a complete training program provides a much wider, sturdier base on which to build performance. In fact, no matter which direction this triangle is tipped, athletes still have a solid base from which to work.

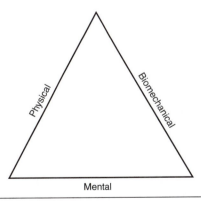

Figure 14.2   A more complete training foundation addresses physical fitness, biomechanical skills, and mental preparation.

In high-pressure, competitive situations, average athletes tend to get too aroused or stressed to perform optimally, which is why they remain average and rarely maximize their abilities. To achieve optimum performance on a regular basis, athletes need to learn how to relax and control the tendency to become overaroused. The performance benefits from relaxation are more than just controlling overarousal. Learning to relax can also improve concentration, control arousal level (stress), improve the athlete's sleep, improve body awareness, decrease recovery time, decrease minor illnesses, and prepare the athlete for effective mental imagery. For our purposes, we will focus especially on this last benefit, preparing for mental imagery.

Relaxation helps prepare someone for mental training by shutting down the rational, conscious mind, which sees things as they currently are. In general, if you try to see things or yourself differently, your rational mind will argue with you. It fights the images that you imagine because it can only accept things as they currently and in reality are.

But you don't want to stay the way you are; you want to improve—and this goes for athletes as well. To get better, athletes must shut down the rational mind and feed new images to themselves of what they want to be. Athletes can learn to relax and use positive mental imagery using the four-step method outlined in the following sections. Performing a relaxation technique (step 1) and using positive affirmation statements (step 2) are the most effective ways to achieve the relaxed and somewhat drowsy state in which an athlete can effectively shut down the rational mind so that the brain is more receptive to the newly visualized images (steps 3 and 4).

I used to break our team into training groups and work on relaxation with them before or following practice, whichever worked best for each group. Since that time, our assistant coaches have become so proficient in these techniques that it is now their responsibility to conduct their own sessions within their respective groups.

Step 1: Relaxed Breathing

The objective of this first step of mental training is to lay the foundation for the rest of the mental training program. In this first step, athletes to learn to relax, and a simple relaxation technique to start athletes with is called the *exhalation exercise.*

To perform this technique, athletes need to know three things:

- Breathe normally. Don't control or alter breathing in any way.
- Concentrate only on exhaling. Breathing out is the phase that allows relaxation.
- Be aware of what you feel only when you exhale. Feel the heaviness, sinking down, slowing down, and other feelings of relaxation only when you exhale.

Athletes should assume a comfortable relaxation position with as much support as possible. The athletes may be lying down, sitting up, or in any position that feels comfortable. They should not cross their arms or legs. During this exercise, have them maintain a passive attitude so that relaxation can occur for the entire body. When ready, the athletes close their eyes and for the first several breaths, quietly concentrate on the air as it enters and leaves their nose.

For the next several breaths, they focus only on the exhalation phase: noticing the warmth of the air as it leaves the nose, *relaxing* as they exhale, allowing themselves to *let go* as they focus on their exhalations, and *relaxing* with each exhalation.

Now, as the athletes exhale, they may feel or sense the body *sinking down* into the supporting environment. They may even notice the body *sinking* more and more with each exhalation.

At this time, they may feel the body *slowing down* as they exhale—the breathing rhythm slowing down, the heartbeat slowing down— just an overall sense of patience. Each time the athletes notice any of these sensations, they allow the body to let go and relax more and more: *letting go, sinking down, and relaxing.*

Athletes may remain in the relaxed state for

© Human Kinetics

Athletes can use their mental training as they prepare for their event.

two to three minutes initially. As they become more proficient with the technique, they can reduce their time to less than a minute. When they are ready to end the relaxation, they take a deep breath while flexing, stretching, and opening the eyes.

Athletes should perform this exhalation exercise two to three times every day for the first seven days of the mental training program. Each session should be three to five minutes. After the first week, athletes can move to the second step, *positive affirmation statements*.

Step 2: Positive Affirmation Statements

Positive affirmation statements are short statements that implant thoughts and images in the subconscious mind. These positive statements help athletes achieve a positive mental attitude, and they are used to overcome the

negative thoughts that athletes may be focusing on when they talk to themselves.

In developing an individual's affirmations, follow these guidelines:

- State each affirmation in a positive manner. For example, say *I am relaxed* instead of *I am not tense.*
- Keep each affirmation brief, no longer than a short sentence.
- Construct the statements using the present tense whenever possible. *I am . . .* rather than *I will be . . . .*
- Develop your own statements, and use words that evoke a feeling within you. The following are a few samples:

  I am calm and relaxed.
  I am strong, confident, and aggressive.
  I am healthy, refreshed, and full of energy.

It takes about seven days for an athlete to perfect his or her own relaxation technique (step 1). On day eight of your program, add positive affirmation statements to the relaxation exercise. To do this, have athletes perform the relaxed breathing exercise first; then, while in a relaxed state, they can silently repeat a personal, positive affirmation statement with every exhalation, 5 to 20 times.

Step 3: Mental Recall

Success breeds success! Each of us has experienced many successes in life. Yet so often when we sit and think about our performances, both past and future, we focus on the negative. We think about what we did wrong or what we are going to do wrong. This counteracts or offsets the success cycle. Negative imagery often leads to inconsistent or low-level performances.

Mental recall reaffirms the positive nature of the mental training program. It encourages the athletes to relive or replay past situations or competitions in which they have been successful. As athletes focus on the positive, they embed in their subconscious the feeling that they can be successful in the future because they have already been successful in the past.

Mental recall is one of the most underused steps of mental training, and it is also one of the most important. Success breeds success, and each of us must learn to capitalize on past successes whenever possible. These past successes help feed the success cycle and move us on to bigger and better things.

Step 4: Mental Rehearsal

Mental rehearsal is a process during which an athlete uses the mind to positively visualize a future event. We've all used mental rehearsal before, but too often we visualize in a negative, destructive manner. When we use the detrimental side of visualization by viewing undesired results, we imprint negative thoughts in our subconscious. Such negative images manifest themselves in our feelings and behaviors that erode self-concept and reinforce negative behaviors.

Mental rehearsal focuses on the positive possibilities to guide the mind and its images. This is the key: rehearsal. Mental rehearsal requires that the athlete be in control and visualize the results that he or she wants to accomplish.

Because they are so similar in nature, the guidelines for implementing successful mental recall and mental rehearsal are discussed together. For mental recall, the athletes use an event they have experienced; for mental rehearsal, the athletes picture a future event and see themselves accomplishing a goal.

Have the athletes begin each session with 30 to 60 seconds of relaxation, enough for them to become relaxed and comfortable but not so much that they feel sleepy. Then have them repeat their affirmations on each exhalation for four to six breaths. Next, athletes should perform their mental recall, focusing on their past successes and recalling them in detail. The athletes continue to do this for approximately one to two minutes. Then, opening their eyes, they flex and take a deep breath (they do this in the middle of the exercise so that they won't fall asleep during the rehearsal stage). Finally, have the athletes close their eyes, relax for one to three breaths, and for one to two minutes, picture themselves performing successfully in an upcoming meet.

Mental training involves knowing several simple yet powerful techniques and practicing them one or more times each day as a supplement to a physical training program. If this is done on a regular basis, each athlete will be rewarded with improved results. Using relaxation in combination with the mental imagery aspect of this program, we have had many athletes actually reach the performance that they were using in their mental training. Once the team is at a competition, the athletes use the relaxation component of this program to control their arousal level. In addition, I have had success with this in the classroom to relieve what I refer to as "test anxiety."

Chapter 15

PREPARING FOR MEETS

© Human Kinetics

In my opinion, preparing athletes to perform in meets is the easiest and most important part of what we do as coaches. The successes of individual athletes, your team, and your coaching career are not measured by the elaborate workouts you have created, but rather by the performances of your athletes in competitions and, especially, in championship meets.

Coaches often approach me and share their workouts, asking for my opinion of their conditioning plan or of a specific workout. My response is simple and can be summed up in a series of questions:

- How did your athletes run or perform in the meets immediately following the workout?
- Did the athletes execute their race plan?
- Did you get the result you were looking for?

If the athletes didn't perform well or the plan didn't achieve the results the coach was looking for, then even the most sophisticated workouts really don't cut it! Success is measured by the athletes' ability to perform in the meet, particularly by how they perform in the most critical situations; those results ultimately give you the answer you are looking for. In this way coaching is a dynamic process. We continue to learn and develop until our final competition.

Preparing athletes to perform well in meets involves solid training—both physical and mental—as well as establishing warm-up and premeet routines. Meet preparation also involves the coach's guidance in selecting the right lineup for the right meet; keeping the big, seasonal picture in mind; establishing meet expectations with your coaching staff and team; and preparing event strategies.

PROVIDING A PREMEET ROUTINE

The practice day before any competition is usually a casual event for our team. While we continue to use the same warm-up as any other practice day, the coach staff and I significantly reduce the volume of work before a meet. The day is really no more than an extended warm-up of the body. It is important, however, to make sure that the athletes break a good sweat and raise their heart rate so that their metabolic rate does not fall below the level it would be at during a normal practice day. If the metabolic rate does fall during the day prior to competition, there is a good

chance that the athlete will experience difficulty in competition. Athletes sometimes refer to this as feeling "flat." As with anything, some individuals need less or more activity than others.

Details, Details

I provide our athletes with a detailed itinerary that outlines every activity we will be doing, when it will be done, and where it will take place. I even provide them with a packing list of what to take to away meets. The opposing coaches who have seen these itineraries often laugh at the level of detail—but they rarely defeat us!

Athletes should also have a precompetition routine that is similar if not identical to the warm-up routine they perform before each practice. By having the same routine, athletes train themselves to be mentally prepared to compete while warming up their bodies. With younger athletes, an event coach may need to direct precompetition warm-up activities for the group to ensure that athletes stay focused. As the athletes mature, however, they can handle warming up for competition on their own.

SELECTING YOUR MEET LINEUP

Track and field provides a great opportunity that is not afforded many other sports—the ability to have a large number of athletes be a part of your program. In fact, team depth is one of the cornerstones of a successful program. Making team cuts or selecting a team should not even be an option in junior high and high school; rather, you should encourage participation by accepting anyone who is willing to be in attendance, do the work, and adhere to the rules.

The largest challenge facing a coaching staff is to get an athlete into the right event. A track and field unit as a part of your physical education program can be an early identifier of athletes well suited for particular events, as are the physical fitness tests that most school districts have as a part of their physical education programs. If you decide to become involved with event-identification testing, there are more specific tests and data available as resources. These test are accurate, yet they are also time-consuming and must be well organized. One of the better sets of identification tests and tables is included as a part of the *USA Track & Field Coaching Manual* (2000).

Each year I ask athletes to choose a primary and secondary event; I also ask them all to select an event they are interested in and are willing to attempt to test their aptitude in. Perhaps the best way to tell whether an athlete has an aptitude in a particular event is to use your eyes while they are trying these events. I have found that with age and experience, I spend less and less time relying on books, tape measures, and watches; instead, I simply use more time just watching athletes. As Yogi Berra once said, "You can observe a lot by just watching."

There are times when I feel that we as coaches spend too much time with our noses buried in coaching materials and not enough time interacting with and watching our athletes. Watching workouts and meet performances can lead you and the athlete to new events if you take the time to watch and break down the videotape. An athlete's conditioning work and strength work may also open your eyes to additional event possibilities.

Once you have found each athlete's aptitudes, establishing a solid team lineup for a meet is going to depend on a few things:

Time of year. The fitness level of your athletes is based on the amount of training they have been able to achieve prior to the time of the season for which a meet is scheduled. Early-season meets may be considered developmental and less important; there are many options available to you to take advantage of such scheduling. You can hold out your better athletes to allow your younger athletes to experience competition, you can place your top athletes into new events to see if they have any promise, or you can evaluate the order of events and run your athletes in a combination that simulates a workout scenario. If you decide to run your best athletes in their primary event, I would recommend that you allow them to just run a single event. That way, they will experience less mental and physical stress and can conserve energy for more important competitions.

Weather conditions. Poor weather conditions in the spring can play a major role in performances contested in the northern tier of the United States, as can extreme heat later in the year in the southern states. Either set of conditions may cause injury or illness that can affect individual athletes and team performances in the more important meets later in the season. I have heard a lot of coaches say that they have to acclimate their athletes to poor conditions because the state or national meet may be contested in these conditions. I believe that you can prepare for this possibility during workouts. In workout settings, not only can you control what is taking place in terms of effort, but you also have the ability to provide the necessary amenities to assist the athlete immediately following such a practice—warm showers, hydration, cool baths, massages, and so on. In a competition setting, athletes may not have the opportunity to stay warm and dry when not competing. Mentally tough athletes perform no matter the conditions if they are healthy and rested; injured and ill athletes give you what they have, but it usually is not enough. In this situation, consider resting better athletes or placing them in only one event to allow them to get into warm, dry clothing as soon as possible following their competition.

Importance of the meet. The relative importance of a meet is the driving force for placing your athletes into a lineup. The less important the meet, the more flexibility you have, and the less I recommend pushing your athletes. On the other hand, the more important the meet is to the athletes and the program, the more events I ask my better athletes to compete in. I have always looked beyond the regular season meets and focused more on the conference, state, and national meets. I also look very hard at what options are available to me in the state and national meets.

Sometimes coaches can get too greedy and ask athletes to do too much in a championship meet. Spreading athletes too thin costs them and their team more than they get in return. The higher the level of competition, the less room there is for error and the greater the mental stress that will be placed on the athletes. In this type of situation, you can get much more with less—as opposed to loading your athletes up. However, if you make the decision to go for it and leave nothing in reserve, you as the coach need to confer with these athletes. You need to outline the best strategy for them to survive the early rounds and to achieve the results you are looking for in the finals.

Goal of the meet. Finally, what is the goal of the meet? First, though, let's ask an important preliminary question: What is the current level of success of your program? In a struggling inexperienced program, every win is important in building success, so it might be important to put a lineup together that allows for that potential victory to take place. However, you will need to allow your athletes to recover from this effort. If you are competing in a low-intensity competition, you may want to rest athletes or have them compete in off events, or in the worst case, have them do a single event. Very few teams can win both early and late in the season. You will be remembered more for the way your team performed at the end of the season than for whether or not you won a specific invitational during the year. Programs and coaches are made or lost based on their success in the major meets at the end of the season.

ESTABLISHING MEET EXPECTATIONS

Having a successful meet depends in part on your athletes' being prepared properly to meet the goal of that particular meet. You cannot expect athletes to win every event at every meet. You therefore need to establish goals for each meet that take into consideration the type and amount of training, the

level of competition, the weather, and the seasonal goal that your intermediate goals will lead you toward.

A big premeet pep talk is in direct contradiction to my mental training program. I have found that a calm conversation about the individual and team goals for a particular competition is much more effective that an emotional talk.

When we compete at multiple-day meets, I no longer talk about the meet at the end of each day; I found that doing so tended to elevate each athlete's arousal level too much before going to bed. We now have a breakfast meeting each morning of the meet to review what has happened and to set up that day's competition. This routine allows athletes to sleep well the night before and to focus on the final outcome of the big meet while still breaking the competition into what has passed (yesterday) and what is to come (today).

If the coaching staff is well prepared for a competition, even a home meet, they will have the details of the meet in place and thereby allow enough time to communicate with their athletes during the meet. However, I also feel that if athletes are properly prepared, little communication needs to take place before or during competition anyway. The most valuable communication between a coach and an athlete occurs postmeet, when you evaluate and critique the performance.

Keep It Simple

It has been my experience that some coaches "overcoach" at a competitions, forcing an athlete to process too much information at once and thereby inhibiting, rather than enhancing, that athlete's performance. Providing supporting words to athletes in competition is plenty. I tell the athletes who need or want input to come to me, and then I will communicate with them. When they do approach me in a meet situation, I make it a point to keep the conversation simple and to the point.

PREPARING EVENT STRATEGIES

As a coach, you must have all of the details prepared in advance of each meet. You must also have thought about as many situations that could arise as possible so that you are prepared with the correct answer or strategy. As an undergraduate, I learned from Buzz Levick, the former head men's basketball coach from Wartburg College, that competition preparation is essential in achieving overall success. In his basketball theory class, Coach Levick shared with the class that he had a small spiral notebook that he carried on the bench with him. It provided the strategy he would employ in various situations, based on time remaining, the score, who had the ball, and where the ball would be put into play.

By using this organizational skill in his sport, Coach Levick could remain calm and focus on the proper call in the most pressure-packed, critical times of a game. This form of organization can also be used in track and field, even though once the race or event starts, it cannot be stopped. Still, race strategies can be changed; field-event athletes can correct errors with each attempt; and the way you put together your relay teams and your meet lineup can reflect your organizational skill.

Perhaps the greatest advantage to being prepared as you enter the meet is that if a problem does arise during the competition, you are prepared to focus on that problem. Because you have prepared in advance for common occurrences, you can address the problems at hand without distress or panic. Too many coaches try to coach on the move or learn on the roll. What usually happens to these coaches is that they do not have the time to deal with small issues, let alone a major problem or a new strategy that comes along, because they are busy putting out so many small fires.

It is important for you and your staff to maintain confidence and tranquility during competition. You must also prepare your athletes for success as well as adversity. Your team members must be able to control the

Team Strategizing

A classic example of how to handle a meet strategy situation took place at our conference (WIAC) indoor track championships in March 2001. With the NCAA championships just six days after the WIAC meet, my staff and I made a decision. Because we had a legitimate opportunity to win a national championship, we would not ask our national qualifiers to "go to the wall" in the conference meet. We thereby allowed them to run fewer meters, incur less stress, and position themselves to have an opportunity to win the more important of the two meets. We also allowed our senior weight thrower to compete at the USA Indoor Championships and not compete at the conference meet, a move that would costs us 10 points. As a result, we lost the conference meet by 14 points, but we became the big winner when the following weekend, we won the NCAA Indoor Championship, which was our eighth national indoor title in 14 years. The ability to think through our options in advance allowed us to make the conference meet competitive, forcing the school who won the WIAC meet to push their athletes for strong performances. We then defeated this same team seven days later for the national championship on their home indoor facility.

emotional highs that come with a great performance, yet they must also be able to work through the disappointment associated with not performing as well as expected. The athletes' ability to maintain their composure is a skill that can be taught on a daily basis. When something happens in a meet setting that tests their composure, athletes can rely on the techniques they have practiced daily to help them deal effectively with their emotions. This is especially helpful in situations in which the coaching staff does not have access to the athletes.

At the 2001 NCAA Outdoor Championships, Mike Koenning, who threw the hammer for us,

202 Coaching Track & Field Successfully

was the second seed going into the meet. He struggled in the trials to make finals, but he did qualify in the seventh position. Our team's championship drive depended on at least a second-place finish by this athlete. After fouling on his first two throws in the finals, Mike tossed a throw that was just off of his lifetime personal best. He moved from seventh to first place and went on to win the individual national championship. During his struggles, he maintained his composure, and he drew upon his experiences. He had confidence that his preparation would allow him to gain personal success while providing momentum for the rest of the team, which went on to win the NCAA team championship.

This is what coaching is all about! Your main goal is to manage your athletes so that they have a positive experience and enhance the overall program. This may mean looking at a season as a two-year proposition for success. I once had an outstanding frosh-soph team, and I was considering moving the best athletes up to the varsity level for the conference meet. By doing this, our varsity would still not have won the meet but would have made a better showing. One of my assistant coaches, who had more years of experience than I did, suggested that we leave the freshmen and sophomores together so that they could win their level of the conference meet by a large margin and experience the feeling of success. Then when the sophomores became juniors, we would move them up along with the freshmen, who would then be sophomores. This was a great suggestion and a decision that allowed us to place third in the Illinois State Track Meet three years later. This group had significant success from that time on, and this suggestion that made all the difference in moving our program forward.

INDEX

Note: The italicized *f* and *t* following page numbers refer to figures and tables, respectively.

ABOUT THE AUTHOR

Courtesy of UW-LaCrosse, SID

Mark Guthrie is the men's track and field head coach at the University of Wisconsin at La Crosse, where he maintains a national championship-caliber program year after year. His teams have won 15 Division III championships and 27 Wisconsin Intercollegiate Athletic Conference titles since he took over the program in 1986. Guthrie began his coaching career in 1975 at the high school level, where he led his teams to three consecutive state cross country championships. Guthrie's success earned him the United States Track Coaches Association's National Coach of the Year Award in 1994, 1997, 1998, 1999, 2000, 2001, and 2002. He was named Regional Coach of the Year seven times and is currently the president of the USTCA for Division III. He and his wife, Dawn, enjoy traveling, boating, and attending their daughters' athletic events.

ABOUT THE CONTRIBUTORS

Josh Buchholtz

Now the head coach at the University of Wisconsin-Stout, Josh Buchholtz was previously an assistant coach at UW-La Crosse from 1999-2002, working with the high jumpers, sprinters, and pole vault specialists. Prior to beginning his coaching career, Buchholtz earned two Wisconsin Intercollegiate Athletic Conference (WIAC) pole vault titles (1998 indoor and outdoor) and three times earned All-America honors in the event, placing third in 1998. During Buchholtz's coaching career, he has had a hand in producing eight individual All-American athletes and five WIAC individual champions. Buchholtz graduated from UW-La Crosse in 1999 with a bachelor's degree in exercise and sport science.

Phil Esten

As head coach of the UW-La Crosse cross country program for 28 seasons, Phil Esten guided the Eagles to 27 national championship competitions. He coached the Eagles to the NCAA Division III national championship in 1996, and he posted 26 consecutive top-10 finishes at nationals. In addition to a national title, UW-La Crosse finished as the national runner-up 8 times, won 20 Wisconsin Intercollegiate Athletic Conference titles, and never finished lower than third in the league during Esten's career. He has coached 28 runners to 46 NAIA and NCAA All-America honors, and he guided Brett Altergott to the individual national title in 1997. An inductee of the UW-La Crosse, NAIA District 14, and Wisconsin Cross Country Coaches' Association Halls of Fame, he was named Division III Co-Coach of the Year in 1996. Esten retired from his coaching duties after the 1998 season but continues to teach as a professor in the exercise and sport science program at UW-La Crosse.

Dennis Kline

Dennis Kline is in his fifth season as a member of the Eagles coaching staff and is responsible for coaching all throwing events. He is credited with developing 5 national champions, 11 All-Americans, and 14 conference champions at UW-La Crosse. Kline also serves as the Director of the Strength Center. Prior to joining the staff, Kline served as the strength director for the Oxford (Ohio) Reconditioning Center located near Miami University. While at Miami University, he received a bachelor's degree in sport studies in 1990 and a master's degree in exercise science in 1992. He had a brilliant collegiate career in the throws. He was the Midwest Athletic Conference champion and participated at the NCAA I championships in the hammer. Kline is the Miami record holder in the hammer. Following his collegiate career, he competed in the 1996 Olympic trials and ranked 15th in the U.S. in the hammer.

EVAN PERKINS

A former assistant coach at the University of Wisconsin-Oshkosh and at the University of Wisconsin-La Crosse, Evan Perkins coached athletes to 13 individual national championships and over 25 All-American awards in the long jump, triple jump, and throwing events. Two of his former athletes are Bill Schroeder, currently in his first year with the Detroit Lions following a seven-year career with the Green Bay Packers, and Mel Mueller, a member of the USA 2000 Olympic Team in the pole vault. Perkins himself won NCAA Division III individual titles in the triple jump during the 1986 and 1987 seasons at UW-La Crosse, where he earned a bachelor's degree as well as a master's degree in human performance. Currently Perkins is the Community Fitness Director for the Marinette School District in Marinette, Wisconsin.

Maximize performance in every throwing and jumping event!

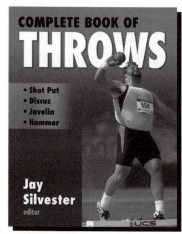

COMPLETE BOOK OF THROWS
- Shot Put
- Discus
- Javelin
- Hammer

Jay Silvester editor

2003 • 176 pages
ISBN 0-7360-4114-1

Complete Book of Throws presents techniques and conditioning programs used by many of the best athletes in the shot put, discus, javelin, and hammer throw.

Shot Put: Master the glide and spin techniques with drills that break down the throwing sequence into individual movements, and then put it back together to establish proper motor patterns.

Discus: Develop a fluid and efficient throw. Find a rhythm, learn the fundamentals and techniques, and practice rhythm drills to accelerate maximally through the throw while maintaining precise control.

Javelin: Perform the technique drills and power training exercises to develop and apply speed, power, and rhythm to the throw, which in turn will help you achieve optimum speed, angle, and height on every delivery.

Hammer: Establish a grip, swing, and wind for a good throwing rhythm and tempo. Then use the drills to develop speed and control to release the hammer at the height of acceleration.

Whether you're preparing your athletes for high-level competition or are helping them learn the basics, *Complete Book of Throws* provides technique drills, conditioning exercises, and detailed sample training programs for building the body, improving form, and perfecting each throw.

Coaches Ed Jacoby and Bob Fraley draw on their combined 60 years of coaching experience to help long jumpers, triple jumpers, high jumpers, and pole vaulters achieve new personal records. They break down each event into key phases—from approach to landing—to teach proper jumping technique and to show jumpers how to avoid common technical flaws. They also provide a strength and development program specifically for jumpers and 16 event-specific workouts that fine-tune skills.

Use the practical, proven techniques in *Complete Book of Jumps* to go higher and farther than the competition.

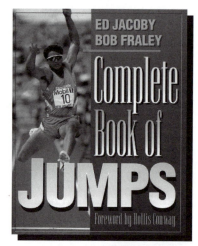

**ED JACOBY
BOB FRALEY**

Complete Book of JUMPS

Foreword by Hollis Conway

1995 • 160 pages
ISBN 0-87322-673-9

HUMAN KINETICS
The Premier Publisher for Sports & Fitness
P.O. Box 5076, Champaign, IL 61825-5076
www.HumanKinetics.com

2335

To place your order, U.S. customers call
TOLL FREE 1-800-747-4457.
Customers outside the U.S. should place orders using the appropriate telephone number/address shown in the front of this book